THE KINGS OF ALGIERS

The Kings of Algiers

HOW TWO JEWISH
FAMILIES SHAPED THE
MEDITERRANEAN WORLD
DURING THE NAPOLEONIC
WARS AND BEYOND

Julie Kalman

PRINCETON UNIVERSITY PRESS

PRINCETON & OXFORD

Published by Princeton University Press
41 William Street, Princeton, New Jersey 08540
99 Banbury Road, Oxford OX2 6JX

press.princeton.edu

Library of Congress Cataloging-in-Publication Data

Names: Kalman, Julie, 1969- author.
Title: The kings of Algiers : how two Jewish families shaped the Mediterranean world during the Napoleonic wars and beyond / Julie Kalman.
Other titles: How two Jewish families shaped the Mediterranean world during the Napoleonic wars and beyond
Description: Princeton : Princeton University Press, [2023] | Includes bibliographical references and index.
Identifiers: LCCN 2023006737 (print) | LCCN 2023006738 (ebook) | ISBN 9780691230153 (hardback) | ISBN 9780691230146 (ebook)
Subjects: LCSH: Jewish merchants—Algeria—Algiers—History—19th century. | Jews—Algeria—Algiers—History—19th century. | International trade—History—19th century. | Imperialism—History—19th century. | Algiers (Algeria)—Commerce—History—19th century. | BISAC: HISTORY / Jewish | POLITICAL SCIENCE / Imperialism
Classification: LCC DS135.A3 K35 2023 (print) | LCC DS135.A3 (ebook) | DDC 965.3004924—dc23/eng/20230214
LC record available at https://lccn.loc.gov/2023006737
LC ebook record available at https://lccn.loc.gov/2023006738

British Library Cataloging-in-Publication Data is available

Editorial: Fred Appel and James Collier
Production Editorial: Sara Lerner
Jacket Design: Heather Hansen
Production: Erin Suydam
Publicity: Kate Hensley and Kathryn Stevens
Copyeditor: Lachlan Brooks

Jacket Credit: View of the Port of Algiers, North Africa, from the Mediterranean. Handcolored lithograph from Friedrich Wilhelm Goedsche's *Vollstaendige Völkergallerie in getreuen Abbildungen* (Complete Gallery of Peoples in True Pictures), Meissen, circa 1835–1840. Florilegius / Alamy Stock Photo

This book has been composed in Miller

Printed on acid-free paper. ∞

Printed in the United States of America

10 9 8 7 6 5 4 3 2 1

For David

CONTENTS

ACKNOWLEDGEMENTS

THIS BOOK WAS RESEARCHED, and largely written, over the course of a four-year fellowship. It gave me the resources, and invaluable time, to immerse myself in thousands of pages of diplomatic and family correspondence. For this, I must express my gratitude, not only to the Australian Research Council, but also to my colleague in history at Monash University, Christina Twomey, who first suggested that I put in a fellowship application, and to the colleagues who read countless drafts until it was ready to submit. At Monash, the historians have fostered a fantastic research culture, and I am grateful to my research group colleagues Alistair Thomson, Nick Ferns, Bernard Keo, Constant Mews, Aydogan Kars, and Andrew Jackson, who read and commented generously on my introduction. Also at Monash, it was Daniel Heller, the very model of a colleague and of a historian, who introduced me to Fred Appel at Princeton University Press. For feedback and encouragement from further afield, I must also thank Francesca Trivellato, David Todd, Jennifer Sessions, Evelyne Oliel-Grausz, Abigail Green, Ira Katznelson, and James McDougall. Peter McPhee and Lisa Leff both brought fresh and critical eyes to the manuscript, exactly when they were needed, giving generously of their time and expertise. Briony Neilson did an expert job of the hard work of checking that the small things were right. The two anonymous readers for the press gave generous, critical feedback. All contributed to making this a better book.

Much of the writing of this book occurred during a global pandemic that will, I have no doubt, much occupy historians of the future. With Australia's borders locked shut, and overseas research impossible, research assistants in the United States, Denmark, Spain, France, and Italy provided an invaluable service, finding and photographing sources. Before the pandemic, I was able to spend time in Algiers, where Nehad Benzeguib was a superb guide. Over the course of the long lockdowns we experienced in Melbourne, my two teenage children, Yekira and Reuben, were wonderful company, and brought all-important perspective to the great challenges we all faced, including the illness and death of my mother. They give me hope for the future, in a time when hope is in short supply.

The last word of thanks must go to David Feldman, to whom it is my great good fortune and joy to be recently married. With his characteristic generosity, as this book has taken shape, he has given unstintingly of his wisdom, insight, and fount of dad jokes. The Kings of Algiers and I have benefited immeasurably from all three, and we dedicate this book to him, with gratitude and love.

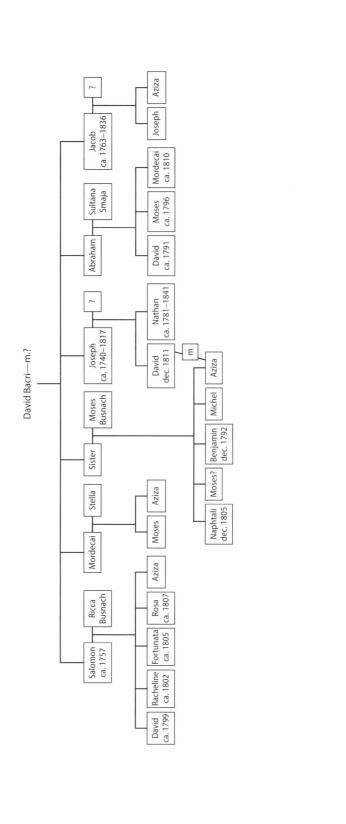

David Bacri—m. ?

Salomon ca. 1757 — **Ricca Busnach**
- **David** ca. 1799
- **Racheline** ca. 1802
- **Fortunata** ca. 1805
- **Rosa** ca. 1807
- **Aziza**

Mordecai — **Stella**
- **Moses**
- **Aziza**

Sister — **Moses Busnach**
- **Naphtali** dec. 1805
- **Moses?**
- **Benjamin** dec. 1792
- **Michel**
- **Aziza** — m — **David** dec. 1811

Joseph ca. 1740–1817 — **?**
- **Nathan** ca. 1781–1841 — **David** dec. 1811

Abraham — **Sultana Smaja**
- **David** ca. 1791
- **Moses** ca. 1796
- **Mordecai** ca. 1810

Jacob ca. 1763–1836 — **?**
- **Joseph**
- **Aziza**

THE KINGS OF ALGIERS

Introduction

STANDING AT THE port of Algiers on a bright day in winter, you look
north, out over the vast expanse of calm blue that is the Mediterranean Sea. The ferry to Marseilles is docked, awaiting its cargo of cars
and passengers. Tall nineteenth-century buildings line the prom-
enade along the water's edge, forming a clean, straight, man-made
line. Once proud and dignified, a marker of French civilization in
Africa, they now stand empty, neglected, and decaying, casting sad
shadows. The port is calm—surprisingly so in this bustling, Mediterranean city. But the port of Algiers is not the city's central focus,
as it once was. In its twenty-first-century guise, it betrays nothing
of the productive chaos that once reigned here. At the end of the
eighteenth century, as the Napoleonic Wars raged, Algiers was a
major trading and corsairing port in the Mediterranean. There was
a constant flow of merchant ships bringing luxury goods, highly
prized by the ruling Turkish elite, and loading raw produce from
the Algerian hinterland, from Europe and the New World. These
same ships would load raw produce from the Algerian hinterland,
for transport to Europe and America. Algerian corsairs roamed
the sea between lands, capturing the ships of enemy powers, and
snatching hapless victims from along its shores. They would tow in
their booty, for sale and enslavement.

The marina was a hive of activity. Slaves, captured from the
merchant ships that ran the gauntlet of the Mediterranean at war,
loaded and unloaded cargoes. The foreign consuls resident in the
city would rush down to the port to welcome any ship flying their

flag, with the hope that it brought news and letters. If one of their ships was captured, they would come to the marina to argue for the release of their countrymen. In the thick of business, at the water's edge, consuls would rub shoulders with traders, who bought and sold everything that came through the port. These traders were the regency's brokers, the vital link between the outside world and the ruling elite. They sourced the raw materials so desired by European regimes, they ordered the luxury goods that came from those same regimes, and if a corsair towed in a captured ship, they would be there, to negotiate purchase of cargo, crew, and passengers, as well as the ship itself, for sale to the highest bidder. Often, the traders were Jews. Elsewhere in the Ottoman Empire, Jews competed with local Christians—Greeks and Armenians, as well as Muslims—for access to trade, and to all the roles brokers could occupy. In Algiers, there was no significant Christian minority to provide competition, and Jews alone could take advantage of this lucrative space. In the late eighteenth century, as the wars of the French Revolution broke out, the most prominent among them was one sprawling family, the Bacris.

The Bacris, and the debt owed to them by France, have long been linked in the historiography to the diplomatic contretemps that set off France's invasion of the regency in 1830.[1] In 1827, on April 29, the French consul, Pierre Deval, had paid a formal visit to the Dey—or ruler of Algiers—Hussein, to mark the festival of Eid al-Fitr, the end of Ramadan. Hussein was not in a festive mood. He was angry with France. He believed that King Charles X and his regime were withholding several million francs that they owed the regency, for deliveries of wheat dating back to 1794. This wheat had been supplied by the Bacris. Hussein was their business partner, and some of this money was owed to him. As France's representative, Deval had been instructed to hold his ground, and not to dignify the Dey Hussein's repeated demands with a formal response from France. But on that day, as Deval stood before him, Hussein saw the consul's refusal to budge as unbearable insolence. Furious, Hussein grabbed a huge fan that one of his slaves was using to keep flies away. He struck Deval across the face with the fan, three times. This was a

1. See the discussion in McDougall, *A History of Algeria*, 50–51.

diplomatic insult, and France responded with a list of demands. They wanted an apology, punishment of the Algerian pirates who had been plaguing France's ships, the right to bear arms in Algiers, a statement that France would enjoy a most-favored-nation treatment in Algerian commerce, and a declaration from the dey that the French government had, in fact, completely liquidated the debt owed to the extended Bacri family for the wheat they had supplied to France. Hussein responded, in turn, with a list of his own grievances, including the money that he believed was still owed. With his response, tantamount to a refusal of France's conditions, French warships commenced a blockade of the Algerian coast on June 12, 1827, and, so the story has gone, the spat simply escalated from there.

The Bacris, and France's debt, have provided an easy, linear narrative of the invasion.[2] But behind the tale of misplaced diplomacy and the French invasion is the fascinating and important story of how the Bacris came to occupy such a central place in international relations. For some four decades, from the outbreak of the Revolutionary Wars to the invasion of Algiers, the five Bacri brothers, their children, and their nephew, Naphtali Busnach, were perhaps the best-known Jewish families trading in the Mediterranean Sea.[3] Their trading house sent prized Algerian wheat around the Mediterranean and beyond, to Northern Europe and America. They brought in colonial goods from the Atlantic, and luxury goods from Europe. They insured boats, and they armed corsairing ships. When captured enemy boats were towed into Algiers Harbor, the Bacris would sell off the cargo. When unfortunate members of the ship's crew, or even its passengers, were enslaved, as was the standard practice, the Bacris would lend money at interest to foreign consuls, so that they might buy back their citizens from the regency. They made loans to consuls to buy luxury gifts for the dey, too, as well as for his extended family and his ministers. So present were members of the extended Bacri family in the lives of consuls that they featured in virtually every letter sent home to the metropole,

2. David Todd addresses this in *A Velvet Empire*, 84–85. See also de Lange, "The Congress System and the French Invasion of Algiers, 1827–1830," 946.

3. Because members of the Bacri family were the main figures in this history, and for the purpose of simplicity, I will refer to the two interrelated families together as "the Bacris."

and they were no less well known in the centers of power. Jacob Bacri—one of the brothers—was invited to dinner with Napoleon, who personally designated the task of supplying his armies to the family. Lord Admiral Horatio Nelson puzzled over how to deal with the Bacris. American Secretaries of Foreign Affairs Thomas Jefferson, James Madison, and James Monroe considered strategies that would allow them to circumvent the Bacris' influence.

The Bacris were everywhere. Yet history writing, siloed into subdisciplines, has not been able to accommodate them. Like the now-silent port of Algiers, their story has been lost in a space between historiographical fields and absolute dates. Histories of the wars in the Mediterranean and its shores are always told from within the bounds of one national narrative, whether British, French, or American. Notwithstanding their involvement in all aspects of trade, including corsairing and slavery, Jews do not figure in the histories of these activities. Nor has space been allowed for trading Jews in the broader histories of the Mediterranean for this period.[4] Jews are always absent from these histories, as though somehow separate from events in which they were involved, and from people with whom they dealt. The history of Jewish trade in the Mediterranean has been told as a stand-alone story, distinct from the histories that surround it. This failure of historians of the Mediterranean to consider Jewish traders and brokers, present throughout the Ottoman Empire, is an opportunity missed. How would these histories change if we let them interact, just as their protagonists interacted? What do we find, and what new questions are we able to ask, if we shift our angle of vision from metropole to periphery, and place these brokers at the center of analysis? These questions lie at the heart of this book.

Periodization, too, has left an empty space where the Bacris exist. In terms of their activity as traders, the family descends from the Sephardic Jews who dominated Mediterranean trade in the sixteenth century. These refugees from the Inquisition established some of the most extraordinary trade networks the world has seen, unprecedented in their scope and spread. Setting up

4. Colley, *Captives*; Jasanoff, *Edge of Empire*; Panzac, *Les Corsaires barbaresques*; Weiss, *Captives and Corsairs*.

new communities all around the Mediterranean and beyond, they took advantage of new shipping technologies and built a global web that crossed oceans, rather than land. It stretched from the Ottoman Empire to the Caribbean, and from Spanish America to Europe. They brought new-world products to eager old-world markets, including sugar, spices, silver and gold bullion, diamonds, pearls, hides, tobacco, cacao, silks and American wood dyes, ostrich feathers, indigo, cochineal, ginger, and coffee.[5] These Jews were in a unique position. They could take advantage of a moment in history that offered full access to the Atlantic for the first time. They could take advantage of their Jewishness, which made them trusted middlemen for the Ottoman powers, and they could make use of their knowledge of European languages, the networks of contacts they had left behind, and those they had created in their new homes.

The historiography of these Jews comes to a halt with the eighteenth century. Indeed, as Francesca Trivellato has noted, the Mediterranean, and Sephardi Jewry, "disappear" from most accounts of early modern European trade after the mid-seventeenth century.[6] According to the historians of these Jews and their trading networks, their unique position allowed for their rise to dominance, and a similar pattern announced their decline. 1750 has been set in the literature as the marker of this latter phenomenon. Portuguese *conversos*—Jews who had converted to Catholicism—gradually stopped emigrating to fertile ports in the new world, and their distinctiveness and significance as a trading community in Portugal and Spain also waned. This meant that their fellow Jews, Jewish or nominally Christian, in Northern Europe and Italy no longer had a network of agents on whom they could rely. These factors led to the steady and certain downturn of Sephardi Transatlantic trade. The Sephardi trading network lost "its momentum and creative drive, and its capacity to adapt." Once-flourishing communities were weakened and impoverished. Sephardi communities dispersed and assimilated, and "not infrequently" crypto-Jews renounced their secret practices of ritual

5. Israel, *Diasporas within a Diaspora*, 4.
6. Trivellato, *The Familiarity of Strangers*, 5.

Judaism.[7] The history of Jewish trade is only picked up more than two centuries later. Between one strain of historiography and the next, lies a gap, as Sarah Stein wrote of the late nineteenth century, "a confluence of significance and silence".[8]

Jewish trading networks never managed to retrieve the extraordinary spread and influence of the networks established by refugees from the Iberian Peninsula, but Jews around the Mediterranean did not stop trading. Sephardic Jews had shown themselves to be wonderfully capable of accommodating change when they left their lives behind them. If we look for the Jews who remained in Mediterranean ports, then we find them adapting to changed circumstances but still active, still trading, and still taking full advantage of their unique position. The networks established by Spanish and Portuguese Jews might have been breaking down, and the once-thriving trading port of Livorno on Italy's northwest coast might have been at the beginning of its stagnation, but France and Britain had entered the Mediterranean, and this presented a new context for trade. We might approach this story anew as a tale of adaptation, rather than decline. The nature and patterns of trade changed, but trading did not stop, and there was no reason for enterprising Jewish traders to stop either. Following their trail leads us to the continuation of this history, through to the Revolutionary Wars, where this story begins.

By the time the Revolutionary Wars broke out in 1793, the extended Bacri-Busnach family was well-established in business. Initially, the Bacris were a family of five brothers: Mordecai, Salomon, Abraham, Joseph, and Jacob. Their father, David Bacri, had set up a trading house in the regency of Algiers in 1774.[9] Within less than a decade, it was prospering. David Bacri brought four of his sons into the business. Abraham, the fifth son, was also involved in family affairs, but seems to have taken the role of fixer, travelling around the Mediterranean as needed. In 1798, the brothers extended the business to include their nephew Naphtali Busnach, the son of an unnamed Bacri sister. The Bacris were independent

7. Israel, *Diasporas within a Diaspora*, 38–39.
8. Stein, *Plumes*, 6.
9. Eisenbeth, "Les Juifs en Algérie," 373."

traders and financiers, or brokers. They belonged to the well-established Jewish communities in the regency of Algiers, where Jews made up around ten percent of the population. This was a loose community, made up of different groups, separated by origin. The original Jewish inhabitants had been present in the region since Roman times. In late antiquity, they had been joined by Berbers who had adopted Judaism. Later came Jews fleeing the Inquisition, and those who had come, or returned, from the port of Livorno.[10] With centuries of cohabitation, distinctions between long-established Arab Jews and the more recently arrived Andalusi refugees became less distinct, although they could still be separated by class. The majority lived modestly as artisans, often beside and in close contact with their Muslim neighbors, "indistinguishable from the other poorer classes of society."[11] A small elite were merchants; among them the Bacris. They were able to gain proximity to state power in Algiers through the position of *muqaddam*, or head of the Jewish community. The *muqaddam* represented the Jewish community to the dey and was given entry into the circle of the regency's elite. As different members of the family became *muqaddam*, they were able to gain the trust of the ruling dey and elite, and become their broker, both in trade and diplomacy. In this sense, in the way it gave them such prized access to power, their Jewishness was central to their success. Deys came to rely on members of the family as intermediaries in both trade and diplomatic negotiations. Mordecai was the first of the five brothers to act as diplomat for the dey. As the trusted advisor to Hassan, he helped negotiate the peace treaty concluded with Holland in March 1794.[12] In early 1795, Mordecai assisted the Swedish consul in a negotiation with the dey for the ransom of approximately one hundred American slaves.

Brokers such as the Bacris were vital for Europeans in the Ottoman Empire.[13] Armenian, Greek, and Jewish minorities, as well

10. Ayoun, "Les Juifs livournais," 663.

11. McDougall, *A History of Algeria*, 36.

12. Mordecai is referred to in French sources as either Mardochée, Michel, or Micaïo, a name that might best translate to Mordecai, or else Michael, in English. Names written in Hebrew characters could enjoy a variety of equivalencies, and spellings, in translation. The most consistent name given this particular brother was Mardochée, which translates to Mordecai. For the purpose of consistency, this is the name I will use.

13. Coller, *Arab France*, 30. See, also, Zytnicki, *Les Juifs du Maghreb*, 21–24, 43–48;

as Muslims, were traders, interpreters, and guides. Trade in the Mediterranean did not experience the "revolution of scale" that occurred in the Atlantic in the late seventeenth century, where a smaller number of actors were able to control ever larger segments of the market.[14] Rather, it was made up of numerous small and medium-sized companies, forming networks between major ports. Nor were European powers able to exert control over production, prices, and transport, as they had done in Southeast Asia and the new world. In the Mediterranean, Europeans were dependent on the negotiation of concessions, and on an array of traders and financiers, including the Bacris: "Local brokers, suppliers, and lenders."[15] In Algiers, Europeans were barely represented. In the eighteenth-century regency, the only French trading house was the *Compagnie royale d'Afrique* (Royal African Company), and there were hardly any English or Dutch traders. This lack of competition from both local and European Christians meant that Jews like the Bacris could occupy multiple spaces in the regency's economic and political hierarchy. They were brokers and dragomen, or interpreters, capable of speaking Italian and Spanish, as well as Turkish. They acted as financial agents for the consulates.

Jewish historians have brought Jewish brokers in North Africa to life. They have shown how Jews, who so often occupied middle spaces, bring to light the nature of relations between states on the ground, in the Barbary States. Daniel Schroeter chronicled the life of Meir Macnin, who traded from Essaouira, Morocco's principal trading port. He was one of a group of elite Jews who monopolized virtually the entirety of Morocco's trade with Europe in the early nineteenth century.[16] These elite Jews were crucial to the ruling elite and foreign merchants who came to seek opportunity in this new town.[17] The absolutist regime within which Macnin operated offered opportunities that were unprecedented, given the regime's hunger for wealth and Macnin's place, as a merchant possessing

Kalman, *Orientalizing the Jew*. On the role of Jews as go-betweens in the Ottoman Empire, see, also, Schroeter, *The Sultan's Jew*, 121; Philipp, "The Farhi Family," 37–52.

14. Trivellato, *The Familiarity of Strangers*, 38.
15. Trivellato, *The Familiarity of Strangers*, 104.
16. Schroeter, *The Sultan's Jew*, 79.
17. Schroeter, *The Sultan's Jew*, 22.

"a network of financial and commercial connections."[18] Joshua Schreier has told the story of another successful Jewish merchant, Jacob Lasry, who traded from the port of Oran, on the coast of the regency of Algiers. Schreier's story spanned the years of invasion and occupation by French forces, and he sought to counter the classic narrative whereby French dynamism reversed decline and brought civilization to the downtrodden and primitive. Instead, Schreier showed how Lasry's activities and his role as middleman during those years served to destabilize binaries such as colonizer and colonized, and to bring to light the messiness of the French project of colonization in Oran. Like Macnin and Lasry, the Bacris' context facilitated their rise. But the Bacris were able to go further than their contemporaries in their pursuit of wealth, notoriety, and power. They operated as a family, allowing them to spread around the Mediterranean, building their own family networks. They were able, too, to profit from the Revolutionary and Napoleonic Wars, which created a situation of chaos and urgent need.

It mattered that the Bacris were Jews, because their Jewishness enabled their entry into the circle of state power. As "insider-outsiders"[19] in the Empire, Jews could claim a fruitful middle space, between Muslim authorities and foreign, Christian powers, seeking ingress and access. As *muqaddam*, they were able to gain access to the circle of state power. Ottoman authorities, of course, understood the place of religious minorities differently from Western Europe. Rather than impose Islam by force, Ottoman rulers accommodated religious diversity, through the Pact of Umar. This pact established the principle of *dhimmitude*, whose purpose was to define the status of non-Muslim minorities in the Muslim state. Jews, and the many branches of Christianity in the Middle East, were seen as People of the Book: monotheistic people who had received divine revelation, but before the coming of Islam. They occupied a middle ground between savagery and full enlightenment.[20] Thus they were subject to certain measures geared toward ensuring separation and subordination, but at the same time, they enjoyed communal autonomy.

18. Schroeter, *The Sultan's Jew*, 3.

19. Trivellato, *The Familiarity of Strangers*, 2.

20. On Jews and *dhimmi* status, see Benbassa and Rodrigue, *Sephardi Jewry*, 2–3. On Jews and *dhimmi* status in Algiers, see Valensi, *Juifs et musulmans*, 25–6.

Muslim rulers in the regencies that made up the empire had to find the balance between holding Western powers at arm's length, and allowing them in. It was a Muslim ruler's duty to protect his community from any ingress of a power beyond the realm of Islam. At the same time, however, it was important to maintain trade with non-Muslim nations, as this could aid and strengthen Islam. This created a space in the Ottoman Empire that both Jews and Christians could fill. Jews did not need to be protected from corruption by non-Muslims in the same way as Muslims did, and they posed no threat in terms of challenges to rule. Across the empire, Ottoman sultans, deys, and beys relied not only on Jewish traders, but also physicians, tax collectors, and administrators.

It was the Bacri family's good fortune to be in the regency. In the Revolutionary Wars being fought in the Mediterranean, Algiers was an important strategic port for all those powers whose ships sailed that sea, but particularly for France and Britain. The regency of Algiers was a semi-independent province in the westernmost reaches of the Ottoman Empire. The Turkish elite that ruled the regency was recruited and imposed from the Empire's center. Both France and Britain had been implanting themselves in the Barbary Coast for some time, and had managed to establish strong trade relationships, particularly in the grain that they both needed. The eighteenth century saw a revival of European trade in the Mediterranean. Britain and France had long-standing diplomatic relationships with the Ottoman Empire. France had been granted concessions—fiscal and jurisdictional privileges that local rulers granted to foreign entities—in the early sixteenth century, allowing them to build and run enclaves along the North African coast. Half a century later, Britain followed, establishing the Levant Company in 1581. This was created by Elizabeth I, who granted a royal charter to a corporation of English merchants, so that they could establish a trading monopoly with the Ottoman Empire (although in fact, their presence in North Africa was weak). In part, the commercial expansion of both powers was a diplomatic move. Both France and Britain hoped that trade relations with the Ottoman Empire would constitute a strong enough alliance to block Spain. But neither France nor Britain wished for the other power to enjoy that protection: France protested the establishment of the Company. From the outset of the establishment of trade relations with the Ottomans, France and Britain were in competition with one another.[21] The Bacris derived enormous benefit from this contest.

In eighteenth-century North Africa, France was the dominant power. France was Algeria's main client, and Algeria was France's main supplier. For fifty years, from 1740, nine-tenths of the wheat brought into Marseilles for distribution throughout France was of Algerian origin.[22] There was constant traffic between Marseilles and various towns along the Algerian coastline. Barbary grain was vital for France. It ensured supply to the Midi, regularly threatened by famine, and it fed France's revolutionary armies in Egypt, and later in Italy. Supplies of grain, meat, and other products from the Barbary States were equally vital for British garrisons on Gibraltar, as well as for Malta, when the latter came under British control in 1801.[23] Minorca, where another garrison was stationed, had never been able to feed itself, and most years it had to import grain from Algiers. This trade was of fundamental importance to the life of the island, and thus to the maintenance of British power in the Mediterranean.

France and Britain were competing for the raw products that the Algerian market had to offer, and over which the Bacris, in effect, had monopolies. Both powers dedicated significant resources to their capture, protection, and exploitation. The Mediterranean and the shores that bordered it were important strategic points during this period, even if that body of water did not become a theater of outright war. French and British actions regarding the regency fit into what Dzavid Dzanic has called "informal imperial tactics," "the extraction of economic, political, and legal concessions from peripheral polities through the erosion of their sovereignty."[24] But this was also mercantile imperialism. In Cornel Zwierlein's formulation, applied to an earlier period, mercantilist imperialism involved the "nationalization of economics," its organizing logic "the distinction between the trade of 'our' nation and that of others."[25] Imperialism, in this time of war, was profoundly competitive, as France and Britain, and their allies

---

21. Gale, "Beyond Corsairs," 39; Vlami, *Trading with the Ottomans*, 15.

22. Touati, "L'Algérie au 'siècle du blé.'"

23. Gale, "Beyond Corsairs," 51. See also Horn, *British Diplomatic Service*, 35.

24. Dzanic, "France's Informal Empire in the Mediterranean," 2.

25. Zwierlein, *Imperial Unknowns*, 20.

and enemies, all competed for preference and preferential access to exports, while also seeking to block the other, in an extension of the war being fought across Europe and in its surrounding seas.[26] Algiers was useful, but it was just as important to maintain good relations with the regency, so as to shut the other out. In much the same spirit, in 1802, shortly before he departed for the Mediterranean, Lord Admiral Horatio Nelson wrote of Malta, "It must never belong to France—Britain does not want it."[27] Algiers was central in both French and British reckoning in the early nineteenth-century Mediterranean.

Consuls had the often-difficult job of representing these competing empires. Consuls were the agents of informal imperialism on the ground, and they all developed relationships of varying closeness and reliance with members of the extended Bacri family. As Joshua Meeks has demonstrated, competition in the Mediterranean during the Revolutionary Wars was a contest of military might, but it also played out diplomatically, through "conversation and negotiation."[28] In late eighteenth-century Algiers, the Revolutionary War and imperial contest played out on the ground, through diplomacy that was, at times, barely diplomatic. Consuls representing France and Britain, but also the United States, Denmark, Sweden, Holland, and Spain, battled to impose a regime of informal imperialism on the regency. This would allow them exclusive and advantageous access to all the precious grain and other primary produce that the regency had to offer, as well as rights to lucrative coral fishing. It would serve to avoid, or circumvent, all the irritations the regency presented, particularly the capture of their boats by its Algerian corsairs, and the enslavement of their citizens. It would deflect this activity onto competitors or enemies. The Bacris were central to these processes in more than one way. As the contest continued and loyalties shifted through the wars, consuls remained convinced that the Bacris always worked to favor their

26. Horn, *British Diplomatic Service*, 35.

27. Nicolas, ed., *Nelson*, vol. 5, 36. Later, of course, in 1803, Nelson stated what Chris Bayly called "the new doctrine": that Malta was "the most important outwork to India, and that it will give us great influence in the Levant and indeed in all the southern parts of Italy." Cited in Bayly, *Imperial Meridian*, 103.

28. Meeks, *The Struggle for the Revolutionary Western Mediterranean*, 4.

competitor, to their own disadvantage. How did this shape their own ambitions?

All consuls in the Barbary regencies were generally required to play a more extensive role than their confreres elsewhere.[29] Consuls were ambassadors in all but name (they could not assume the title, as Western states officially had diplomatic relations with the sultan, in Istanbul). In North Africa, their responsibilities extended beyond the economic (seeking new products and markets), and into the domain of the political.[30] British consuls on the Barbary Coast were treated differently from most other consuls in the British service. They were managed by the Home Office, separated from the main branch of the British consular service, which was under the direction of the Foreign Office. In the sense that they essentially worked as diplomats, undertaking political as well as the normal economic duties of the "merchant-consul," they did, indeed, have different responsibilities from the standard posting for the average British consul.[31] French consuls in North Africa, too, played a more extensive role than their confreres elsewhere. It was only in the Ottoman Empire, in fact, that French consuls had "a truly political role to play."[32] In the Barbary regencies in particular, part of the consul's responsibilities was to negotiate treaties, and this required the establishment and maintenance of good relations with the dey and his entire ministry, or divan. This was not easy.[33] As the Revolutionary and Napoleonic Wars progressed, and islands in the Mediterranean were gained and lost, treaties had to be constantly renegotiated. Each new treaty required the regular presentation of sumptuous gifts, and deys could choose to reject anything that they considered to be insufficiently luxurious. There was always a Bacri in the middle of these transactions, managing both finances and

29. Much of the scholarship of consular studies has focused on postings in the North African states of Tunis, Tripoli, Algiers, and Morocco, because of the unique demands of these positions for both French and British consuls. See Pennell, "The Social History of British Diplomats in North Africa," 348; Platt, *The Cinderella Service*; Marzagalli, "American Shipping into the Mediterranean," 43–62.

30. Lee, "The Supervising of the Barbary Consulates," 191. De Goey, *Consuls and the Institutions of Global Capitalism*, 36.

31. Lee, "The Supervising of the Barbary Consulates," 197.

32. Ulbert, "A History of the French Consular Services," 308.

33. Anderson, "Great Britain and the Barbary States," 95.

diplomacy, and thus placing themselves at the center of relations of power in the regency.

For the consuls of both nations, the broadening of their responsibilities was due to their isolation, both from the ambassador in Constantinople, and their minister in Paris or London. Consuls along the Barbary Coast were distanced from the metropole. Corsairing and piracy, but also—in the late eighteenth and early nineteenth centuries—war, interrupted the passage of mail. With no instructions arriving from the metropole, these consuls, who often had a very detailed and long-standing knowledge of the world of their posting, were forced to adapt, on their own initiative, to changing circumstances and diplomatic expectations; to create diplomatic policy "on the hoof."[34] Foreign consuls in Algiers had a wide remit.

Among consuls' tasks was dealing with the consequences of corsairing, the practice whereby enemy ships would be captured, with ship and cargo sold, and passengers taken into slavery. Corsairing was sanctioned and often directly funded by the state. The goal of corsairing was to make money through spoils and prisoners, so unlike pirates, corsairs did not kill. Rather, they sought to bring their booty into a safe port in the best possible state, so as to maximize their profit. At sea, corsairs would capture enemy boats carrying goods and people. The captured boat would be taken to port, and there, both the boat and its cargo would be sold, and passengers and crew enslaved, either to be sold or ransomed. These were the established and accepted parameters of the practice. All the states of the Barbary Coast had corsairing ships: not just Algiers, but also Tunis and Tripoli, and the short-lived seventeenth-century city-state of Salé, established by Moriscos from Spain, and located on today's Moroccan coast. Corsairing ships from the Maghreb stole thousands of men from ships, but also from shores. From lone shepherds to entire villages, none were safe from them. Many thus stolen never returned home.[35]

Algiers was a corsairing port. Corsairs, sponsored by the dey, would regularly capture the ships of French and British allies,

34. Pennell, "The social history of British diplomats in North Africa," 348. See also Clancy-Smith, *Mediterraneans*, 344.

35. Weiss, *Captives and Corsairs*, 1, 7.

towing them into port, distributing their riches, and enslaving their crew and passengers. Corsairing had declined over the course of the eighteenth century, but in the shipping chaos caused by the Revolution, it enjoyed new impetus. Algerian, but also French and British corsairs, roamed the Mediterranean, often capturing ships carrying Bacri goods. The Bacris would charter the ships of neutral powers and load them with goods for non-neutral ports, such as Marseilles. Woe betide any corsair that captured a Bacri ship. The Bacris always involved the dey in their trading ventures, and he would angrily demand restitution and compensation for any ship caught for which the Bacris sustained a loss. Over the years of the war and beyond, the Bacris drew various powers into long drawn-out battles for restitution of goods or the payment of their value. Due to the involvement of deys in the Bacris' business, these spats were often elevated to the level of state relations, and consuls were inevitably the messengers.

Consuls were also required to maintain almost constant trade negotiations, a process in which members of the Bacri family played a central role.[36] Every consul had a dragoman, or interpreter, but they would often find that a Bacri would interpose himself in the middle of negotiations, whether they be economic or political. Bacris did not make a distinction. All the consuls interacted with the brothers and their nephew regularly, whether for trade, financial, or diplomatic negotiations. If they didn't quite socialize, they nonetheless spent considerable time in one another's company and homes, discussing strategies and making deals. The diplomatic correspondence is rife with tales of the exploits of Mordecai, Jacob, Joseph, his son David, and Naphtali Busnach. Consuls reported conversations verbatim; they gave close descriptions of physique and character. The Bacris bring these separate sets of diplomatic correspondence together. They become a focal point of the contest between France and Britain in particular, and they shine light on it from an external, nonnational perspective. Thus they, and the dynamic of contest that they reveal, are the focus of this book.

36. See Kämpe, "Competition and Cooperation," 37; Calafat, "Les Juridictions du consul."

Consuls were the agents of imperialism in Algiers. Imperialism in the regency was informal, in more than one sense. It was informal, because those powers that sought imperial influence did not seek to formalize their relations of power, but instead, for the most part, allowed consuls to act as representative agents. But it was informal, also, because it was mediated by personal relations. It was here that the Bacris were expert. The world in which they operated was governed by personal relationships: between the Bacris and the dey, as well as his ministers, and between the Bacris and various consuls. This was why the Bacris always sought to establish a personal relationship with any new consul in the regency. Those representing the lesser powers in the regency, such as American and Swedish consuls, tended to acquiesce in these relationships. French and British consuls would react to overtures with astonishment and outrage. It was an insult that one often levelled at the other, that they were in league with the family. It would not do for the representatives of these great, competing nations to be drawn into the Bacris' web.

The newly created United States of America, a particularly significant latecomer to the Mediterranean, understood the contest in different terms. The signing of the Declaration of Independence did not mark the beginning of US shipping to the Mediterranean. Ships from New Britain, protected by the crown, had been sailing to the Western Mediterranean since the seventeenth century. They had immunity from attack by corsairs bought by the British government, which paid tribute to the Barbary States for protection. In the ports of Southern Europe, British-American colonists found willing buyers for their cod and grain.[37] With the independence of the United States in the late eighteenth century, this shipping met new challenges as the new republic sought to assert itself as an independent trading power. After 1783, US ships could no longer rely on the security provided by the cover of the British flag. Indeed, in a practice it was to use widely throughout the years of war, Britain used Barbary corsairs as proxies in the trade contest, both stifling US trade and leaving the sea clear for British merchantmen. It was

37. This discussion draws on Silvia Marzagalli's important and groundbreaking work on American shipping in the Mediterranean, as part of the larger Navigocorpus project. Marzagalli, "American Shipping into the Mediterranean," 43.

effective. US vessels became easy prey to the depredations of Barbary corsairs. They were frequently raided, and trade suffered terribly. In 1785, Algerian corsairs took two US ships: the *Maria* and the *Dauphin*. By December 1795, there were approximately 150 US slaves in Algiers.

The United States, too, had to deal with the Bacris. In the final years of the eighteenth century, pressure from US shipowners to continue and extend trade in the Mediterranean did not abate. US grain, naval stores (resin-based components such as tar, pitch, turpentine, pine oil, and rosin, used in building and maintaining wooden sailing ships), as well as dried cod, and rum were in demand in Europe's Mediterranean ports, and the number of US ships passing through the Straits of Gibraltar was increasing. In March 1794, Congress narrowly approved the creation of a navy, authorizing the building of four forty-four-gun and two thirty-six-gun ships of war. In a test of the new republic's abilities on the world stage, Congress also sought peace with Algiers, the busiest corsairing state.[38] Bacris were at the center of negotiations. Joseph Donaldson Jr. was employed to bargain with Dey Hassan. After some discussion, they reached terms: the United States would pay Hassan $642,500 in cash, as well as an annual tribute in naval stores to the value of $21,600. This was equal to an extraordinary seventeen percent of the annual US budget. It was Mordecai Bacri who supplied the necessary gifts for the dey and his family, at a value of approximately $21,000.[39] This was a peace bought dearly, but as Jefferson saw it, "when the Barbary States threatened American trade in the Mediterranean, they threatened the well-being of the American Republic."[40]

The US Senate ratified the treaty in early 1796. This did not mark the end of US efforts to ensure the safety of its shipping in the Mediterranean. Peace could be fragile, if the annual tribute was late, or if a ruler chose to dislike the diplomatic presents. But the Revolutionary War presented too good an opportunity to pass up. US ships, neutral in the war, could offer their services for

38. Peskin, "The Lessons of Independence."
39. Parker, *Uncle Sam in Barbary*, 103.
40. Cogliano, *Emperor of Liberty*, 7.

intra-Mediterranean trade, and the Bacris were always ready with a cargo. With French ports blockaded, and British ships stopping and seizing any ship flying the French flag, or carrying French cargo, the need for neutral ships to keep maritime trade alive was great. The wars began a period of unprecedented growth and great prosperity for US shipping. Between 1790 and 1807, US shipping into the Mediterranean grew by five to six times.[41]

In order to help ships' captains and merchants deal with local authorities, the United States established consular posts in Tangier, Algiers, Tunis, and Tripoli. In Algiers, Richard O'Brien, master of the ship *Dauphin* when it had been captured in 1785 and captive in Algiers since that time, became US consul for the port city, and consul general for all of the Barbary States. It was O'Brien who named the Bacris and Naphtali "The Kings of Algiers."[42] Consuls were to help secure US shipping by providing assistance to US ships and acting as intermediary in any interaction with local authorities. They were also required to provide information on the local economy and trade possibilities. Secretary of State Timothy Pickering was a keen reader of this information. He believed "the enterprise of American merchants and navigators would prompt them to visit the ports of the Barbary powers" if they were well-informed, and able to do so safely.[43] He estimated that Mediterranean trade before independence had counted for one-sixth of the wheat and flour, and one-quarter of the fish traded from the American colonies. This trade loaded "outwards from eighty to one hundred ships, annually, of 20,000 tons, navigated by about 1,200 seamen."[44] The goods came from all parts of the United States. The Mediterranean did not take the bulk of US trade and shipping. It was nonetheless considered important enough to warrant a costly, drawn-out war against Tripoli. In the Mediterranean, Marzagalli argues, the US

41. Marzagalli, "American Shipping and Trade in Warfare," 23–24.
42. National Archives and Records Administration (NARA) Atlanta, State Department Consular Despatches, Algiers Series, M23, roll 3, vol. 2, n.p., August 24, 1797, O'Brien to Secretary of State Pickering.
43. Cited (but not referenced) in Wright and Macleod, *The First Americans in North Africa*, 29.
44. Jefferson, "Report of the Secretary of State Relative to the Mediterranean Trade." Also cited in De Goey, *Consuls and the Institutions of Global Capitalism.*

government "cut its diplomatic teeth."⁴⁵ But this was the different diplomacy of a new nation seeking to establish its credentials on an international stage. The United States did not seek to compete with France and Britain to gain influence in the regency. Nor did it try to block powers it saw as hostile. Like their fellows, US consuls dealt daily with members of the Bacri family. But the United States' different investment in the regency means that US consuls could generally stand outside the imperial contest between France and Britain and see it for what it was. Their letters and reports provide us with an important external view of the relationship between the Bacris, the French and British consuls, and the Dey of Algiers.

The Bacris sit at the center of this history. It is a history of what it was to be a Jewish trader in this volatile world: the opportunities and constraints they faced, the challenges of devising business strategies in the face of these,⁴⁶ and the ways in which the different contexts in which they operated—strategic port city, secular republic, semi-independent regency of an Islamic empire—contributed to and complicated their fortunes. It is a history of Jewishness, too, and the ways in which this was perceived and understood by those who dealt with the Bacris. Jewishness is a presence throughout this book: it is central to the Bacris' story. At times, this is a positive attribute, one that allowed the family to reach levels of great influence in the regency by virtue of being neither Christian nor Muslim. But in the regency, all of the advantages of being a Jewish broker in Algiers could also be vulnerabilities. Deys, chosen by the elite Ottoman infantry that was the janissary corps, came and went. Many did not die in their beds. When a dey was deposed, his trusted advisor would be left exposed. Two of the Bacris were murdered either because of or by their dey. Naphtali's extraordinary rise to power engendered disquiet and jealousy among the broader population, alarmed at the power vested in one Jew. He was assassinated by a janissary. David, Joseph's son, was to be the victim of the vicious jealousy of the Duran family: trading Jews who also sought the advantage of the post of *muqaddam*, and bitter rivals to the Bacris. David was killed on the dey's orders, after the

45. Marzagalli, "American Shipping into the Mediterranean," 62.
46. Trivellato, *The Familiarity of Strangers*, 266.

Durans spread rumors about him. Jews in the regency who sought advancement could be seen to be too powerful, and this could have serious consequences.

At other times, the Bacris' Jewishness was the reason behind great hostility from the Europeans with whom the Bacris dealt, who brought ideas of Jews and Judaism from their own societies. In the eyes of Europeans and Americans, Jews were the deicide people, and their lowly position in most Western societies was fully deserved. Jews in France had been emancipated, but as Napoleon's partial reversal of this emancipation suggests, they were held to a very high standard of behavior. For foreigners in the regency, it was an affront to Christianity—and for the French in particular, an affront to the nation—that Jews could act assertively, as the Bacris did. It is perhaps because of their confidence and ambition that they were perceived to be inordinately powerful. It is impossible to know whether the Bacris were as powerful as consuls made out, but it is important that consuls perceived them to be so. It is rare that the Bacris' voices can be heard unmediated. For the most part, they come to us by way of consular letters, as well as a precious handful of letters that they themselves wrote, to various ministers in Paris, when the French government placed the family and their assets under sequestration. The Bacris' Jewishness—with all of its baggage and connotations—was the lens through which they were perceived and understood, and this book traces the implications of these perceptions, both for consuls and the powers they represented and for the Bacris themselves.

This is also a family story, and the book is structured chronologically, following the extended Bacri family's heady successes, and their equally dramatic failures. Family ties were no guarantee of cohesiveness, trust, or protection; family loyalty lasted only as long as each family member did their job well. Much of the drama that drives this book turns around the youngest brother, Jacob. His business correspondence reveals the breakdown in relations and growing acrimony between the brothers and their Busnach cousins. A massive fraud committed by a Busnach against a Bacri would echo down the generations, as family members pursued one another through the courts of Europe for money, and family disputes played out on a wide stage.

The Bacris were Jewish traders. As we have seen, their identity and status as Jews was essential to access the politics and economy of the regency. It also allowed them to force their way into events taking place around them. When their story is allowed to interact with the surrounding histories—just as they themselves interacted with their patchwork, varied world—it brings to life a history of war, competitive imperialism, corsairing, slavery, and global trade in the nineteenth-century Mediterranean. It expands and enriches British imperial history, bringing Britain back into the Mediterranean, in a time when their presence there has been lost to the historiography. It gives shape to an early, self-conscious United States, seeking to be recognized as a national player on the big stage of international diplomacy and trade. It tells the story of France and Algiers from a perspective where the invasion marks an ending, rather than a beginning, giving depth and nuance to the story that follows. By starting at the periphery, rather than in the metropole, by taking a perspective that looks north, across the Mediterranean, we see the formal history of French imperialism in a new way. The Bacris bring these histories together.

The Bacris sat between the representatives of an old, weakening empire and the nascent nations that wished to expand into it. They give us new access to and perspective on relations between the two. They allow us to revisit old stories and pose new and important questions. We know that in war, imperialism, and diplomacy, policies were formed in the metropole. But how did they play out on the ground? What happened when a nation's representatives came up against others, whether competitors or independent brokers, who had conflicting ambitions? The relations between consuls and members of the extended Bacri family allow us to explore how the imperatives of the Napoleonic war, imperialism, and international relations played out, and were adapted and reshaped, "through incessant concession and sparring," far from the metropole.[47] They show how people's interactions in distant ports could determine paths chosen and directions taken in the great history of the imperial world.

47. Clancy-Smith, *Mediterraneans*, 344.

CHAPTER ONE

The Rise of the Bacris

THE REVOLUTIONARY AND Napoleonic Wars in the Mediterranean provided the setting and circumstances that allowed for the extraordinary rise and success of the Bacris. Very much at home in their world, they were able to take full advantage of the possibilities that the war offered them. As Jews in Algiers, they could be close to the center of power. They could draw on the nature of power relations in the regency to their advantage, establishing personal and business relations with the regency's elite. Their skills and methods—already established—lent themselves to the circumstances of the war: the dire need for raw materials and the intense contest to obtain them. They were perfectly placed to profit from the shipping chaos that the Revolutionary War brought to the Mediterranean in the form of blockades, battles, and the reinvigoration of corsairing. It was the war that allowed them to rise to unprecedented heights. It was the war, too, that set the stage for the way they were understood, as inordinately powerful.

In 1793 the Revolutionary War came to the Mediterranean. France declared war against Britain and the Netherlands on February 1 of that year and soon afterwards against Spain. Britain entered the Mediterranean, and the sea became a major theater of war. Britain put in place a close blockade of France's Mediterranean coast, and there was fighting in the Western Mediterranean and the Ligurian Sea near Corsica, between French and British naval forces, the latter supported by the navies of Spain and several Italian states. While the British had no colonies or naval bases in the Mediterranean, except for Gibraltar and Mahon, they did have significant trade interests there. As well as maintaining the blockade, Britain sought to protect their trade routes. Warships or small squadrons were sent to accompany merchantmen, and these would clash with corsairs. Trade and communications ran the gauntlet of conflict and criminality. In the absence of reliable shipping, demand for supplies increased, as not just populations, but forces in foreign lands, needed feeding. The increasing demand and shipping chaos offered an unprecedented opportunity to the enterprising trader. Into this chaos came the Bacris.

The origins of the Bacri family are unclear. They spoke Judeo-Arabic—the dialect of the so-called Arab Jews—a Jewish language whose base language is Arabic, with Hebrew and Aramaic content, written in Hebrew characters. But some of the Jews who had settled in the Maghreb after fleeing Spain adopted Judeo-Arabic over time.[1] It is uncertain which language the Bacris used to communicate with foreign consuls, although we know that they had French. Whatever their beginnings, by the time this story begins, the Bacri and Busnach families had become Livornese, because their ancestors had taken advantage of a trade opportunity. In 1591, Ferdinand I, the grand duke of Tuscany, delivered the Livornina (an expanded version was issued two years later, in 1593). Wishing to develop his port of Livorno, Ferdinand invited Jews, Turks, and Muslims to settle there, in the hope that they would establish trading businesses. In order to make the invitation attractive, Ferdinand promised that those Jews who settled in Livorno would be protected from the papal inquisitors, still active in Italy.[2] Unsurprisingly, many Jews, and particularly recent refugees fleeing the Inquisition, took up this invitation. So, too, did long-established families of Jews from the Maghreb. They came to a "bustling free port" on Italy's northwest coast, and Tuscany's main commercial center.[3] In the mid-eighteenth century, the city was also home to the second-largest Jewish community in Western Europe, after Amsterdam, and the largest in the Mediterranean. It was a diverse and thriving

1. On the Jews of the regency of Algiers, see Valensi, *Juifs et musulmans*; Taieb, *Sociétés juives du Maghreb moderne*; and McDougall, *A History of Algeria*, especially ch. 1.

2. On the Livornina, see Bregoli, *Mediterranean Enlightenment*, 20–23.

3. Bregoli, *Mediterranean Enlightenment*, 2.

trade hub, at the heart of the celebrated trading networks built by Jews from the Iberian Peninsula, seeking places of refuge from the inquisitorial powers. It was probably the most important port in the Mediterranean, until it was eclipsed by Marseilles in the eighteenth century.

By the time Livorno entered its decline, the Bacris and Busnachs had either returned to or settled in the port of Algiers to take advantage of the burgeoning trade relationship between the regency and France. In 1716, a Jacob Coen Bacri was newly arrived and busy in the port of Algiers, receiving a consignment of precious stones from Tunis. In 1721 a Busnach, also named Naphtali, moved from Livorno to Mahon, a British naval base on the island of Minorca, in the Western Mediterranean. By 1723, he was established, or reestablished in Algiers, shipping various goods. The Arab version of his name—*Boudjenah*—means "he who has wings," and this was certainly appropriate, given this Naphtali's business acumen. Already wealthy, Naphtali quickly planted roots in Algiers and, in 1724, the shipping registers find him sending ribbons, paper, and mirrors to Tetouan in Morocco, as well as cargoes to Livorno and, in 1728, wheat to Marseilles. In Algiers, he was buying Christians out of slavery, to sell them back to their home states. In 1726, he shipped a cargo of wool and elephant tusks to a client in Livorno, on a ship that was rather incongruously named the *Jesus Mary Joseph.*[4] Naphtali Busnach was indeed making himself comfortable in a diverse world. A year later another Busnach—Abraham—followed his relative to Algiers and joined him in import and export, as well as the ransoming of Christian captives. By the late eighteenth century, the two families had joined, through the marriage to a Busnach of a Bacri sister. They became one extended family: the Bacris.

The five Bacri brothers—Mordecai, Joseph, Abraham, Salomon, and Jacob—worked in loose concert, through their trading house. The business had its headquarters in Algiers, but members of the family also set up office in Livorno, Marseilles and Paris. Joseph, the eldest Bacri brother, stayed in Algiers to run things there, together with his brother Mordecai, and his handsome, talented son David. It is not possible to know whether they truly worked

4. Haddey, *Le Livre d'or des israélites algériens*, 41.

in partnership. Abraham never joined the company formed by the brothers and seems to have worked behind the scenes. Salomon was perhaps the most successful of the brothers. He had left Algiers around 1787 to settle in Livorno, and he ran a branch of the family business there, receiving goods and moving them on, insuring cargoes, and acting as banker when needed. Salomon implanted himself in the Livorno community and became a respected member of its elite. Jacob, the youngest brother, was sent to Marseilles, to try to persuade the French regime to pay for the wheat that the Bacris had been supplying on credit to revolutionary—and cash-strapped—France. When Jacob found himself deep in debt, it was to Livorno and the brother he called Shlomo that he went, to beg for a loan. Jacob's correspondence, some five hundred letters preserved in the departmental archives in Marseilles, gives an insight into the minutiae of the family business, and of the dynamic (if not the actual business arrangement) between the brothers. His older siblings clearly did not trust Jacob: Joseph formally dissociated himself from him, and Salomon bailed him out a first, but not a second time. When Jacob found himself in terrible financial trouble, his brothers left him to cope on his own. Jacob was to have his revenge.

It was thanks to the position of *muqaddam* that the Bacris were able to enjoy the proximity to power that enabled their rise in Algiers. The *muqaddam* was always drawn from one of the community's few elite families. And within this elite, competition to occupy the seat at the dey's right hand was intense. The Bacris, and their bitter rivals, the Durans, would launch intrigues against one another, even drawing, at times, on local law to have rivals deposed or beheaded. This was a role that conferred great opportunity. It gave access to the regency's elite, and with the input of their capital and influence, the *muqaddam* could amass great riches. The *muqaddam* could thus play a vital role, offering the elite an investment in trade, and creating a virtuous circle of mutual enrichment. But the role of *muqaddam* also brought great risk. At the very height of his power, the *muqaddam* could also be deeply vulnerable. He was only protected and rewarded as long as his elite business partner remained in power. Mordecai was a close advisor to the dey, Hassan. It was Mordecai who first negotiated the wheat deal with France that gave the brothers the monopoly over this trade, with a percentage of the profits to go to the dey. This was wheat derived mostly from tithe payments to the dey, thus allowing him—and the Bacris—to make money out of a resource that had been freely given.[5] Under this arrangement, the Bacris were to supply France with as much wheat as the country in upheaval needed, on credit. This was the deal that would tie the family to France for the decades to follow and write the family into legend.

On May 15, 1798, Hassan succumbed to an untreated foot infection that became gangrenous. With Hassan dead, Mordecai found himself without his protector, and was arrested. Hassan had been succeeded by his nephew Mustapha, the finance minister. For reasons that are unclear, Mustapha put Mordecai in prison, and threatened to burn him to death. A pyre was prepared by the Bab el Oued, or River Gate, near the Jewish quarter. Mordecai was only saved by the payment of a large sum of money to the new dey, which may well have come from the Bacris.[6] After all, one reason behind the Bacris' success was that they always made sure the ruling dey benefited from their business. Having narrowly escaped death, Mordecai promptly left Algiers for Livorno, to join his brother Salomon. Still reeling from his terrible fright, Mordecai died shortly after he landed.

Back in Algiers, the Bacris did not miss a beat. Joseph took over from his brother. He worked closely with his nephew Naphtali Busnach, and business continued. Naphtali soon became trusted second-in-command to the new dey, Mustapha. He reached a level of influence never before seen in the regency. The brothers' investment in their nephew Naphtali, in bringing him into the business, was to pay off. Naphtali enjoyed unprecedented trust and influence in the palace. According to all the consuls (and commentators since), the relationship of intimacy and trust that Naphtali built with Mustapha was unrivalled. So, according to the same sources, was his power. Naphtali made himself the first point of contact in the palace for any foreign visitor, representative, or dignitary. Anyone who wished to deal with the dey had to go first to Naphtali. Nothing happened in Algiers without Naphtali's knowledge, whether that be the appointment or

5. Abun-Nasr, *A History of the Maghrib*, 167.
6. See NARA Atlanta M23, roll 5, vol. 4, p. 186, July 19, 1799, O'Brien to Pickering.

dismissal of senior officials,[7] the arrival and departure of ships, or the declaration of war with one or other of the Western powers present in the Mediterranean. His renown was such that an official from Constantinople, who had travelled to Algiers on an important mission, sought an interview with Naphtali before he had even presented himself to the dey.[8]

Naphtali was a figure who divided opinion. Consuls regularly accused him of being calculating and unscrupulous, shrewd in his management of Mustapha and without boundaries in his quest for power. Many in the community, on the other hand, called him modest, learned, pious, and charitable, drawing on his power to help the poor and oppressed in the community.[9] In the elegy published after his death at the hands of a janissary, the community lamented the loss of "Naphtali, diadem of our city."[10] Resentment at his power from janissary troops was the cause of his assassination. Joseph, on the other hand, was a survivor. Naphtali had worked closely with his uncle: while he acted as Mustapha's advisor and a middleman in diplomacy, Joseph took care of the business side of the family's affairs. After Naphtali's death, Joseph brought his son, the handsome and charismatic David, into the business. There was always another Bacri to step into the shoes left by the untimely decease of his relative.

The Bacris were agile, and this skill helped them to adapt to and profit from the circumstances of the war. The Mediterranean was a complex, many-faceted world. As brokers and traders in the regency, handling "a hodgepodge of goods,"[11] they had to keep track of constantly changing currency values, demand, and prices. They needed to keep abreast of shipping laws that varied with the changing circumstances of the war, as well as finding the loopholes that allowed them to continue trading. They operated in a world governed by multiple currencies, and ever-shifting exchange rates. They had to play the game of diplomacy, calculating and constantly recalibrating risk against success. They needed to guard their

7. Hirschberg, *A History of the Jews in North Africa*, 32.
8. Bloch, *Inscriptions tumulaires*, 95.
9. Bloch, *Inscriptions tumulaires*, 95.
10. "Elegy of Algiers," in Fenton and Littman, *Exile in the Maghreb*, 106.
11. Trivellato, *The Familiarity of Strangers*, 104.

position in the Jewish community against those who would usurp it and keep the dey and elites happy. The price of failure was very high; indeed, Naphtali's story served as a cautionary tale.

With the war playing out in the Mediterranean, shipping became more unpredictable than ever. The transport of mail was desperately slow and often completely unreliable. But the Bacris would make quick decisions. If too many vessels were waiting in the regency port of Arzew to be loaded with wheat, as happened in early 1802, then a boat in the harbor at Marseilles would be commandeered and set on a revised course, destined "either for America or for the Mediterranean."[12] In 1801, Jacob wrote to Giordani, his agent in Cadiz, asking to be kept advised, along with the Algiers branch, on the price of wheat, "so that if it were agreeable we could have a few loads shipped to you, given that prices in Lisbon have dropped, that France, far from being able to export wheat, needs it to be shipped there, and the storms that they have experienced have destroyed the sprouting of the next crop."[13] A week later, on December 7, he sent the same request to the family's agents in Alicante, Dié Brothers. Grain was clearly in short supply in Spain, since a month later, Jacob was responding to Giordani's reply—obviously sent with alacrity— that he had no doubt that given the drop in prices in Lisbon, the Algiers branch would "make considerable dispatches to you."[14]

The Bacris had widespread contacts, and this meant that they could find ways around the restrictions brought on by the war. Mediterranean ports would be placed under blockade by opposing forces, and French and British authorities gave themselves the right to search any ship and confiscate goods carried for the enemy. Both Jewish and Genoese trading networks sought nonetheless to find advantage from the shared space that was the Mediterranean. Brilli notes the "widespread Genoese custom of flying French, Spanish, English, Austrian, Papal and Tuscan flags according to convenience and itinerary."[15] Similarly, the Bacris owned several ships, which they

12. Archives Départementales des Bouches-du-Rhône (ADBR) 39 E 21, p. 80, 5 pluviôse an 10 (January 25, 1802), Jacob to Jacob Gozlan, Marseilles.

13. ADBR 39 E 21, p. 62, 5 frimaire an 10 (November 26, 1801), Jacob to Giordani and Sons, Cadiz.

14. ADBR 39 E 21, p. 75, January 8, 1802, Jacob to Giordani and Sons, Cadiz.

15. Brilli, "Coping with Iberian Monopolies," 31.

would sail under whichever flag was neutral, and therefore, in theory, safe from attack by corsairs or enemy powers. As Brilli observes, this expedient allowed for these traders to reach regions otherwise inaccessible to them because of corsairing or conditions of the war. It also meant that they could avoid having to pay the taxes that consuls in the landing ports collected.[16] The Bacris also chartered boats belonging to powers that were neutral in the conflict; those departing Algiers were generally Danish or Swedish. This, paired with the Bacris' Algerian nationality, was aimed at protecting ships from British capture.[17] To maintain this practice successfully, the Bacris needed knowledge of a series of shipping laws that could change regularly. They would switch flags, obtain safe passes, and place ships under different trading houses, either to comply with, or circumvent particular laws.[18] But the use of neutral ships was a risky practice, and it did not always turn out as the Bacris wished, particularly when one of their vessels was taken by a corsair.

The Bacris were helped by their network of agents all around Europe: in Paris, Malaga, Alicante, Madrid, Genoa, Cadiz, Lisbon, London, Amsterdam, and Barcelona. Many of these were the same Genoese who formed their own trading networks through the Iberian Peninsula.[19] Alicante was a port that the Bacris and Busnachs used regularly, and here they relied on Dié Brothers, for both business and news. They carried cargoes from as far away as Philadelphia, and shipped goods to the West Indies.[20] In 1805, they were even exploring the possibility of bringing grain from the plains of Russia through the Black Sea (the Russian ports offered the incalculable advantage of not freezing over in the winter).[21] There were great riches to be had from there too: once Britain was able to access the Black Sea, they brought back corn, tallow, and timber for shipping.[22] Where they saw the potential for profit, they extended

16. Brilli, "Coping with Iberian Monopolies," 31.
17. Hildesheimer, "Grandeur et décadence," 393.
18. ADBR 39 E 21, p. 74, 11 nivôse an 10 (January 1, 1802), Jacob to Jacob Gozlan, Marseille.
19. Brilli, "Coping with Iberian Monopolies."
20. NARA Atlanta M23, roll 5, vol. 4, p. 101, April 2, 1799, O'Brien to Pickering.
21. Archives du Ministère des Affaires Etrangères (AMAE) 8CCC/37, p. 307, 3 nivôse, an 14 (December 24, 1805), Thainville to Ministre des relations extérieures Charles-Maurice de Talleyrand-Périgord.
22. Wood, *A History of the Levant Company*, 181.

their reach. Grain was in demand from all of the regencies, not just Algiers. So the Bacris expanded the possibilities for trade by funding the building of a depot for the storage of corn in Benghazi, in Tripoli,[23] and they hired an agent there to transact business on their behalf.[24] In Tunis, Salomon Azulai, banker to the English consul, kept the Bacris updated. The Bacris were well-connected in the Jewish world. When in 1814 Raynal Keene, an American living in Spain, was instructed by his government to travel to Algiers and negotiate the freedom of American sailors, he took letters of introduction to the Bacris from Aaron Cardoza, the wealthy and highly regarded Gibraltarian Jew.[25]

Corsairing was both a practice and a bugbear for the Bacris, as it was for all parties in the Mediterranean. But corsairing was fundamental to the regency's identity. It brought specie to the regency and facilitated the growth of a merchant class. With corsairing, too, the Bacris positioned themselves right in the middle of the interactions between Western powers and the regency that corsairing provoked. They armed boats, but they also tried to keep trading as the war went on, using whatever loopholes or advantages they could find, including making the dey their business partner. When their schemes went awry, this could have greater diplomatic consequences. Corsairing was also part of the war of religion against the Christian enemy, and this, as Daniel Panzac has noted, gave corsairing "a dimension that was both legitimate and religious."[26] This also gave the state clear reasons to control the practice, and the dey was its almost exclusive overseer. Corsairing ships could capture vessels flying flags of regimes with which the regency was at war. Deys would, if necessary, declare war, so that their corsairs would have a greater choice of targets. In 1791, the Dey Hassan declared war on Sweden, and even though the corsairs did not take a single Swedish ship, the Swedes paid him 350,000 francs for a new agreement and promised to deliver annual gifts. Corsairing could bring income in myriad ways, and it allowed the regency to amass great wealth. It allowed them to

23. Perrin, ed., *The Keith Papers*, vol. 2, 365. Extract from Wickham's Dispatch to Lord Grenville forwarded to Keith, Vienna, January 25, 1801. In Gale, "Beyond Corsairs," 108.

24. Wright and Macleod, *First Americans*, 42.

25. Noah, *Travels in England, France, Spain, and the Barbary States*, 149.

26. Panzac, *Les Corsaires barbaresques*, 8.

build "a metallic treasury that might probably sustain them for many years to come," in Shaler's estimation.[27]

In the West, the idea of so-called Barbary piracy struck terror in the hearts of Europeans and fired the European imagination. Corsairing was so present in the lives of all who travelled this particular sea that it worked its way into the popular imagination. Lord Byron made a romantic figure of the corsair in his popular tale of the same name, published in verse in 1814. French composer Hector Berlioz wrote his overture *Le Corsaire* while on holiday in Nice—on the Mediterranean—in 1844. The memoirs of those who had been enslaved and rescued were bestsellers in seventeenth-century France, Portugal, and England. But corsairing was a two-sided affair. Catholic countries on the northern shores of the sea between lands maintained this intense maritime war with the Muslim countries to the south, and the sponsored galleys of the pope and of the other Italian states, as well as Spain, Portugal, and Malta, could be just as terrifying. The work of Christian-sponsored corsairs was to steal Muslim men, together with their merchandise. In fact, anyone from the Maghreb was fair game: thousands of Muslims—as well as some Ottoman Jews and Orthodox Christians—languished in the galleys of the French king Louis XIV.

The heyday of corsairing came early, in the seventeenth century. In 1623, Algiers armed no less than seventy-five ships. In 1627, equipped with English and Dutch-style square-rigged sailing ships, which allowed them to travel further than before, Algerian corsairs had made it all the way to Iceland, where they raided coastal towns, carrying off several hundred captives. By the end of the eighteenth century, corsairing was in full decline. The fleet sat, neglected, in the harbor. Deys turned to other sources of income, increasing and diversifying taxes.[28] Some ninety percent of the population of Algiers derived their living from the land during this period, and wealth could be drawn from taxes on agricultural production.[29] This was important, because after Spain made peace with the regency in 1786, Algerians could only pursue Portuguese, Neapolitan, Genoese, and Hamburg

27. Shaler, *Sketches of Algiers*, 33.
28. Abun-Nasr, *A History of the Maghrib*, 166.
29. McDougall, *A History of Algeria*, 13.

ships, to which were added US ships, which since the Declaration of Independence by the United States, no longer had the protection of the British flag. In 1785, the Algerians had taken their first US ship. But the decrease in income underscored the decline of corsairing. From 200,000 francs in 1785, the yield decreased to 140,000 francs in 1786, and only 77,000 francs in 1787. With the Revolutionary Wars and the disruption to commercial shipping in the Mediterranean, corsairing increased spectacularly. The Algerians took the greatest possible advantage. Armed with new copper-lined boats well-equipped with cannons, for two decades, Algerian corsairing ships roamed the Mediterranean once again. In two particularly lucrative years, 1798 and 1799, Algerian corsairs captured forty-two and thirty-one ships respectively. Each year brought in more than one and a half million francs.[30] Throughout the years of the war, corsairing maintained its regained momentum. Overall, Algerian corsairs captured 211 boats between 1798 and 1815.

With corsairing came disputed captures and the enslavement of crews. This then increased the risk of confrontations, varying from the diplomatic to the outright military. When the Bacris found themselves in the middle of such confrontations, diplomatic spats would ensue. The fate of the rather ironically named *Good Hope* provides one example of what could go wrong, and how the Bacris would respond. The *Good Hope* was a Danish brig chartered by the Bacris to bring merchandise to Algiers from London for the Dey Hassan. In March 1798, the *Good Hope* was taken by a French corsair, *Le Requin* (the Shark). The vessel was escorted to the port of Fécamp in Normandy, where it was judged to be a valid prize by the commercial court in that town. The Bacris protested, and when French authorities rejected the premise of the Bacris' protests, the dey was drawn into the dispute. The question of what should be done about the taking of the *Good Hope* became one of diplomacy between France and the regency. The story of the *Good Hope* shows how the Bacris were able to first create a diplomatic spat, and then insert themselves into it, a business method they would continue to use.

The *Good Hope* was deemed a valid prize by the French court in Normandy because the law of January 18, 1798 had ruled that

30. Panzac, *Les Corsaires barbaresques*, 92.

any ship carrying British merchandise could be captured by French corsairs. The Bacris' agent in Paris, Simon Abucaya, had sought to forestall French capture, writing to the naval minister in Paris to request a letter of safeguard for the ship, on the basis that it was loaded for the dey's account. The safeguard was granted, but not-withstanding this letter, the vessel was taken. The executive directory intervened in the process: the directory and ministers of the navy, justice, and foreign affairs all believed that the letter of safe-guard had been rightfully granted and gave the boat protection. By May, however, it had become clear to all that the *Good Hope* had not, in fact, been loaded for the dey's account. Rather, as Foreign Minister Charles-Maurice de Talleyrand-Périgord (Talleyrand) set out, in angry detail:

1. That the boat the *Good Hoffnung*[31] was freighted and loaded by Raphael Abraham Cohen Bacri, Jew from Algiers, then in London, for the account of several Jewish merchants established in Algiers, Livorno, and Marseilles.[32]
2. That only a minor part of the cargo, approximately ten thousand piasters, was destined for Algiers.
3. That the surplus was destined for a Jewish house in Livorno under the name of Salomon, brother of Raphael Abraham Cohen Bacri.
4. That in this major part destined for Livorno there were a small number of effects, destined for Jacob, other brother of Raphael Abraham Cohen Bacri, established in Marseilles, where they were to be sent from Livorno.[33]

The directory, having decided that the potential for any diplomatic contretemps with the regency was so negligible as not to warrant

31. This was the mixed translation of the Danish name given to the boat by French authorities.

32. This was the fifth brother, Abraham.

33. AMAE 8CCC/34, n.p., 17 floréal an 6 (May 6, 1798), Talleyrand to Moltedo. The courts themselves appear to have become exasperated by the Bacris'—and by extension, Mustapha's—claims. A later judgement opened by asking, "does the Algerian flag enjoy the astonishing prerogative of neutralising an enemy ship, with an enemy crew, loaded for an enemy account?" *Au conseil des prises: Mémoire pour les capitaine et armateur du corsaire français le* Brutus: *Contre les capitaine et propriétaires de la cargaison du navire soi-disant le* Rachel. The *Rachel* was a Bacri boat.

consideration, sent the case back to the courts for judgement. But Bacris were devoting considerable energy to the return of their cargo, as was the new dey, Mustapha, who in June 1798 wrote to the executive directory to announce his ascension to the throne. He took advantage of the occasion to list some demands, namely: the restitution of the cargo from the *Good Hope*, as well as the return of 200,000 piasters loaned to France by the regency, wheat from another Bacri boat that had been captured, and payment for a load of wheat delivered to France by a Muslim Algerian, Mollah Mohammed. Mustapha was concerned, he stated, although his concern could also be read as a veiled threat: these affairs, he wrote, were causing "coldness and deterioration" in the Franco-Algerian relationship. And continuing the same, slightly dangerous tone, Mustapha signed off, wishing happiness and glory in perpetuity, for France.[34] Mustapha, and other deys, only ever saw themselves as the full equals of the other states with which they dealt.

Mustapha—or perhaps Naphtali—was manifesting the close business relations between the Bacris and the dey. He was also drawing on the close and complex relationship between France and the regency. Since 1740, the *Compagnie royale d'Afrique*, or Royal African Company had enjoyed a virtual monopoly over wheat exports from Algiers. Marseilles, where the Company was based, was the principal importer of Algerian wheat, and the Company's representatives in Algiers were the main middlemen of the Algerian wheat trade. This trade had stopped with the revolution, and the advent of the Bacris. By 1794, France found itself in desperate need of grain. The years of 1792–94 had been harsh in France. Quite apart from the Terror, the uprising in the Vendée, and the war, the country had been hit by a famine that reached its zenith during the spring and summer of 1794. "Hail, hard rains, and then a drought plunged yields by as much as a third."[35] With wheat shortages looming, the French government instructed the consul in the regency, Césaire-Philippe Vallière, to seek another means of access to this precious resource. Vallière approached the Bacris, "extremely wealthy and all-powerful in Algiers, then, as now,

---

34. Plantet, *Correspondance des Deys d'Alger*, vol. 2, 478. Mustapha to executive directory, June 1798.

35. Miller, *Mastering the Market*, 164.

businessmen for the dey and the main heads of the regency," as an 1818 report on the deal put it.[36] After several requests from the French consul, they agreed to supply France with all it needed. Mordecai negotiated the "quasi-monopoly" over the wheat trade with the Dey Hassan, who was busy centralizing control.[37] The agreement from the Bacris—that grain from the regency would make its way to ports on France's Mediterranean coast—came just in time. By April 1795, grain prices had soared to almost nine times their 1790 price.[38] The Seine River froze over, and soil hardened to a depth of half a meter. Nor were difficulties to end. The harvest of autumn 1795 was "arguably the worst of the century," and it was followed by another severe winter, bringing on a severe subsistence crisis lasting two years, from 1795 to 1796.[39] The French were so desperate to secure their supply of grain that as the Revolutionary Wars were going on, they parked one part of the already stretched fleet off the coast of Bona (Annaba), on the northeastern coast of Algiers, to try to stop others from buying the corn that would be exported from there.[40] That the Bacris had agreed to supply the wheat on credit was a great relief for the revolutionary regime, forced to finance wars, both external and civil, that had been fought on every border. This ensured control, supply, and funds. But it also made the sale, and ensuing debt, an issue between states. This relationship of need, established in war, would govern relations between France and the regency for decades to follow.

The *Good Hope* was part of this dynamic. In July, Talleyrand responded to Mustapha's letter regarding the ship, in the name of the executive directory. He refused to address Mustapha's concerns, because, as he stated, perhaps making a point, "such questions" were not appropriate in a friendly letter, such as he was writing.[41] He did, however, undertake to have the new consul, Dominique

36. AMAE 8CCC/44, p. 89, October 1818, Pierre Deval, *Mémoire analytique de la correspondance du département des affaires étrangères depuis 1794 jusqu'en 1818, concernant les réclamations des Sieurs Bacri et Busnach, sujets algériens, sur le gouvernement français.*

37. Touati, *Le Commerce du blé*, 337.

38. Miller, *Mastering the Market*, 164.

39. McPhee, *The French Revolution*, 66–67.

40. The National Archives, London (TNA) FO 3/7, p. 90, April 7, 1793, Charles Mace to Henry Dundas, Secretary of State for the Home Department.

41. Plantet, *Correspondance des deys d'Alger*, vol. 2, 479. Talleyrand to Mustapha, July 12, 1798.

Moltedo, pay a visit to Mustapha, to respond to his concerns in person. This letter did not reach its destination, and in September, Mustapha wrote again, to reiterate his request that his demands be met, as proof of France's friendly intentions. This time, there was no mention of Mollah Mohammed, and Mustapha's demands on behalf of the Bacris were made in much greater detail, their consequences much clearer. "In attacking them, or their funds, one attacks us or our treasury," he wrote. He offered a solution too: simply by paying the Bacris what was owed them, France could restore "our partiality, confidence, and good will for the republic."[42] This is a letter that could well have been dictated by Naphtali, all the more so since Mustapha was illiterate. To France, the entanglement was clear: as an 1818 report put it, France could not reconcile "the obligations resulting from our laws regarding corsairs, and those resulting from our treaties with the dey of Algiers."[43]

Naphtali and his Bacri uncles, too, were well aware of the ways the debt entangled France with the regency, and with their trading house. In their efforts to obtain repayment, the Bacris took advantage of their close personal relationship with Mustapha. In the regency, business and diplomacy were conducted by means of the establishment of personal relationships and the ability to make direct appeals. This was one of the many reasons why the post of *muqaddam* was so important, since it gave the direct access the Bacris needed. In the case of the *Good Hope*, because of their standing in the regency, they were able to have the *khaznadji*, or prime minister, write to reiterate and clarify Mustapha's veiled threats. "Do not be surprised," he wrote, "if many of your consul's requests to the dey have been refused up to now, when you have had so little regard for what he, a new sovereign, has asked of you."[44] This was the type of approach that placed the debt at the highest level of diplomatic relations, not that this was any guarantee of repayment.

As their relationship with the regency's elite suggests, the Bacris were very much at home in Algiers, and this contributed

42. Plantet, *Correspondance des deys d'Alger*, vol. 2, 480–81. Mustapha to executive directory, September 17, 1798.

43. AMAE 8CCC/44, p. 92, October 1818, Pierre Deval, *Mémoire analytique*.

44. Plantet, *Correspondance des Deys d'Alger*, vol. 2, 483–84. Khaznadji or prime minister of Algiers, to Talleyrand. September 22, 1798.

significantly to their success. The Bacris' implantation in the regency meant that they dealt with everyone there—Jew, Muslim, and Turk alike. The Bacris' dealings, which traversed cultures and religions, serve as a reminder of what is lost when the history of Jews in the Mediterranean is considered as somehow separate from other histories. The Bacris did not operate on the basis of division. They simply occupied any space that they perceived to be available and profitable. They undertook trade on behalf of members of the Algerian elite, and also acted as agents for them. Jacob saw to the needs of Algerian dignitaries himself in Marseilles, and ensured they were taken care of in other ports where the Bacris had agents. The Bacris did business for and with various deys. They always had papers from the dey, often acting as his agent, exporting goods for his account, or bringing in luxury products on his orders. When Jacob moved to Marseilles in 1795, Hassan sent a letter of recommendation to the convention, urging the French government to regard Bacri with favor, since he was his "merchant in charge of the dey's commissions."[45] In 1798, Joseph loaded 1,362 barrels of brandy, 150 barrels of Malaga, and 630 measures of canary seed for Lisbon on behalf of the new dey, Mustapha. In the same year, again acting as the dey's agent, he shipped 102 barrels and 20 half barrels of wine, 341 barrels of brandy, 154 reams of paper, 68 crates of soap and 18 barrels of Malaga wine. This was on Joseph's own boat, a polacca named the *Vekilargy* after the office of naval minister in the regency—perhaps a strategic gesture of deference. This ship was to return to Algiers, with merchandise that the dey had ordered.[46]

Members of the Bacri family also served as diplomatic brokers. The Bacris were not entirely unique in these dealings. Many Jewish traders in Algiers took advantage of their local knowledge and the lucrative opportunities available to offer their services as diplomatic go-betweens, helping consuls find their feet in this foreign world. The Jewish elite of Algiers had a long tradition of acting as brokers in this game of diplomacy.[47] Consuls would appoint Jews as official

45. Plantet, *Correspondance des Deys d'Alger*, vol. 2, 455–56.
46. Haddey, *Le Livre d'or des israélites algériens*, 68.
47. See, for example, Heinsen-Roach, *Consuls and Captives*, ch. 6, "A True Public Minister: Consuls and Jewish Mediators," 118–37.

brokers.[48] Such was the case with Isaac Bensamon, a faithful servant to Britain for several years. He was even acting consul at times when there was no Briton in Algiers to fill the post. Isaac Saportès had been in service to the French consul, like his father before him, until he was ousted by Naphtali.

In the scope of their activities, the Bacris were doing what the community's elite had always done. Their networks around the Mediterranean, their ability to communicate with Europeans, and their status in regency society made them ideal brokers. But it was the timing of their cornering of the wheat market in Algiers that catapulted them into an unprecedented negotiating position, and thus into new fields of renown. Key to their notoriety, also, was the fact that, unlike their predecessors, rather than attach themselves to just one consulate, they worked between all comers and the dey. This is what singled them out from their fellow trading Jews and made them equally well-known by all. It was also what placed them right at the heart of the war as it played out in Algiers. All those powers with pretensions in the Mediterranean had consuls present in the regency: France, Britain, and the United States, but also Spain and Portugal, Holland, Denmark, and Sweden, and various Italian states, often represented by other consuls already present. Once again, it was Mordecai who laid the way for his brothers. One evening, on March 22, 1794, a Dutch squadron, commanded by Rear Admiral Pieter, Baron Melvill van Carnbee, from a military family of Scottish descent, laid anchor in the Bay of Algiers. The dey sent Mordecai to find out what the Dutch wanted, but a highly offended Baron Melvill gave Mordecai very short shrift. The normal custom was to send one of the European consuls as intermediary, and here, instead, was the dey's Jew. Melvill must have come around, though, as just a few days later he concluded a peace treaty, negotiated by Mordecai. It did not come cheap: Melvill paid cash and naval munitions as an addition to the annual tribute, as well as gifts to mark the peace. Later that same year, in November, Carlos IV, the King of Spain, paid the Bacris the sum of forty thousand Spanish reals, in recognition of the "loyalty and zeal" that they had shown as censals

48. The word used to describe Bensamon and others like him was *censal*, a Spanish word signifying broker, or middleman.

to his consulate in Algiers. When Hassan sent Charles Mace, the British Consul, away in disgrace, Sir Gilbert Elliot, British viceroy in Corsica, dispatched Lord Frederick North to Algiers to clear up the diplomatic mess that Mace had left behind. North reported that he was able to profit "very considerably" from Mordecai Bacri's "great influence" over the dey. But while Hassan initially agreed to North's requests, he soon changed his mind. It was Mordecai who "threw himself at the Dey's feet," persuading the fickle Hassan to recant. North plied the dey with gifts to mollify him, purchasing "a most magnificent pair of diamond earrings for the dey's wife, a beautiful pearl and diamond necklace and earrings for his daughter and four diamond watches and as many rings for the dey's wife's two uncles, his chief secretary of state, and his Jew broker"—none other than Mordecai Bacri.[49] North spent fifteen thousand Spanish crowns, and it is entirely possible that this sum was advanced to him by a member of the family firm.

In the eyes of the Bacri family, all were equal in the world of business, perhaps because they understood this in terms of personal relationships, rather than hierarchies of need or status. Everyone was a potential client, including foreign consuls. In Marseilles, Jacob dealt with consuls from all over Europe, as well as from America, as a matter of course. He would act as a financial and trade agent, as well as a fixer. He sent bills of exchange for Tunis to the long-standing French consul there, Jacques-Philippe Devoize, effectively using Devoize as his agent.[50] He acted as a financial intermediary for the longest-serving French consul in Algiers, Charles-François

49. TNA FO 3/8, p. 11, January 3, 1796, Frederick North to the Duke of Portland, Secretary of State for the Home Department.

50. ADBR 39 E 21, n.p., 30 germinal an 12 (April 20, 1804), Jacob to Devoize, Tunis. Traders operated using a financial instrument called the bill of exchange. Once trade reached beyond personal networks, "in an environment dominated by private information, spatial separation, and limited communication," the bill of exchange allowed for the establishment of trust. With this bill, a merchant in Algiers could request his agent or bank in Paris, Amsterdam, London, Malaga, Livorno, or any other distant city, to pay a certain amount to a third party, at a set date in the future. The agent had to endorse the bill—that is, to sign it and agree to pay—for it to become valid. Endorsement also made the agent liable to pay, according to a mechanism called the joint liability rule. This rule, legally enforceable across most of Europe, "tied merchants together in joint liability." The joint liability rule, therefore, protected the merchant, and enabled long-distance trade between strangers. Aoki Santarosa, "Financing Long-Distance Trade," 691, 694.

Dubois-Thainville.[51] It is worthy of note that the Bacris dealt closely with Spain, when the state was generally seen as the enemy by the descendants of those Jews who had been forced to leave there. Jacob was clearly very much at ease with the Spanish diplomatic network. He made use of the Spanish ambassador's mail delivery from Paris to Madrid, holding it up for a day in Marseilles, so that he might include his own letters to his agents in that city, Pierre Baille and Co.[52] He worked with the Spanish consul in Marseilles to help another Spaniard, who was stuck and unwell near Paris.[53] In 1801, Pedro Téllez-Girón, ninth Duke of Osuna, and a Spanish military commander in the Revolutionary Wars, wrote to Jacob, asking him to arrange to send wheat to Spain.[54] In Algiers, Joseph acted as commercial agent for the Spanish consulate for some years, and such was the relationship of trust and closeness, that the Spanish consulate was where he chose to register important documents for posterity, including the one denouncing his brother, Jacob.

The Bacris dealt regularly with the minor powers too. Matthias Skjöldebrand had been appointed Swedish consul in Algiers in 1792 (Sweden had signed a treaty with the regency in 1729—the Mediterranean was the main destination of its merchant fleet, seeking raw materials to import and new markets for Swedish products).[55] In 1801, Skjöldebrand had left Algiers and was in Paris. Johan Norderling had taken up the Algiers post. In Marseilles, Jacob worked as go-between. He wrote on behalf of his "friend," Skjöldebrand, advising of the issuing of bills of exchange and payments due,[56] and then wrote to Skjöldebrand himself, to keep him informed of the transactions' progress, as well as to remind him of funds Skjöldebrand owed him.[57] At the same time, he was making loans to the new consul, Norderling, about to depart Marseilles for Algiers. Norderling asked him, also, to make funds available to his wife, who was to remain in

51. ADBR 39 E 21, p. 79, 3 messidor an 10 (June 22, 1802), Jacob to Hervas, Paris.
52. ADBR 39 E 21, p. 29, 18 thermidor an 9 (August 6, 1801), Jacob to Pierre Baille and Co., Madrid.
53. ADBR 39 E 21, p. 82, January 8, 1802, Jacob to Dié frères, Alicante.
54. ADBR 39 E 21, p. 36, September 4, 1801, Jacob to Duke of Osuna, Madrid.
55. Kämpe, "Competition and Cooperation," 37.
56. ADBR 39 E 21, p. 17, July 1, 1801, Jacob to Jean Janssen, Hamburg.
57. ADBR 39 E 21, p. 20, 20 messidor an 9 (July 9, 1801), Jacob to Matthias Skjöldebrand, Paris.

Marseilles.[58] His agents in Lyons—Seguin and Poujol—had already advanced funds to the new Swedish consul as he passed through the city.[59] Clearly, Jacob had been in touch with Norderling before he reached France. Specie was in short supply in the regency, and the Bacris, who bought the different currencies that came in on captured ships, were always available to act as banker. As US consul Richard O'Brien put it, "for the good of the nation if you want money to carry a point you must go to B&B." And, according to O'Brien, the French, Spanish, Dutch, Swedes, and Americans regularly did just that.[60]

Mordecai worked particularly closely with the Americans, who needed to make peace with the regency. David Humphreys, the US Minister to Lisbon, was charged with negotiating a treaty. Richard O'Brien had remained in Algiers after his manumission, in order to use his familiarity with the regency to assist his government. In 1794, as negotiations were beginning, O'Brien wrote to Humphreys to advise that the dey had rejected the terms of the peace offerings made by the United States, and was instead making his own, much inflated demands. In O'Brien's opinion, the United States needed "willing, trustworthy participants" who could negotiate on their behalf. French diplomats might be prevailed upon to help, but if they would not, then "the Bockeries, Jew Merchants is a good house for Algiers of influence with the dey and Ministry, and for their own interest, or to serve themselves, if commissioned, they will make the greatest exertions to bring about the peace for the US."[61] But James Monroe, the US Minister to France, was concerned at the lack of progress in peace negotiations, so he sent his friend, the

58. ADBR 39 E 21, p. 60, 19 and 20 brumaire an 10 (November 10 and 11, 1801), Jacob to Jacob Gozlan, Marseille.

59. ADBR 39 E 21, p. 78, 28 frimaire an 10 (December 19, 1801), Jacob to Seguin and Poujol, Lyons.

60. NARA Atlanta M23, roll 6, vol. 5, p. 244, January 10, 1801, O'Brien to Secretary of State Marshall.

61. *Naval Documents Related to the United States Wars with the Barbary Powers*, vol. 1. *Naval Operations Including Diplomatic Background from 1785 through 1801*, 83, O'Brien to Humphreys. O'Brien was known for his colorful turn of phrase. Joel Barlow wrote to Monroe to recommend O'Brien for the position, noting, "The blemishes that arise from a defect in the rudimental arts of education will appear only in his correspondence, the jargon of this country called 'lingua franca' in which all business is done by word of mouth, puts the scholar and sailor on a level, and the University of Algiers is better for certain purposes than that of New Haven." Cited in Parker, *Uncle Sam in Barbary*, 109.

businessman Joel Barlow, to settle matters in Algiers. By the time
Barlow arrived in the regency, in March 1796, negotiations had
indeed been progressing, and then stalling, while Joseph Donaldson, special envoy on the ground in Algiers, waited for the funds
that were to come from London, to ransom 150 enslaved American sailors. The government was concerned that a failure to free
the sailors could threaten its "still fragile authority."[62] Mordecai,
"a warm friend," stepped into the breach, offering to lend Barlow
the funds he needed, meaning that the American slaves could be
released.[63] A Bacri boat bore them away from Algiers. But the
United States delayed honoring its financial pledges, and Hassan's
patience wore thin, so that even Mordecai who, as Barlow wrote,
had "as much art in this sort of management as any man we ever
knew, [and] more influence with the dey than all the regency put
together," was barely able to maintain the dey's good humor with
regard to the Americans.[64] Barlow, in the hope of reestablishing
goodwill, summoned Mordecai, and instructed him to go to the dey
on behalf of the United States to offer a new American ship of twenty
guns, to be presented to his daughter. Mordecai observed to Barlow
that twenty-four guns would make a more attractive prospect. Barlow agreed, and Mordecai went to the dey, to return sometime later
with the message that the ship must have thirty-six guns. In gratitude for his success, Barlow and Donaldson gave Mordecai eighteen
thousand dollars, which he was to distribute among the officers of
state as he saw necessary and keep the balance for himself.[65] After
all, in Barlow's eyes, Mordecai "had saved the Americans countless
times from disaster."[66]

The ship, named the *Crescent*, arrived in early 1798. After Barlow's departure, and in the absence of a new consul, the Secretary
of State Timothy Pickering wrote to "Joseph C. Bacri and Company"
to appoint them US Agents, along with the brother of the Swedish

---

62. Buel, *Joel Barlow*, 1.
63. NARA Atlanta M23, vol. 1, part 1, p. 121, April 3, 1796, Barlow to Humphreys.
64. *Naval Documents*, vol. 1, 144, cited in Rosenstock, "The House of Bacri and Busnach," 348.
65. *Naval Documents*, vol. 1, 143, April 5, 1796, Barlow and Donaldson to Humphreys.
66. Buel, *Joel Barlow*, 209.

ambassador, Pierre Eric Skjoldebrand.[67] He reported to Congress that Barlow and Donaldson had made "such arrangements with the house of Messrs Bacri [. . .] as will doubtless ensure the payment" of the funds owed the dey.[68] They were trusted sources of information too. Joel Barlow reported that Mordecai was able to give him the latest news—"fresher" than that supplied by a French consular official—regarding the capture and release of a US vessel.[69] The Bacris became major trading partners of Barlow, shipping goods to and from the United States, and around the Mediterranean. Mordecai was still working for the Americans in 1798, when, as O'Brien reported, "our friends the Jews here" sent funds to Tunis and Tripoli, again on their behalf, to settle America's accounts there.[70]

The Bacris provided a reliable source of specie when this was in short supply due to unreliable shipping, but it was their control of the wheat trade that was their bargaining chip in the war. For France and Britain, the contest in the regency coalesced around this primary resource. Britain wanted the wheat too. Already in 1790, the English consul Charles Logie, following orders, set out the state of the grain market in Algiers, and the possibilities for Britain of accessing that grain. The situation was not promising: demand was increasing following the peace with Spain, he reported, and the French and the Jews had a monopoly over exports.[71] Britain had permanent garrisons in the Mediterranean, on Minorca and Gibraltar, and both needed to be provisioned. Hassan's favorable attentions, and goodwill, were vital. Standing behind Hassan were the Bacris.

In terms of this contest, the Bacris' agreement with France had pleasing outcomes for the latter beyond the fact of the supply of wheat on credit. The wheat that the Bacris were to ship to France was all the more precious because Britain, now at war with France, did not want the enemy to have it. This was the nature of the contest in Algiers. Both powers sought advantage in the wheat trade, as

67. *Naval Documents*, vol.1, 214, August 31, 1797, Pickering to Joseph Bacri.

68. *American State Papers*, 553.

69. AMAE 8CCC/32, p. 412, 24 messidor an 4 (July 5, 1796), Algiers, copy of a letter from Barlow to Louis-Alexandre d'Allois d'Herculais, Special Envoy to Algiers.

70. *Naval Documents*, vol. 1, 239, March 1, 1798, O'Brien to Humphreys.

71. TNA FO 3/7, p. 12, April 27, 1790, Logie to ?

well as with the other raw products the regency had to offer. Both sought to establish exclusive agreements with the regency, including shutting the other out. The Dey Hassan himself told Vallière that the English consul, Charles Mace, "had begged him, in the name of his king, not to supply any aid, of any kind, to the French."[72] Keeping the wheat out of French hands was a priority of high order for Britain: Mace had arrived in Algiers just two weeks before, but as he explained to Home Secretary Henry Dundas, he made straight for the palace after landing and within an hour, he had an audience with Hassan.[73] Happily for Vallière, Hassan was resistant to Britain's "monstrous appeals." In early 1794, Vallière could report that the dey was faithful to his friends, that his "good disposition towards us, the essential service that he is working to render us, his expressions regarding the republic, the interest he takes in its fates, and his behavior, candidly and publicly pronouncing in our favor, are sacred premises for our attachment and our recognition."[74]

In 1794, when Vallière was confirming the wheat supply for France, Hassan had held the British off. But Hassan's goodwill fluctuated, and fortunes changed with his moods. Eighteen months later, in mid-1795, Mace wrote triumphantly to William Cavendish-Bentinck, 3rd Duke of Portland, and the new home secretary, that he had succeeded "beyond [his] utmost expectation" in negotiating terms with Hassan that were favorable to Britain. Britain had invaded and occupied Corsica, intending to use the island as a central Mediterranean base. British authorities wanted to be certain that the coral fishermen of Corsica would not lose the exclusive right to the Algerian coastline that they had enjoyed as French citizens. Coral fishing was highly lucrative. His Majesty's British subjects had also been granted the choice of raw products from Algiers, including hides, wool, and wax, at the same price paid by France; freedom to enter all of the regency's ports to purchase corn; and, perhaps most importantly, that "the rights and privileges which the French African company have hitherto enjoyed shall be entirely annulled and abolished," and transferred to Britain. These were "eminent privileges," which the

72. AMAE 8CCC/32, p. 87, 10 pluviôse an 2 (January 29, 1794), Vallière to François-Louis Deforgues, Ministre des affaires étrangères.

73. TNA FO 3/7, p. 132, January 12, 1794, Mace to Dundas.

74. AMAE 8CCC/32, p. 87, 10 pluviôse an 2 (January 29, 1794), Vallière to Deforgues.

French had "boasted of" for many years.[75] This was indeed a victory, given that Mace faced difficult diplomatic challenges, including interceding on behalf of Portugal after their navy burned an Algerian ship and continued to block the Strait of Gibraltar to the regency's corsairs, and trying to persuade Hassan of Britain's claim to two hundred Corsican fishermen, captured while fishing for Algerian coral. (The dey had been slow to accept Corsica as British, and this recognition had not yet been granted.)

French and British consuls wrote the Bacris into their conflict, and this set the stage for the way they were to be perceived over the years to come. This was war, and to the parties in it, it was beyond outrageous that the Bacris dealt with both sides as it suited them. Mace, for example, complained that he had to work in the face of "most of the consuls, and every Jew merchant here" attempting everything against British affairs, and the French, showering Hassan with gifts.[76] As Mace's complaint suggests, the Bacris came to sit in the middle of the Franco-British contest in Algiers. Not only did relations with the dey, and thus the fortunes of trade, depend largely on them, but both French and British diplomatic representatives believed that the Bacris were working against them, in favor of their competitor. Even the *Good Hope* could be seen in this light. Indeed, Talleyrand considered the affair of the *Good Hope* to be simply another example of the "intrigues that [the Bacris] use to favor English trade," and new proof of their devotion to the English cause.[77]

The belief that the Bacris were at the heart of the contest for produce and favorable relations in Algiers established a basis for perceptions of the family as malign and inordinately powerful. They appeared so to foreign consuls because of their refusal to acknowledge the authority and power of others. This was, in part, because of the nature of relations in the regency. Because Mordecai, and after him, Joseph and Naphtali, had personal relationships with the dey and ruling elite, or divan, and because they treated foreign consuls in the regency equally personally, consuls perceived them as being in positions of great power. This explains the sometimes hyperbolic,

75. TNA FO 3/7, p. 191, June 21, 1795, Mace to Portland.
76. TNA FO 3/7, p. 160, January 6, 1795, Mace to Portland.
77. AMAE 8CCC/34, n.p., 17 floréal an 6 (May 6, 1798), Talleyrand to Moltedo.

even hysterical nature of their accusations. The Bacris did not care about the priorities of different states, and only gave attention to their needs when prices motivated them to do so. This did not go down well with foreign consuls, trying to secure a reliable food supply in the midst of war. Thus, for example, in late 1796, the Bacris began sending wheat to Gibraltar, rather than to France. Demand in France had dried up, and the Bacris sought a new market. In June 1796, Vallière had been replaced by Jeanbon Saint-André, a Protestant priest who had embraced the revolution and voted for the death of King Louis XVI. Saint-André was obsessed with maintaining the honor and dignity of the nation he represented; honor and dignity that, as he saw it, were regularly trampled underfoot by Bacris. For Saint-André, the diversion of wheat to Gibraltar was an example of the Bacris' untrustworthiness, a plot against France, driven by the Bacris, together with Britain, Sweden, and the United States.[78] In the context of the war, a purely economic decision became, from the perspective of the French agent, an act of undiluted politics.

In late 1796, Saint-André reported home that the English were busy establishing trading companies in Algiers and Oran. They were being given "powerful" help by the Swedish consul Matthias Skjöldebrand, an enemy of France, and by "the Jews of the country," Mordecai Bacri and Naphtali Busnach.[79] France needed to bring the Bacris and Naphtali under control. They posed a danger to French trade. If peace were brokered, nothing would prevent them from making Algiers their warehouse, reestablishing their Italian branch, and "driving French trade out of Africa."[80] They were enriching themselves "at the nation's expense."[81] The Bacris, Saint-André explained, were powerful. Their goal was to make money and, to that end, they had developed significant political clout in Algiers.

> They promise the small states of Europe peace, and make it; if they are
> discontented, they declare war on them. A question of the redemption
> of slaves? They are the mediators in it. A European merchant offends

78. Touati, *Le Commerce du blé*, 351.
79. AMAE 8CCC/33, p. 96, 1 nivôse an 5 (December 21, 1796), St André to Charles-François Delacroix, Ministre des relations extérieures.
80. AMAE 8CCC/33, p. 96, 1 nivôse an 5 (December 21, 1796), St André to Delacroix.
81. AMAE 8CCC/33, p. 96, 1 nivôse an 5 (December 21, 1796), St André to Delacroix.

them? They chase him out. . . . The cause of our loss of influence in Barbary is the growth in credit of the Jews.[82]

It would be a good thing for France to "humiliate these Jews a little,"[83] and Saint-André knew how this might be done. He proposed that France take advantage of what he called "their financial interest." If the government withheld funds it owed to the Bacris, it could be sure of their submission.[84] If France did not "push the English aside, and crush the Jews," he stated, then its chance would be lost forever. Thus Saint-André made clear what he saw to be the vital, linking triangular relationship in Algiers: France's fortunes against its eternal competitor, and the Bacri family. Saint-André's suggestion was taken up by the foreign minister, Charles-François Delacroix, and relayed to the executive directory. Using the debt, Delacroix explained, France could prevent the Bacris from losing sight of France's interests and force them to be more circumspect in their dealings with the English.[85] Clearly, he trusted Saint-André's judgement.

The Bacris' "financial interests" were to loom large over Franco-Algerian relations, and over the Franco-British contest in the regency. From Saint-André's perspective, the two great threats to French ascendancy—the Bacris and the English—were linked. In late 1796, he wrote to Paris that (Mordecai) Bacri "wants to add to French gold that of Britain, without reflecting on the gratitude he owes the former."[86] The Bacris were organizing hunting outings for the naval minister, Skjöldebrand, and the British consul. This was a concern because they were capable of arranging preferential trade arrangements for the British.[87] But the latter also baulked at the Bacris' "entrepreneurial cupidity."[88] In 1795, Charles Mace wrote to the Duke of Portland, complaining that the House attempted "everything against the British affairs in this place."[89] His successor,

82. Cited in Esquer, *Les Commencements d'un empire*, 20.
83. AMAE 8CCC/33, p. 96, 1 nivôse an 5 (December 21, 1796), St André to Delacroix.
84. AMAE 8CCC/33, p. 96, 1 nivôse an 5 (December 21, 1796), St André to Delacroix.
85. Delacroix to Ramel, 6 floréal an V (April 25, 1797), cited in Plantet, *Correspondance des Deys d'Alger*, vol. 2, 463.
86. AMAE 8CCC/33, p. 100, 3 nivôse an 5 (December 23, 1796), St André to Delacroix.
87. AMAE 8CCC/33, p. 100, 3 nivôse an 5 (December 23, 1796), St André to Delacroix.
88. AMAE 8CCC/33, p. 100, 3 nivôse an 5 (December 23, 1796), St André to Delacroix.
89. TNA FO 3/7, p. 160, January 6, 1795, Mace to Portland.

John Falcon, continued to insist that Bacri—now Joseph—was "certainly a very active agent of the French government," and had always been so.[90] Britain, too, looked to its dignity. It was unthinkable that it might be reduced "to the same servility and degradation" as other European powers. But good relations were important, not just for the sake of dignity, but also for trade, and Britain was prepared to go to striking lengths to maintain good relations.[91] Their own dealings with the Bacris and the *Good Hope* demonstrate this.

The fate of the *Good Hope* in the hands of the French judicial system is unclear. But just over two years after it was taken by the French corsair, the ship reappeared in the record once again, this time, as a vessel owned by the Bacris and taken by an English corsair. It is possible that the Bacris took ownership of the *Good Hope* from the Danes. When their cargos, shipped on Danish vessels, were lost to corsairs, the Bacris would commonly demand recompense. Von Rehbinder, the Danish consul, had asked Hassan not to ship goods belonging to Algerian subjects in Danish vessels without first ensuring full safety at sea. The dey initially granted this request, but then changed his mind, and as a Danish inquiry reported, this was at the instigation of none other than Joseph Bacri. Algerian cargos (belonging to the Bacris) set forth from Algiers in Danish ships, and they were indeed confiscated by the British. Around the same time as the first taking of the *Good Hope*, and over a period of three years, on several occasions, the Danes had to pay compensation to Joseph. Joseph's demand, on one occasion, that the Danes pay 10,000 Spanish pesos for the loss of cargo on their ship *Enterprise*, was described by a Danish inquiry as "perhaps the most unreasonable of all made in this epoch, except perhaps by Bacri's last. "The consul," the report went on, "entered into negotiations with the Jew, not because he believed he was right, but because it was in [the Jews'] power to disturb the peace at any given time."[92] Eventually, in 1800, after two years of wearying negotiations, agreement between the Danes and the dey was reached. On that occasion, Naphtali was the

90. TNA FO 3/8, p. 140, April 26, 1799, Falcon to Home Secretary William Wickham.

91. TNA FO 3/8, p. 59, March 19, 1797, Richard Masters to Portland.

92. Danish National Archives (Rigsarkivet), Ministry of Foreign Affairs, Algiers, Cases concerning Baron Rehbinder's inauguration as Danish Consul in Algiers, serial number 2867, pp. 61–62.

intermediary between the dey and the Danish delegation, of which the Danish consul was an active member.

In early August 1801, Jacob wrote to the Algerian Ambassador in Britain to confirm that his mail had been forwarded to the dey, but he needed a favor also. A Bacri boat, the *Good Hope*, had been taken by a British corsair. Could the ambassador, Jacob asked, protest to the British government in the strongest terms?[93] Later that same month, the Algerian ambassador made Jacob's protest to Home Secretary Lord Pelham.[94] Pelham sought information, and a month later, he was in a position to respond to the ambassador. Pelham reminded the ambassador that all vice admiralty courts in the Mediterranean had been directed to pause any proceedings, of any type, that concerned the Dey of Algiers or any of his subjects, until the consul in Algiers had been informed. Any funds owing in a case that should not have gone to the vice admiralty court would be returned to Algiers as soon as was possible after the verdict. And Pelham was pleased to add that the King had ordered gifts to be taken to the dey when the ambassador returned to Algiers and was "graciously pleased" to release the ambassador from taking leave of the King. His Majesty was, as Pelham explained, "unwilling to give you the trouble of going so far as Windsor."[95] As well as revealing much about the way the Bacris worked, the story of the *Good Hope* shows us, also, that for the sake of their respective nations, French and British diplomatic staff felt that they had no choice but to pacify the significant irritant that was the Bacri family.

Foreign representatives and their governments were prepared to accommodate the Bacris because they understood them to be powerful. It was French and British, as well as US perceptions, at all levels, of what Naphtali Busnach, as well as Mordecai, Joseph, and Jacob Bacri could do, that determined the behavior of these nations in the regency in the midst of a war that made the contest for Mediterranean resources intense. Consuls anticipated difficulty and understood difficulties that arose through the lens of their conviction that the Bacris enjoyed inordinate power in the regency. In

93. ADBR 39 E 21, p. 25, August 2, 1801, Jacob to Algerian Ambassador, London.

94. TNA FO 3/9, p. 72, August 28, 1801, Algerian Ambassador to Home Secretary Lord Pelham.

95. TNA FO 3/9, p. 96, October 10, 1801, Pelham to Algerian Ambassador.

the early years of the Revolutionary Wars in the Mediterranean, Mace, Falcon, and Saint-André were convinced that Joseph and Naphtali were working for the other, frustrating their ambitions, needs, and desires.

The Bacris thrived in the regency, and in the war, because they were deeply enmeshed in systems and networks that they—for the most part—knew how to manipulate to their advantage. If they lost the occasional cargo, as happened when the *Good Hope* was taken for France, they could have the dey pressure foreign powers to recoup the value, or to insist that the ship be returned. In the regency, their relationship with the state was deeply personal, a matter of establishing close links with the dey and his ministers and cultivating and maintaining these. This was the nature of relations in Algiers, and the Bacris were skilled in this particular art. But the decades ahead were to present constant challenges to the Bacris: the war was to come to the regency, and the Bacris would suffer crippling sequestrations, assassinations, and massive fraud. How they were able to continue their business through all the vicissitudes and difficulties they faced, whether others continued to see them as powerful and why, and how this determined the path of imperial contest in the regency is the subject of the chapters to follow.

CHAPTER TWO

War Comes to
the Regency

FOR AS LONG as Algiers remained neutral in the Revolutionary
Wars, the Bacris had been able to profit. But in 1798, Napoleon
invaded Egypt. The Sultan, furious, forced Mustapha to declare war
on France. This chapter is set in this time of war between France
and the regency, and the fragile peace between the two that followed. Rather than standing aloof from conflict, and profiting from
it as well, the Bacris now found themselves at its heart. Through the
deepening of contest, and the diplomatic successes and failures of
Britain and France, the centrality of the Bacris becomes clear. As war
came to the regency, and thus to the Bacris, we see the ways in which
the Bacris were able to influence and manage diplomatic relations, as
well as the limitations of their capacity to do so. And we see, equally,
the consequences of consuls' inability—sometimes willful—to understand the culture of relations of power in the regency.

In one sense, war was fundamental to the functioning of the
regency. Over the centuries when corsairing constituted its major
source of wealth, it maintained hostilities with smaller powers, so
that its ships might legitimately attack their merchantmen. The
French, the British and the Spanish were aware of this system. They
sanctioned it, implicitly, and each made use of it to their own advantage. So long as ships belonging to the Italian States, to Denmark,
or to Portugal, for example, were under attack, French, British,

and Spanish boats could sail the Mediterranean freely. The Revolutionary Wars in the Mediterranean changed this. Where before the regency had made war and peace at will, now it was pulled into a dispute that it did not want. In May 1798, with what Boyd Hilton termed his characteristically "audacious rapidity," Napoleon set sail from Toulon on France's Mediterranean coast with an army of forty thousand men.[1] Headed for Egypt, his so-called Army of the Orient landed in Alexandria on July 1. French troops captured the city quickly, and on July 3, they set out for a two-week journey across the desert to Cairo. At the pyramids on July 21, the French army subdued the sultan's soldiers, and three days later, they marched into Cairo. The British fleet had withdrawn from the Mediterranean at the end of 1796, after Spain had joined France in the war, and at the beginning of 1798, there was not a single British battleship east of Gibraltar. Rumors that France was preparing a massive armament in the Mediterranean brought the British sailing at speed back into that sea. The goal of the armament was unclear, but the British were always sensitive to any possible threat to their trade routes to India. The commander of the Mediterranean fleet, Lord St. Vincent, was ordered to send a few ships, under command of Rear Admiral Nelson, to ascertain the expedition's intended destination. Nelson reached Toulon on May 31, but he was too late; the French fleet had sailed twelve days earlier. He promptly set out to find it. On August 1, Nelson came upon the French fleet in Abu Qir Bay, near the mouth of the Nile, and in a stunning victory for the British navy, Nelson's ships completely destroyed the fleet. Soon after, on September 11, the Ottoman sultan Selim declared war on France. He sent orders to his regencies to do the same.

In Algiers, Mustapha resisted the order to declare war on France, and Joseph and Naphtali focused all their efforts on ensuring that he did not change his mind. They had considerable interest in doing so: if France and the regency were at war, the payment of the funds owed to the Bacris could not help but become a more distant prospect. Mustapha could not deny a direct order, however. On December 19, a bailiff sent by the sultan arrived in Algiers, bringing the silk ceremonial caftan that commemorated and confirmed

1. Hilton, *A Mad, Bad, and Dangerous People?*, 88.

Mustapha's appointment. The sultan's bailiff had also brought the order, effectively forcing the dey to make the declaration marking the outbreak of hostilities between the regency and France.

The French consul in Algiers was Dominique-Marie Moltedo. Moltedo had succeeded Saint-André, who had been named to the prized posting of Smyrna. Notwithstanding the formal demands coming from the Sultan's court, Moltedo had reason to believe that the regime in Algiers had no desire to declare war against France. He had employed Joseph and Naphtali to ascertain the regime's attitude toward France. They had assured him, as had others with contacts in the palace, that he had nothing to fear. Thus reassured, Moltedo proceeded to the official welcoming ceremony for the bailiff, took part in the ceremonial kissing of hands, and went home. Moltedo had not long before received orders to return to France, to take up a new post. He remained in Algiers only to await the arrival of his successor, Charles François Dubois-Thainville. But with the declaration of war, all French citizens in the regency were vulnerable, as events were to show. Moltedo was to be forced to wait longer than he would have thought reasonable, and to do so in unpleasant circumstances.

Early in the morning of December 21, two days after the arrival of the sultan's bailiff, several more bailiffs paid a call on Moltedo. Forcing open the front door of his home, they entered. Moltedo, roused from his bed, had to dress hurriedly, as did all those present in his home: his nephew Jean-Luc; his personal secretary Michel Lecointe, and this man's son, also Michel, aged just ten; Moltedo's domestic servant, a Corsican named François Ucciani; and Joseph Charles Astoin-Sielve, the consular secretary. All were taken to the prison. At the same time, other bailiffs were also visiting the home of Dominique Joseph Paret, a French merchant living in Algiers, as well as any other French known to be present in the town, including several other men of business, and three priests: seventeen unfortunates in all. The bailiffs also arrested five women, the wives of the merchants, and Astoin-Sielve's sister Marie Victoire, taking them all to the home of Antoine Pierre Fraissinet, a Frenchman, merchant, and consul of the recently established Batavian Republic.[2]

2. The Batavian Republic was created in the Netherlands on January 19, 1795 through a popular revolution, with the help of French revolutionary forces.

When all the French men were gathered together, they were taken to the forge to be shackled, and then delivered to the *bagnio*, or slave quarters. There they spent the first night of their imprisonment with the other Christian slaves, on beds of straw, with nothing but the clothes on their back, unable to sleep comfortably because of the iron rings around their ankles. After five days, on December 26, Moltedo was able to send the first news of their arrest to his foreign minister Talleyrand. In a letter headed "from the galleys of Algiers," written in haste, Moltedo traced "the pathetic picture of the punishment that I suffer, along with the rest of the nation, seventeen in number."[3]

From the misery in which the French now found themselves came a stirring tale of republican courage. When news of their arrest broke in Algiers, the Spanish ambassador and his consul, as well as the consuls of Denmark and the Batavian Republic, had rushed to help. The Spanish ambassador, Don Manuel de las Heras, had asked the Algerian authorities to remove the chains from the boy Michel Lecointe, and this request had been granted. But the young boy refused to accept any relief until his father had the same, and if this were denied him, the ten-year-old stated, then he would suffer as his father did, and with courage. The boy's defiant stand was reported by all who witnessed it: Moltedo was greatly admiring of the way the boy expressed his "budding patriotism."[4]

For all the detained Frenchmen, including young Michel, a routine of work and waiting set in. During the day, the men were taken to forced labor, while the boys and Moltedo remained in the slave quarters. And in this routine they awaited news. When would the sultan's bailiff leave? Would they be allowed to return to their homes once he was gone? (French subjects in Tripoli had been released immediately after the departure of the sultan's messenger.) Was their harsh treatment simply Mustapha's way of pleasing the sultan's messenger? If, as Moltedo wrote bitterly to Talleyrand, "they could count on nothing," they were at least consoled by the "infinite number of honest people," who sought to improve their situation, and who took turns to keep the prisoners fed.[5] Among this infinite number, as well as the

---

3. AMAE 8CCC/34, p. 298, 6 nivôse an 7 (December 26, 1798), Moltedo to Talleyrand.
4. AMAE 8CCC/34, p. 298, 6 nivôse an 7 (December 26, 1798), Moltedo to Talleyrand.
5. AMAE 8CCC/34, p. 298, 6 nivôse an 7 (December 26, 1798), Moltedo to Talleyrand.

consuls, were Joseph and Naphtali. It was largely due to Joseph and Naphtali's efforts that six days after their arrest, on December 27, the prisoners' chains were removed altogether, and replaced with an iron ring, which they were allowed to take off to sleep.

It was to be a long time before Talleyrand received Moltedo's letter. The news of the arrest and imprisonment of his consular staff and all French citizens in Algiers did not reach him until late January, almost a month after the event. Word came to him from various sources. Augustin Guys, an agent in Talleyrand's own ministry stationed in Marseilles, received and forwarded the news from the French consul—Poiret—in Alicante, who had received word from de las Heras. Thus it was by means of letters from the Spanish ambassador, but also the Spanish consul, Michel de Larreu, and Joseph Bacri, that Talleyrand finally heard the terrible news.

From de las Heras, Talleyrand learned that the consulate, and the homes of the other French arrested had been locked, and the keys taken to Mustapha; that Sielve's sister, Paret's wife, and another Frenchwoman had been taken to Fraissinet's home; that on hearing the news, Don Manuel had rushed to see the minister of the navy, and had begged him to be allowed to supply the prisoners with their daily needs, and that the next day, it was agreed between the representatives of Spain, Denmark, and Sweden that they would take turns bringing food to the prisoners. The evening before he left Algiers, de las Heras paid a last visit to his unfortunate colleague. The Spanish ambassador described how Moltedo embraced him with tears in his eyes, and assured de las Heras that he, and all his companions, bore their punishment with the true republican courage shown by the youngest among them.

It was in these first letters that Talleyrand came to know, also, that Joseph and Naphtali had done all in their power to relieve the prisoners' suffering. Through repeated entreaties and gifts, they were able to persuade Mustapha to remove the prisoners' irons at night so that they might sleep, and, three days later, to replace the iron and chain with a simple ring. On December 28, they retrieved the keys to Paret's home and the consulate, and were able to return these to the prisoners, so that they might send people to fetch clothing. They had themselves made guarantors for any funds owed by the prisoners. It was thanks to Joseph that the prisoners' belongings had not been confiscated. "This same Bacri," wrote the Spanish consul de Larreu, "has not stopped working to obtain their complete freedom."[6] Joseph confirmed all that had been written about him. The tasks he had given himself, he wrote, had come to fruition.

By early February, Talleyrand had the final version of a full report on the situation in Algiers, ready to present to the executive directory. In this, he noted for his superiors that "the Jews"—his shorthand for Joseph and Naphtali—had given the victims "evidence of the most lively interest." Whatever might have been their motives, he went on, they were zealous in their efforts to protect the French citizens in Algiers, and indeed, they had been successful. For this reason, they had earned the right to what he called national recognition. This, Talleyrand suggested, could entail an invitation to the Jews to use their influence to have the French released from Algiers. "It could even be useful," he felt, "to express some confidence; they would be flattered by this, and would become even keener to serve us."[7]

By mid-March, it would seem, Talleyrand finally had word from Moltedo himself. The French consul had continued to write, each letter entitled "from the prisons of Algiers," updating his minister on his situation, and giving assurances of his continued loyalty, and his regard for national dignity. On January 22, it was his sorrowful duty to inform Talleyrand that three weeks after the departure of the sultan's bailiff, he and his fellows had not been allowed to return home as promised. Not only were they still being held in prison, but their treatment had worsened. Put to work loading and unloading cargoes from ships, the French prisoners were made to undertake labor done, as Sielve complained, "by the lowliest slave."[8] None of their friends had been able to bring about a change in their situation, and now this was becoming desperate. While the consuls who had taken it upon themselves to supply food had indeed done so, they could not continue indefinitely, and Moltedo had experienced the humiliation of begging, first Larreu, the Spanish consul, to commit to feeding the prisoners, and then Talleyrand, to supply funds.

6. AMAE 8CCC/34, p. 309, 1 pluviôse an 7 (January 20, 1799), Michel de Larreu to Talleyrand.

7. AMAE 8CCC/34, n.p. (322a), 18 pluviôse an 7 (February 7, 1799), "Rapport au directoire exécutif."

8. AMAE 8CCC/34, p. 347, 19 pluviôse an 7 (February 7, 1799), Astoin Sielve to Vallière.

By early February, Moltedo's suffering, seeing his fellows taken away to work each morning while he, left behind in the slave's quarters, was unable to share their punishment, had reached its peak. Then, in the morning of February 2, his interpreter arrived, together with Busnach. Moltedo was taken to the minister of the navy, or *vekilardji*, together with the three young Frenchmen. The *vekilardji* announced that the four were free to return to Moltedo's home. Moltedo reported carefully to Talleyrand that he "did not hesitate" to demand that the other prisoners be liberated also, or that those with him be freed, and he sent back to work with those still held prisoner. His protestations, while virtuous, would ultimately prove needless, since shortly afterward, all the French were released.[9] Back in their homes, all their belongings intact around them, they were nonetheless confined in daylight hours on the advice of the prime minister, who suggested that it might be dangerous for them to be seen during the day in the city's streets. But while Ramadan continued, they did not dare go out at night, either, since after dark the same streets were similarly full of people.[10]

War with the regency had brought great misfortune to the French in Algiers, but it was also disastrous for France. It cut off the supply of food to the south, just as the region was hit by drought. It made the supply of Malta, blockaded by the English, infinitely more difficult, and interrupted communication with Egypt.[11] For two centuries, France had enjoyed a practical monopoly over the export of Algerian wheat. The Revolutionary and Napoleonic wars were "fatal" for this trade.[12] When war broke out in 1793, the consequences for French shipping were immediate.[13] The destruction of the French navy at Abu Qir Bay only compounded French misery. For Britain, on the other hand, their goal, of assuring maritime security in the war had been achieved.[14] Their navy was once more ascendant, and their merchant marine could ply British trade in the

9. AMAE 8CCC/34, n.p., 18 pluviôse an 7 (February 6 1799), Moltedo to Talleyrand.

10. AMAE 8CCC/34, p. 349, 2 ventôse an 7 (February 20, 1799), Astoin Sielve to Vallière.

11. AMAE 8CCC/34, p. 360, 14 ventôse an 7 (March 4, 1799), Vallière to Talleyrand.

12. Touati, "L'Algérie au 'siècle du blé.'"

13. Marzagalli, "Le Négoce maritime et la rupture révolutionnaire," 189.

14. Duffy, "British Policy in the War against Revolutionary France," 11.

Mediterranean once again. Nelson imposed a blockade on French-controlled Alexandria to prevent the French army from escaping or being supplied. In September, he put in place a blockade around Malta, and in November, British forces captured Minorca. In a matter of months, the Mediterranean was transformed: it had become a British sea. French trade, in contrast, faced new insecurity. After war was declared, Mustapha sent out six corsairing ships, with express instructions to cruise France's Mediterranean coast and take any French ships they might find, as well as any neutral vessels bound for, or having left from a French port.

The response from France to Mustapha's decree was immediate. The executive directory decreed, in turn, that any vessel of the French navy, as well as any French corsair, should attack, capture, and confiscate the cargo of any ship sailing under the flags of Algiers, Tunisia, or Tripoli, or any merchandise from these regencies carried on a neutral ship.[15] But the game of reprisals did not stop at goods. It also expanded to include people. French citizens had been arrested in Algiers, and on January 26, the directory also ordered similar measures to be taken against Algerian subjects in France. All Algerian subjects were to be imprisoned, and all Algerian goods and properties in the Bouches-du-Rhône department, of which Marseilles was the capital, sequestered. On February 12, police in Marseilles placed seals over the home of Jacob Bacri, and over his warehouses in the same city. An embargo was placed over seven of Jacob's boats that were sitting in the harbor, loaded, ironically, to take supplies to French troops in Malta. Jacob himself was now living in Paris, and his fate was announced on March 1, in the *Moniteur universel*, the official national newspaper of the directory. "As a reprisal, in response to the atrocities which have been committed against the French in their country," Jacob, together with Simon Abucaya, Mustapha's *chargé d'affaires*, were in the Temple (once the headquarters of the Knights Templar, now a state prison), where enemies of the regime were held.[16]

15. AMAE 8CCC/34, p. 341, 27 pluviôse an 7 (February 15, 1799), "Arrêté: Droit de représailles."

16. *Le Moniteur universel*, 11 ventôse an 7 (March 1, 1799).

Jacob had been in France since 1794. The most reliable of his chroniclers, Françoise Hildesheimer, found mention of him in Marseilles shipping registers in January 1795, and in documents of the city's commercial court in June of the same year. Hildesheimer surmises that Jacob most probably came to Marseilles in the previous year, shortly after the deal was arranged for the supply of wheat. His task would have been to act as the family's representative in France, "to safeguard the family's interests and ensure the smooth running of business."[17] It helped in establishing his business that the most prominent members of the merchant class had largely fled the city, in the face of the Terror.[18] In April 1798, Jacob moved to Paris. By that time, France had been in foment for almost a decade, and the capital was at the very heart of all the tumult. Popular uprisings and brutal executions had taken place in the city's streets. In the words of François-Antoine de Boissy d'Anglas, a moderate member of the revolutionary parliament, France had lived through "six centuries in six years." By 1798, however, the situation had started to settle and stability had begun to reimpose itself. France was now ruled by the executive directory, a group of moderate republicans who reacted against the radicalism and violence of preceding years and who believed in privatization, morality, and authority. Their aim—to instill strong, stable government—was helped by several bountiful harvests, which brought to an end the economic crises and rampant inflation of previous years.

Jacob came to a Paris that was, now, relatively becalmed. Here he found Simon Abucaya, the regency's representative, and a fellow Algerian Jew. He joined a growing community of Arabic speakers. Muslims, Christians, and Jews, they came from Egypt, Syria, Algeria, Morocco, Tunis, Tripoli, and sometimes further afield. A handful of them, including Abucaya, had been living in the French capital before and during the Revolution. As France became increasingly stable, and especially following Napoleon's foray into Egypt, this community continued to grow. Its members were strongly connected, across the bounds of region and religion. Life in Paris was expensive, and doing business was difficult. Those who shared a background in Arabic,

17. Hildesheimer, "Grandeur et décadence," 391.
18. Guiral and Amargier, *Histoire de Marseille*, 191.

and the Islamic culture of the Ottoman Empire, came together to help one another. The letters of Mordechai al-Najjar, a Tunisian Jewish writer living in Paris, "often referred to others, whether Muslim, Christian or Jewish, as *min baladina*, 'of our country,' if they came from a common Arabic-speaking and Islamic culture."[19]

Thus, in moving north from Marseilles, Jacob was following an already-established trail. But his mission in coming to Paris was unique. For France now owed the Bacris several million francs, and Jacob's job was to find a way to recoup the money owed. In Paris, Jacob, together with his wife, set himself up in the Maison du Nord, in the rue de la Loi, one of the city's streets that had been renamed during the revolution in an effort to wipe away the old regime. Previously known as the rue Richelieu (a name it would resume again in 1806), this was one of Paris's most fashionable streets. Here, Jacob established a network of contacts, including bankers and agents, and he maintained and enlarged the Bacri web, which reached across the Mediterranean, and beyond. Jacob set up an office and directed operations, while the Bacris' French warehouses remained in Marseilles, under the direction of Michel Busnach, Naphtali's brother. With Napoleon's conquests in battle, Paris was fast becoming the center of Europe, and business could extend its reach: proximity to the directory, and later to the first consul, was power.

Jacob's stay in France has become the stuff of legend, with rumors swirling around his wealth. One historian of France's relations with Algiers has described Jacob frequenting Parisian dives, and keeping a mistress, a singer from the opera chorus called la Piccini, who cost him dearly. It was la Piccini, the author suggests, who was behind Jacob's great need for money.[20] In December 1798, while Jacob was in Paris, his home in Marseilles, the Hôtel Samatan, was burgled. The police minister's report stated that a group of fifty "brigands" systematically emptied the house of jewels, diamonds, gold, and money to the value of 400,000 livres.[21] The same historian who had Jacob living the high life in Paris claims that the police report "raised doubts about the truth of the burglary," effectively hinting

19. Coller, *Arab France*, 84. On al-Najjar, and the population of philologists in Paris from North Africa during this time, see Fenton, "Mardochée Najjar," 77–114.

20. Esquer, *Les Commencements d'un empire*, 32–33.

21. Hildesheimer, "Grandeur et décadence," 396.

that Jacob might have organized it.[22] But Jacob was in Paris with his wife and his older brother Abraham, who had received special permission from the directory to come across from London to join his younger sibling. More believable is the portrait painted by Françoise Hildesheimer of Jacob circulating "in directory society, among the parvenus of politics, trade and finance, eager to enjoy their wealth."[23]

For the regime, Jacob's presence had a different significance and meaning. In the war with the regency, Jacob and Simon Abucaya served as a guarantee. This was the aim of sequestration, and the reason why the Bacris in France were the primary target. Sequestration was a tit for tat; the holding in France of something precious to the regency, as a way of ensuring the safety of French citizens and property in Algiers. Very early, warnings had started coming from Algiers, that given the situation of the French in the regency, to treat Jacob Bacri and Michel Busnach too harshly would be at best unwise, and at worst, frankly unsafe. Well before the March 1 announcement in the *Moniteur* of Jacob's imprisonment, both Marie-Victoire Sielve and Moltedo himself had written, to beg that French reprisals against Algerians in France be muted, or, as Sielve put it, "there would be as many victims as there are French here."[24] In a letter dated February 6, after his release, Moltedo took care to warn Talleyrand that if they had been freed, this had much to do with the perception in Algiers that its subjects in France had been left alone, a piece of information he coincidentally received from Busnach. But news of the measures taken against Jacob Bacri and Michel Busnach in Marseilles had already reached Algiers, as Marie-Victoire wrote, and this had "shocked and hurt" Joseph, Naphtali, and their relatives in the port city. Marie-Victoire hoped that the regime would rectify their mistake, implying in her letter that the actions taken in France could threaten the newfound freedom of the French in Algiers. But it was clear, also, that she felt these actions to be unfair. Busnach, she noted, reassured her that the Algiers Bacris were happy. In her assessment, they had "taken the news as well as possible," and did not appear to have changed in

22. Esquer, *Les Commencements d'un empire*, 32.

23. Hildesheimer, "Grandeur et décadence," 396.

24. AMAE 8CCC/34, p. 292, 3 nivôse an 7 (December 23, 1799), Marie-Victoire Sielve to Vallière.

their attitude toward France. Their constancy, she wrote, in a gentle remonstrance, merited "some acknowledgement."[25]

Talleyrand did not agree. For him, the question was rather how to achieve the right balance in punishing them. Charles-Maurice de Talleyrand-Périgord, former bishop of Autun from an ancient noble family, had quickly become involved in the revolution. But he was no radical revolutionary. Although he supported the claims to citizenship made by the Sephardic Jews of the southwest and southern France on the basis of their historical rights, granted in royal letters patent,[26] he did not intervene to support the cause of the Jews of Alsace, whose path to emancipation was longer, and more fiercely disputed. Talleyrand's attitude might be characterized as ambivalent at best. When in early March, former consul Césaire-Philippe Vallière wrote from Marseilles to complain that Jacob and Michel's treatment elevated them to a height they had no right to occupy, he found a sympathetic audience in Talleyrand. It pained him, Vallière wrote, to see how the Jews had been treated. Measures enacted against them were entirely fair, even restrained, but they might also appear to be directly proportionate to the treatment of the French in Algiers, and this, he felt, wounded "the republic's dignity." Bringing all his prejudices to bear, Vallière described the Bacris as "vile, despised Jews," who enjoyed no esteem in Algiers. Nonetheless, he went on, it was vitally important to be aware of the damage that their detention in France could do, in ensuring that the French in Algiers would be safe, and that the Bacris in the same city would remain "favorable to us in their domestic and political intrigues."[27] Talleyrand borrowed Vallière's words in his report to the executive directory: "The manner in which the Algerian subjects have been treated resembles retaliation too closely and that wounds the dignity of the Republic," he told his masters. "It would have been sufficient to secure them by locking them up in a healthy and convenient house. Their families, through attachment to them and given our debts to them, must be favorable to us, not in terms of their influence, but in terms of their domestic

25. AMAE 8CCC/34, p. 349, 17 pluviôse an 7 (February 5, 1799), Marie-Victoire Sielve to Vallière.

26. Schechter, *Obstinate Hebrews*, 184.

27. AMAE 8CCC/34, p. 360, 14 ventôse an 7 (March 4, 1799), Vallière to Talleyrand.

and political intrigues,"[28] thus reinforcing the notion that the Bacris could choose to work against France in the regency.

This was as far as Talleyrand was prepared to go in allowing the Bacris any power, although the question of how powerful they were, and whether France ought to fear their power, was vexed. In mid-March, on receiving the news that seals had been affixed to the offices of Bacri and Busnach in France, Moltedo wrote that "justice and recognition" obliged him to declare "that it is public knowledge that these Jews did everything they could to stop Mustapha from declaring war on France, and although unsuccessful, they did not stop using their credit to soften the fate of the French as much as was in their power to do so, and that if we have not been despoiled at all, we are once again obliged to them."[29] Moltedo was using the shorthand for the Bacris that was to become common, as though they only had to be called Jews for something specific to be understood: the fatal combination of their untrustworthiness and their power. Perhaps that was why Talleyrand clearly found it difficult to believe that Joseph and Naphtali had sought to help the imprisoned French. He instructed his staff to forward any information to do with the facts given by Moltedo to him from everywhere, "without delay." He wished to determine whether the information given in Moltedo's letter was in fact true, and if so, the effect of this information, so that he might draft a report on the mode of reprisal. It was clearly tempting to believe that the Bacris' power was overstated. Falcon, the British consul who had previously been secretary in the regency, was also dubious. He told Wickham, in the Home Office, that he was

> not at all surprised the French imprisoned at Algiers should write to their friends in great spirits, flattering themselves soon to be liberated, whether true or false, the Jew Bacri inspires them with those ideas, and urges the writing of such letters in order to prevent any retaliation on the part of the government of France, upon his brothers established at Marseilles, Genoa, and Leghorn.[30]

28. AMAE 8CCC/34, p. 359, 25 ventôse an 7 (March 15, 1799), "Analyse d'une lettre du citoyen Vallière ex-consul de la République à Alger." Original emphasis.

29. AMAE 8CCC/34, p. 330, 26 ventôse an 7 (March 16, 1799), Moltedo to Talleyrand.

30. TNA FO 3/8, p. 138, April 26, 1799, London, Falcon to Wickham.

It is striking that those in Algiers itself, who had experienced the great trauma of imprisonment and forced labor, and who had personal relationships with Joseph and Naphtali, were so much more comfortable with the idea that these two, as Jews, could be trusted as a source of succor. They had witnessed, and understood, the importance of the Bacris to the regime. In Algiers, Moltedo, more aware of how Joseph and Naphtali could serve the republic, had asked Joseph to write to Tunis to enquire about buying all ships that could take provisions to Malta.

It is true, nonetheless, that the Bacris in Algiers were deep in intrigue of a sort. For if Naphtali was putting on a happy face, behind the scenes, he and Joseph were clearly drawing on all their networks to have their relatives in France freed. The war might have been disastrous for France. But the imprisonment and sequestering of their relatives and goods in France and the now-occupied Livorno was equally disastrous for the Bacris. In accordance with their standard practice in the regime they inhabited, they began a concerted campaign of direct personal appeals in Algiers, Paris, and Marseilles. In late February, Joseph sent a letter to their agents in Alicante, Dié Brothers. Three separate translations of this letter were made and forwarded to three different collectors of news from Algiers to send on to Talleyrand. This was most probably no coincidence. Vallière received one copy from his own business correspondents in Alicante. Poiret, the French consul in that town, received another. The final copy went direct to Marseilles, to a relative of one of the prisoners of Algiers, who took care to pass it to the newly appointed consul, Charles-François Dubois-Thainville, still stuck in that city, awaiting transport to Algiers. The letter, slightly different on each occasion, had Joseph reporting that "by dint of powerful work and efforts," he had finally been able to get the French prisoners taken off public works. He would, he wrote, "continue to work diligently to make things easier for them, whatever they may be." After all, France was of "immense" interest to him.[31]

In late March, as though by chance, a copy of a letter dated February 18 from the Bacris in Algiers to Michel Busnach in Marseilles appeared in the *Moniteur universel*. Joseph and Naphtali confirmed

---

31. AMAE 8CCC/34, p. 353, 4 ventôse an 7 (February 22, 1799), Joseph Bacri to Dié, Alicante.

to Michel that they had received his letters, "which expressed all your desire to see us try to obtain for the French all the alleviation that their misery asks for. You see," they went on, "that your expectations have not been disappointed." But they took care to add that this had not been achieved without pain or sacrifice. Now they hoped that the French government would reciprocate with regard to their situation.[32] Not only were they writing letters clearly calculated for a wide audience, they sought to increase the possibility of achieving their aims by drawing on personal relationships and having others write, also, on their behalf. Early in April, Talleyrand received an extraordinary letter from the Marquis d'Azara, Spain's ambassador in Paris. The dey had written to the King of Spain, Azara wrote, asking him "to take an interest regarding the executive directory and the House of Bacri in Algiers." In his letter, Mustapha argued that the Bacris had "very good reason to believe themselves exempt" from the sequestration order. After all, they had "done the Republic some very precious favors," both before the sequestration order was issued, and after. It was thanks to them, "and their influence with regard to the dey" that Moltedo and his fellow prisoners had been freed, "all their possessions, which had been confiscated, returned."

> It is the Bacris who broke their chains and who pulled them out of the most atrocious slavery, despite the orders of the Ottoman Porte, which ordered that they be kept and treated as inhumanely as possible.
>
> By means of Algerian ships, the Bacris fed Malta, with a generosity whose merit the republic should fully appreciate. And it is thanks to the Bacris that the Spanish obtained highly important services several times in Algiers.
>
> All these considerations, and the interest of maintaining the friendship of the regency of Algiers, which in the current circumstances can do very important favors to France and Spain, or do us much damage, persuaded the king my master to request that the sequesters on the Bacris' goods be lifted, and that they be treated as friends, and I beg you to explain them to the executive directory, explaining, also, all the interest that his majesty takes in the success of this request.[33]

32. *Le Moniteur universel*, 6 germinal an 7 (March 26, 1799).
33. AMAE 8CCC/34, p. 379, March 23, 1799, Azara to Talleyrand.

This is a letter where one does not so much read as *see* between the lines: Naphtali and Joseph, dictating perhaps, or simply handing Mustapha a pre-written letter, needing only the official seal. In May, with no word reaching Algiers of any change in circumstances for Jacob, they allowed another letter to make its way into the *Moniteur*. In this letter, emblazoned across the national journal's front page, they left out not one single act of loyalty and friendship. They had, they explained, sent their own boat to help the French stuck in Bona (Annaba) to transport their goods, they forwarded the latest happy news of supplies reaching Malta, and went on to describe how, on hearing of the financial difficulties suffered by the consul and French citizens in Tunis, they immediately instructed their agent there to offer a loan of seven thousand piasters, on top of the nine thousand already lent. Their letter grew to a great crescendo in its final paragraph, where they described how the English, seeking to rob the French of their establishments in Africa, had sent boats to Bona to that end, and established a contract with the bey in Constantine. "But," they triumphantly stated, "as soon as we knew of it, we rushed to see our sovereign the Dey of Algiers, who deigned to listen to our pleas in favor of the French, and who not only cancelled the commitment made by the Bey of Constantine, but also then ordered that the English be driven out." Joseph and Naphtali did not stop to enjoy their victory, but "immediately," went to share the good news with the French, offering to keep the business in Bona going on their account, since they were unable to ship goods while the war continued.[34] Not only did they draw on personal relationships to make appeals, but the very content of their appeals constituted tales of personal favors done. And they knew, too, how to play on the contest. But while it would be incorrect to state that clientelism played no role in Revolutionary and Napoleonic France, the Bacris did not understand that they could not access the power this clientelism could convey.

Joseph and Naphtali's letter made its appearance on May 22. There had been no more letters sent in April, perhaps because the second half of the month was taken up with Passover. The two families observed the Jewish festivals and wrote to one another at

---

34. *Le Moniteur universel*, 3 prairial an 7 (May 22, 1799).

this time to ensure that any cousins, or children, who might be travelling, would be with family. In 1801 after his release, Jacob, still
in Paris, sent his nephew Nathan to Marseilles, instructing Jacob
Gozlan, his agent there, that Nathan would arrive in time to spend
the Jewish New Year in that city.[35] If for consuls and men of politics,
Jewishness was an identity, and one that carried particular qualities,
for the Bacris, Judaism was a matter of the ritual observance of Jewish law. But in April 1799, now imprisoned in his home, Jacob was to
spend Passover moldering in detention. In May, he too took up the
job of writing direct, personal letters, starting with the police minister. "On your orders I was arrested and taken to the Temple. I am
unaware of the motives; I wish," he went on, in carefully enunciated
outrage, "to respond to those I am reduced to imagining."[36] After
all that his family in Algiers had taken care to do for the French
imprisoned there, how could Jacob not be treated the same? With
no immediate response, and fearing, as he put it, that his letter
must have been lost, he wrote again, five days later. Wouldn't the
police minister have been pleased to see justice done, and Jacob
released? Why, Jacob asked, was he being treated differently, and
more harshly, than his fellow countrymen? Maintaining his pointed
politeness, Jacob asked that the police minister "be so good as to
make me aware of the motives that have necessitated this rigor, so
that I might draft my claims to the directory."[37]

   In line with family practice, though, Jacob left nothing to chance.
On the same day, he directed another letter to Talleyrand, attach-
ing a copy of his second letter to the police minister. This time,
Jacob's tone was markedly different. With Talleyrand, Jacob was
conciliatory and understanding: he lamented the lack of news from
Algiers that would constitute more official proof of the actions of
his relatives in that city than the accounts that they themselves
had sent. Jacob could only hope that letters would come soon from
the French consul, to "confirm to the government that all I have

   35. ADBR 39 E 21, pp. 33–34, August 24, 1801, Jacob Bacri, Paris, to Jacob Gozlan,
Marseilles.
   36. AMAE 8CCC/34, p. 412, 4 prairial an 7 (May 23, 1799), Jacob Bacri to police
minister.
   37. AMAE 8CCC/34, p. 431, 9 prairial an 7 (May 28, 1799), Jacob Bacri to police
minister.

said was pure truth." Jacob had no doubt that then the directory would free him and return all his possessions.[38] Jacob's confidence would prove misguided. Talleyrand knew that the French in Algiers had been released—this news had reached him in late March, two months before Jacob's letter. He had reported it to the directory soon after. (Jacob may well have been aware of this, given that the family had been intercepting mail between Algiers and Paris for some time, and even, according to Saint-André, had a spy in Talleyrand's ministry.) Jacob tried again in June, this time sending an appeal. He had, he began, with stiff dignity, resolved not to bother the government until proof that he did not deserve to be treated so harshly might come from Algiers. But circumstances had now become urgent: Simon Abucaya was dangerously ill, and Jacob was his only friend in Paris. He appealed for permission to visit Abucaya. He was duty-bound to do so, he wrote, and "justice and humanity" did not allow that anyone could "deprive me of the capacity to fulfil it."[39] Jacob did not lie: Abucaya was indeed unwell, and he died in Paris two months later, on August 10. Talleyrand, who had allowed Jacob to remain in detention, his business in shutdown, was so good as to forward Jacob's request to the police minister.

Jacob had made a further attempt, addressing a petition to the nation's highest authority, the executive directory, a copy of which he then forwarded to Talleyrand in early July, with a request that he write a report for the directory. Jacob, like Joseph and Naphtali, listed all that the Bacris had done for France. Unlike their letter, however, his was a complaint. Jacob had maintained his outrage, but a note of weariness crept into his letter also. Jacob had, he reminded the directory, supplied large quantities of grain, saving France from famine, and allowing France to build up a debt that remained unpaid. He had come to Paris with the express purpose of settling the debt. On the basis of a pledge from the finance minister, however, he continued to supply grain, and although he was promised a cash payment for this new supply, he received only a partial deposit. As Jacob told it, the regime now sought to hold him hostage: in order to be repaid, he first had to take on the supply

---

38. AMAE 8CCC/34, p. 432, 9 prairial an 7 (May 28 1799), Jacob Bacri to Talleyrand.
39. AMAE 8CCC/34, p. 437, 23 prairial an 7 (June 11, 1799), Jacob Bacri to Talleyrand.

of Malta, in provisions as well as cash. In an agreement he negotiated with the finance minister, his trading house would receive a
payment of 160,000 francs for this undertaking, as a guarantee for
further payment. In fact, Jacob went on, he had been forced to agree
to a low price, and to take on what was universally recognized as a
dangerous venture. French boats had difficulty reaching Malta, as
enemy ships blockaded the island. It was a venture, Jacob stated,
that offered only "the view of a real loss." Seven more boats were sitting at Marseilles, loaded and ready to leave, when war was declared,
and rather than allow these boats with their much-needed cargo to
depart for Malta, the government sequestered them. Sealed, too,
were Jacob's homes in Marseilles and Paris. The deposit that stood
as the guarantee for the supply of Malta was removed from Jacob's
account, and Jacob himself was placed under arrest, where, as he
explained in the third person, "he has found himself for the last six
months."[40]

When Mustapha was informed of actions against his subjects
in France, Jacob continued, he immediately released all French in
Algiers, Bona and La Calle (El Kala, on the Mediterranean coast
by Algiers' eastern border), and returned all their belongings. The
only continuing privation imposed upon them was the inability to
depart. So Jacob issued a challenge to the directory: could it allow
the dey the upper hand in justice and generosity? Or would it take
up the challenge and exercise reciprocity? Covering all bases, Jacob
finished with a threat. Reminding the directory that this was not
the first time he had written, Jacob insisted that his requests were
worthy of their consideration, since if Mustapha were not

> persuaded that his subjects are treated with justice and humanity in
> France, and if he were not unaware of the captivity and privation of
> their possessions that they have suffered for a long time, he would with-
> out fail exercise reprisals and would plunge the French in his states,
> once again, into the unhappy situation from which the prudence and
> the credit of the House of Bacri removed them.[41]

40. AMAE 8CCC/34, p. 445, 14 messidor an 7 (July 2, 1799), Jacob Bacri to Talleyrand.

41. AMAE 8CCC/34, p. 455, messidor an 7 (June/July 1799), Jacob Bacri to executive
directory. The order was given for the sequester to be fully lifted on August 19.

Jacob's—and indeed, Joseph and Naphtali's—mistake was to imagine that the way they had always dealt with power in the regency was a model to be applied universally. Thus, they made repeated personal appeals. Imprisoned in his home, Jacob had clearly been conferring with his older brother Joseph in Algiers. In mid-July, Joseph and Naphtali wrote a second letter, this one addressed to the executive directory. Both of their letters are very rare surviving examples where their own voices can be heard. In less polished French than Jacob's letter, they set out a very similar exposition of services rendered in the face of adversity to a thankless French nation, of love and loyalty nonetheless unabated, culminating in a humble request that some of this loyalty now be repaid, by freeing Jacob and releasing his ("our," they noted, in their letter, signaling the family dispute that was to come) belongings.

If the letters from Jacob, imprisoned in France, are revealing of his weariness after six months of detention, in contrast, beyond the poor French, Joseph and Naphtali were clearly in control of themselves. They were secure in the familiar comfort of Algiers. Adopting a tone they imagined to be carefully and cleverly calculated to achieve their ends, they made no accusations. They understood, they stated, why the regime might have felt it necessary, in the circumstances, to treat "us" harshly. Perhaps the directory was not certain of the strength of their attachment to France. But if the French government would only be so good as to seek reliable information on all that Joseph and Naphtali had done, "and had not ceased doing," then they could not but seek to repay the debt ("or at least half of it") and lift the sequesters in France. Their business was suffering, but they could not believe that France would seek to ruin them. And, conclusively establishing their martyrdom, and playing on the contest once again, they ended:

> The English are running all over us to excess, on the pretext that we are the friends of the French, and do them favors. The Algerians humiliate us constantly on the same pretext, and lately the French government lands the final blow![42]

---

42. AMAE 8CCC/34, p. 458, July 18, 1799, Joseph Bacri and Naphtali Busnach to executive directory.

The Bacris did not see the different structures of power around them. They did not appear to comprehend why their appeals, so fruitful in the regency, fell on deaf ears in France. They saw people, with whom they simply had to form relationships, whose weaknesses and peccadilloes they set out to discover, all the better to manipulate them. Members of the two families wrote to one another in a local dialect of Judeo-Arabic, known as Vulgar Algerian. A purported translation of one letter, undertaken more than a century ago from documents deposited with the Spanish consulate in Algiers, has Jacob writing in 1803 from Livorno to his brother Abraham in Algiers. Abraham had been sending Jacob letters, voicing his concern over his brother's failure to recover the moneys owed to the family by France. Jacob wrote to reassure his brother that he would have his money, with interest. He told his brother that "the lame one," presumably Talleyrand, had gone to great trouble to obtain a letter from the dey, to end the affair.[43] Could Abraham, Jacob asked, organize for Naphtali "to have our master [the Dey Mustapha] write a letter to the little one, where he will tell him that the money claimed by Bacri and Busnach is his, and that he begs him to pay, for his sake." He warned his brother that only he had the means to obtain the funds, since the lame one was, as he stated, in his hand. And Jacob had indeed discovered the weaknesses of those with whom he dealt. He reminded his brother that the "little one" did not like requests to be put to him forcefully. He preferred, as Jacob explained, to be asked nicely.[44] If the lame one was Talleyrand, then the little one was none other than Napoleon. Jacob's letter, striking in its confident tone (and, given the tone of Talleyrand's own letters, possibly stretching the truth), is also revealing of the limitations of the family's reach. The Bacris' refusal to respect power structures did not mean, necessarily, that they themselves were powerful. There were situations that they could not better or overcome. Jacob's extended imprisonment and sequestration, as well as his misguided appeals,

43. Talleyrand was born with a severely deformed right foot that caused him to limp all his life.

44. Jacob to Abraham, December 12, 1803, cited in Bloch, *Inscriptions tumulaires*, 111. Bloch, originally from Alsace, served as a rabbi in Algeria during the 1880s. He had access to the Spanish consular records that were left in Algiers.

provide an example of this. Their story lies, in many ways, at the juncture between their bravado and their poor judgement.

The former led some to believe they were all-powerful. Indeed, in the characteristically colorful language of US consul Richard O'Brien, they had "the devil's impudence."[45] For others, the Bacris' inability to understand the world beyond their immediate context was both challenging and confusing because of how it determined their actions. They appeared to have nothing but disdain for structures of power. Where the Bacris saw a world of personal relationships to be established, others saw contempt. But did this mean they were powerful? In a sense, this is also a tale of moments of French and British inability, or perhaps unwillingness, to understand power relations in the regency. It is telling that the French could not decide where the truth of the Bacris' power should lie. Were they truly as powerful as Saint-André's letters had insisted? Even Talleyrand, who consistently insisted on their lowly status, had their mail intercepted and read, as though to cover all possibilities nonetheless. Talleyrand had written to Moltedo as Jacob's campaign to be released was picking up pace. He asked his consul to gauge Joseph and Naphtali's attitudes to France, because this would indicate the attitude of the regency. "Show the Jews some marks of satisfaction for the steps they undertook in your favor," he instructed. "Try to discover the true motive for their behavior, to penetrate their views, and by means of them, those of the regency."[46] Moltedo replied in code, a series of numbers on a page, that only the prime minister still maintained "some feelings of friendship" toward France, and this was because he was "very much attached" to the Jews. Where Joseph and Naphtali themselves were concerned, "they did all they could to spare us the annoyances that happened to us and they would make great sacrifices to reconcile things, their interest obliging them to, but I believe that that is not in their power."[47]

The question of just how powerful Joseph and Naphtali were was not resolved by this exchange, for Jacob's threat to the directory that the news of his imprisonment would not go down well

45. NARA Atlanta M23, roll 5, vol. 4, p. 20, July 22, 1800, O'Brien to Secretary of State Marshall.

46. AMAE 8CCC/34, p. 408, 23 germinal an 7 (April 12, 1799), Talleyrand to Moltedo.

47. AMAE 8CCC/34, p. 451, 20 messidor an 7 (July 8, 1799), Moltedo to Talleyrand.

was to come true. In late August, Moltedo wrote to Talleyrand to inform him of a rather unpleasant meeting that he, together with agents from the African Agency, had had with the prime minister. This minister was upset that, having used his influence to have the French freed and their belongings restored to them, the French government had not acted in kind. The prime minister, who Moltedo knew to be a good friend of Joseph and Naphtali, laid out his complaint in detail, repeated in Moltedo's letter: they were locked up at home with a guard, the cargoes of their ships in the port of Marseilles had been sold, and the rest of their belongings were sequestered. Jacob's warning came to fruition: the prime minister threatened that if, after a month and a half, he had received no word of an improvement in their situation, he would send the French back to the prison and to public works.[48]

It was not only the Bacris who suffered from their inability to adapt to different contexts. Consuls and states also showed themselves to be unwilling or unable to recognize and accommodate the difference in relationships of power in the regency. This contributed to diplomatic outcomes for them. In the experience of foreign consuls and their bureaucrats, Jews were a lowly, despised population. Jews in France were having to prove themselves worthy of the rights and privileges that had been newly granted. The situation in Britain was less clear-cut. Jews found themselves in a grey area, where they were not excluded as a corporate group, and a handful of wealthy Jews enjoyed broad social integration, but they still faced forms of exclusion, both civil and economic, due to the nature of British society that sought to block non-Anglicans from full participation.[49] In Algiers, the Jews were a minority in a state that acknowledged difference and minority, dhimmi status. Their relations with their neighbors did sometimes devolve into violence, but they also enjoyed communal autonomy and proximity to power that was not the case in Western Europe. The Bacris dealt with France and Britain as though they were the equals, and

---

48. AMAE 8CCC/34, p. 466, 3 fructidor an 7 (August 20, 1799), Moltedo to Talleyrand. Talleyrand resigned in June 1799 because of pressure due to military losses. He was replaced by his close colleague, Reinhard, and reappointed ten days after Napoleon's coup.

49. See Alderman, *Modern British Jewry*, 7–8; and Endelman, *Radical Assimilation in English Jewish History, 1656-1945*, 20–22.

even, at times, the superior, of these two nations and their representatives. They expected to establish personal relations, since that was the way of business. For both the French and the British, it was, quite simply, an outrage to think that the Bacris might be seeking to trade with both nations, or to favor one over the other, in a time of war. Their outrage in the face of the Bacris allowed them to articulate their new ideas of state power and dignity, and to bring clarity to what it meant, in the context of the Revolutionary Wars, to be French, or British, far from the metropole. For all of the Western powers in Algiers, their nation was paramount, and ever increasing in stature. All understood their role in Algiers in terms of national strength. To win international contests was to demonstrate the same. Overseas influence and domestic power fed into one another. In order to win in Algiers, they had to understand and accommodate the place of the Bacris. Unlike France, Britain repeatedly refused to see the Bacris as being linked to British relations with the regency. They were to suffer the consequences of this approach.

In early 1800, consuls for both France and Britain were on their way to take up their respective posts in the regency. The British consul was John Falcon, former secretary to the previous consul, Richard Masters. There had been no British consul in the regency since Masters had left in June 1798. Masters returned, briefly, in late March the following year, only to organize himself a more attractive post, as governor of Tobago, and to arrange for Falcon to take his place. But in his absence, there was no one in the regency to advocate for Britain in the obtaining of supplies at a time when the field would have been open to British needs, given the state of relations between the regency and France, and British ascendancy in the Mediterranean. In June 1799, consuls in the region had all received a circular, direct from Whitehall, instructing them to extend every effort in supplying British military forces there.[50] Falcon had lived in Algiers previously, and his experience was put to the service of his judgement. The moment was propitious, he assessed, to "procure the whole of the trade carried on by the French in Barbary," including the coral fishery and necessary supplies. From London, he wrote that Bacri, busy doing all in his power "to effect a reconciliation

50. Gale, "Beyond Corsairs," 91.

between Algiers and France," would seek to prevent any agreement with Britain. Bacri was, Falcon knew, "a very active agent of the French government," but if he could be made to see an interest for himself in an agreement with Britain, he could be brought around. The threat of war provided the means: both Bacri and Mustapha lived in "dread of going to war with Britain." With war, Bacri had "a great deal to risk and nothing to gain." If the port of Algiers were blocked, in all probability this would, in Falcon's view, "cause an insurrection, and endanger both the dey's life and his own"—a possibility of which both Joseph and Mustapha were "very well aware."[51]

Richard O'Brien, the ship's captain who became US consul, held Falcon in "sincere regard and esteem,"[52] and like Falcon, he believed that the Bacris supported French interests in the regency. O'Brien had dealt closely with Mordecai and spoke very highly and warmly of him. "Miciah," as he called him, was America's "best friend."[53] But after Hassan's death, and decline of Mordecai's influence, O'Brien found that he was obliged "on hard terms to purchase the influence of Naphtali Busnach."[54] With Naphtali, his—and, by extension, America's—position became more difficult. Under Naphtali's stewardship, the Bacris became "mercenary," duping both Western nations and regency elite.[55] O'Brien did not dare to oppose them publicly, as this "would be to declare war against Algiers."[56] Whatever his feelings, however, he was obliged to continue to work closely with the Bacri family. Without their credit, which they were always ready to extend, there would be an end to US affairs in the Barbary States.[57] (By mid-1800, the US was in debt to the Bacris for one hundred and ten thousand dollars.)[58] O'Brien, like the other consuls, would make visits to the homes of various Bacri family

51. TNA FO 3/8, p. 138, April 26, 1799, London, Falcon to Wickham.
52. TNA FO 3/8, p. 196, January 29, 1800, O'Brien to Falcon.
53. NARA Atlanta M23, roll 6, vol. 5, p. 14, July 22, 1800, O'Brien to Marshall.
54. NARA Atlanta M23 6.5, p. 14, July 22, 1800, O'Brien to Marshall.
55. NARA Atlanta M23 5.4, p. 81, April 5, 1799, O'Brien to Pickering.
56. NARA Atlanta M23 6.5, p. 20, July 22, 1800, O'Brien to Marshall.
57. NARA Atlanta M23 6.5, p. 27, July 22, 1800, O'Brien to Marshall.
58. NARA Atlanta M23 6.5, p. 100, August 16, 1800, O'Brien to Humphreys.

members, in order to negotiate terms of a loan, or even propose revisions to a US-Barbary treaty.[59]

O'Brien felt the war would be in America's interest. Algerian corsairs would be otherwise occupied, drawing attention away from American affairs. Moreover, war would serve "to scare and diminish the French corsairs, to prevent Frenchmen from bringing Americans into the Barbary ports, and by all these points to give Americans more safety in entering and navigating the Mediterranean."[60] After the arrest of Moltedo and other French, O'Brien told John Marshall, his new secretary of state, that Joseph and Naphtali had used their influence to obtain the liberation of the consul and merchants from the prison and hard labor, and had seen them returned to their homes.[61] In fact, as he continued to insist, Joseph and Naphtali had worked assiduously to prevent any declaration of war on France. In the face of support by the corps of janissaries for the sultan, they were unable to prevent war from being declared. The war was short-lived, however, as the Bacris had managed to restore peace—it was they who had "made" it. Now, they kept the dey "in hot water with the British," submitting to French influence, and ignoring orders from Constantinople, where British diplomats urged the sultan to force war on France once again.[62] For O'Brien, who, like Falcon, was increasingly obsessed with the Bacris and their power, the entirety of American affairs, not only in Algiers, but also in Tunis and Tripoli, were "dependent on the Bacris and Busnachs, to give us credit, and to pay those just debts our negotiations incurs."[63] The Bacris were "the real and sincere friends and advocates of the nation of anarchy."[64]

For Falcon, Joseph and Naphtali's power was malign: as agents of France, they worked, effectively, to undermine Britain's ambitions in the regency. In Falcon's view, as he explained to William Wickham, now home secretary, the "avaricious" Joseph Bacri

59. NARA Atlanta M23 5.4, p. 55, February 25, 1799, O'Brien to Pickering.

60. NARA Atlanta M23 6.5, p. 29, July 22, 1800, O'Brien to Marshall.

61. NARA Atlanta M23 6.5, p. 29, July 22, 1800, O'Brien to Marshall.

62. NARA Atlanta M23 6.5, p. 151, January 10, 1801, O'Brien to William Smith, Minister Plenipotentiary for the United States at Lisbon.

63. NARA Atlanta M23 5.4, p. 123, May 6, 1799, O'Brien to Smith.

64. TNA FO 3/8, p. 166, November 8, 1799, O'Brien to The British Admiral or General at Mahon.

would do "everything in his power to effect a reconciliation between Algiers and France."[65] (Falcon would have found a sympathetic audience in Wickham, who had established British foreign secret service activities during the French Revolution.) Now waiting to return to Algiers to take up his post, Falcon, perhaps in anticipation of difficulties to be faced, felt it necessary to inform the British envoy extraordinary to Constantinople, Thomas Bruce, the seventh Earl of Elgin, "of the intrigues and machinations of two Jews, Bacri and Busnach, living at Algiers, subjects of the dey, and who are not only the secret, but avowed agents of the French." Bacri, he went on, was "a cunning man," who governed the dey, who carried on an illegal commerce with France, and who adopted "every method in his power to cause a misunderstanding between His Majesty and the dey." The dey found it "so much in his interest to protect [Bacri] scarce any means can be devised to destroy his credit."[66] So certain was Falcon of this that he ended his letter by asking Elgin to keep his complaints secret from Mustapha and the regency, as his "person," as he put it, "might otherwise be endangered."[67] In Falcon's eyes, British competition with France for influence in Algiers was woven tightly together with the Bacris' activities. Britain did not wish for a French peace. John Falcon had been given instructions to obtain full and free export rights to grain.

Falcon arrived in early June, the first of the two new consuls for Britain and France to reach Algiers. Falcon's appointment had not been welcomed by the regency. Thainville reported to Talleyrand that as Richard Masters's secretary, Falcon had spoken out strongly against the system in Algiers and had "debased" other national representatives. He had, Thainville said, made himself powerful enemies.[68] While Falcon is generally described by his British contemporaries as having been "of unimpeachable character," Mustapha protested his appointment, claiming that Falcon "had rendered himself obnoxious" during his previous stay in the regency.[69] The

65. TNA FO 3/8, p. 138, April 26, 1799, Falcon to Wickham.

66. TNA FO 3/8, p. 180, January 7, 1800, Falcon to Elgin.

67. TNA FO 3/8, p. 180, January 7, 1800, Falcon to Elgin. The Sultan of the Ottoman Empire was known to the English as the Grand Signor.

68. AMAE 8CCC/36, p. 368, 5 floréal 11 (April 25, 1803), Thainville to Talleyrand.

69. Playfair, *The Scourge of Christendom*, 229.

bad feeling surrounding Falcon's appointment was to set the tone for his posting. He had a first negotiation with Mustapha regarding the release of enslaved citizens, and the supply of raw goods. But the dey blocked these requests, and Falcon returned to his boat, intending to go to Lord Admiral Keith, commander of the Mediterranean fleet, to discuss matters with him, before returning to Algiers. Notwithstanding the determinations he had set out when in London, once in Algiers, Falcon found Joseph and Naphtali's power to be "so great," that he "deemed it most politic to make friends with them."[70] As Falcon explained it, if British aims were not being met, this was due to the undue influence of the Bacris. A Ragusan ship, owned by the Bacris and loaded for Mustapha's account, had sailed from Marseilles, when it was seized by British privateers, taken into Mahon, and condemned, the boat and cargo declared a valid prize. Mustapha insisted that until this boat was released, all slaves—including those whose release was sought by Falcon—would remain in Algiers. This was, predictably, the fault of Joseph Bacri and Naphtali Busnach, who, in concert with the "passionate" Mustapha, carried on an illicit commerce "beyond conception." If one of their ships was taken, Falcon explained, "his highness immediately supports them in their claim and by this means the French and Spanish are supplied with a principal part of their grain in the Mediterranean." In the face of this power, Falcon assured the home secretary, the Duke of Portland, that he would continue, "by every means consistent with the honor of my king and country, to conciliate the minds of the dey and his favorites, however great the obstacles."[71] The new French consul, Charles-François Dubois-Thainville, was quickly to become yet another obstacle.

Thainville had entered the diplomatic service in 1792, and had already held posts in Holland, Constantinople, Smyrna, Cairo, and Syria. In May 1800, Thainville received orders from Talleyrand, his minister: he was to proceed to Algiers, and negotiate a peace treaty, with full backing from Napoleon. Thainville arrived in Algiers on July 13. At one in the afternoon, his ship entered the port, and shortly after his arrival had been announced, he received

70. TNA FO 3/8, p. 222, June 2, 1800, Falcon to Portland.
71. TNA FO 3/8, pp. 227–28, July 24, 1800, Falcon to Portland.

permission to disembark. He wrote to his minister that as soon as the ship had dropped anchor, Joseph and Naphtali came to see him on board.[72] On July 23, a clearly piqued Falcon informed Keith that

> The French Ambassador was received with the greatest triumph and honors; he has been with the dey at his country house, and persuaded him that in a very few months the English will not have a ship in the Mediterranean. They do not believe there are any English ships to do them harm, and appear by this man's report so completely led by the nose (that is, the dey and his ministers) by Bacri and Busnach, that there is nothing the most improbable and preposterous they do not believe.[73]

The great expectations resting on Falcon's shoulders may well explain the height of his hysteria regarding Naphtali and Joseph.

Notwithstanding Richard O'Brien's claim that they were "the peacemakers, and also them that disturbs the peace,"[74] Naphtali and Joseph had failed to prevent war in 1798, despite their best efforts. When it came to France, the Bacris needed peace above all so that they could focus on the repayment of their debts. By early 1800, with a new French consul on his way to the regency, the Bacris had a chance to right that particular wrong, and help to broker peace. France, too, was keen to renew the relationship on good terms, and the French were prepared to make concessions to achieve this. As Talleyrand acknowledged to Napoleon, now First Consul, peace with the regency, as well as opening access to a supply of grain, would also allow France to restart its activities related to the African concessions, "coveted by the English for so long."[75] The French government also saw Algiers as a point of communication with the French army in Egypt, and a means to send desperately needed provisions to the blockaded forces on Malta.[76] It took Thainville just six days to successfully negotiate an unlimited armistice. As he explained to Talleyrand, in his negotiations, Thainville dealt with Naphtali rather than

---

72. AMAE 8CCC/35, p. 31, 26 messidor an 8 (July 15, 1800), Thainville to Talleyrand.

73. TNA FO 3/8, p. 232, July 23, 1800, Falcon to Keith.

74. NARA Atlanta M23 5.4, p. 174, November 22, 1799, O'Brien to Smith.

75. AMAE 8CCC/35, p. 58, 27 thermidor an 8 (August 15, 1800), "Rapport au premier consul de la République."

76. AMAE 8CCC/35, p. 98, 11 vendémiaire an 9 (October 3, 1800), Thainville to Talleyrand.

Mustapha. The dey, who was not capable of any political understanding, could not be easily swayed from the avidity that dominated his passions, even when "all the advantages to the regency of a
prompt accommodation with us" were explained, carefully but with
strength. Busnach and Bacri, on the other hand, "were very powerful," and Busnach "entirely directed the dey."[77] It was to Busnach
that Thainville made the high-handed speeches of which he was
so fond, and which he would relay, word for word, to his minister.
(Thainville would commonly describe not only the words he used,
but the way he delivered them.) For Thainville, it was important to
maintain a narrative of national ascendancy, and he only ever used
language that he felt to be worthy of the republic he served. "The
dey calls himself our friend," Thainville reported himself pronouncing to Busnach, and yet the English were able to draw provisions
from Barbary ports, refused to France. "In the eyes of the French
government," he asked Busnach, rhetorically, why would the regency
deserve to be reconciled with France, "when we will command peace
over all peoples by the force of our weapons?"[78]

The money France owed to the Bacris and Busnachs was at the
heart of the peace negotiations between Thainville, on the one
hand, and Mustapha and Naphtali, on the other. In mid-August,
Talleyrand wrote to Napoleon, seeking a decision to do with the
negotiations. In the process of discussions, Mustapha had asked
Thainville how much money he had been told to offer; a question that Joseph and Naphtali had forewarned Thainville would
be raised. The dey was requesting 200,000 piasters, or one million
francs. Upon Thainville explaining that he was not authorized to
"buy peace," Naphtali was reported by Thainville to have replied:
"Well! to come to an agreement, we will present the sum to be
agreed as an act of gratitude on our part to the dey, who, in settling
peace lets us recover considerable sums. We will advance the sum:
only give us authorization to do so in the name of the government
and tomorrow the cannon at the fort will announce peace."[79]

77. AMAE 8CCC/35, p. 74, 9 fructidor an 8 (August 27, 1800), Thainville to Talleyrand.
78. AMAE 8CCC/35, p. 42, 13 thermidor an 8 (August 1, 1800), Thainville to Talleyrand.
79. AMAE 8CCC/35, p. 46, 25 thermidor an 8 (August 13, 1800), "Rapport au premier
consul de la République."

Should national dignity stand in the way of making this pecuniary gift? Ever the pragmatist, Talleyrand thought not. Indeed, if France took up the Bacris' offer to advance this sum, then, Talleyrand stated hopefully to the First Consul, rather than being central to this arrangement, "the Jews," as he called them, "would only do the job of banker."[80] But Talleyrand was clearly aware that in seeking to minimize the importance of the Bacris in France's negotiations with the regency, he was indulging in a fit of wishful thinking. Talleyrand was convinced, in fact, that where France's needs and desires were concerned, the Bacris and Busnachs *were* the regency. He made this clear in a letter he wrote to the finance minister in early 1801, pursuing a decision regarding the loan. "I cannot insist enough on the swiftest possible execution of this decision," he stated; Mustapha was becoming unhappy with the way France was managing negotiations, and had written to Talleyrand, making his complaint in "very pressing terms." Talleyrand could not ignore Mustapha's repeated requests that France pay Naphtali and Joseph the money they owed them. France understood their debt to be linked to relations with the regency. The question of the debt, he wrote to his ministerial colleague, had to be understood as an "affair of state."[81] Mustapha, as well as most of the regency's elite, was involved in the monetary affairs of "these Jews," and therefore took an interest in it. It was essential that the French allow the truth of this

> to take root in their minds. It explains how the solidity of our agreement with Algiers is subject to the least satisfaction given the Jews. They have contributed much to the success of citizen Dubois-Thainville's negotiations, but these are not fully completed and in this sense, we are still dependent on them.[82]

France was indeed dependent. Barbary grain continued to be vital for the Midi. In October 1800, after a poor harvest, Talleyrand wrote to Thainville in October 1800 that "only Barbary" could offer the resources that the south needed. France required nothing less

80. AMAE 8CCC/35, p. 58, 27 thermidor an 8 (August 15, 1800), "Rapport au premier consul de la République."
81. Cited in Plantet, *Correspondance des Deys d'Alger*, vol. 2, 491, n. 1.
82. AMAE 8CCC/35, p. 190, 27 nivôse an 9 (January 17, 1801), Talleyrand to finance minister.

than an exclusive right to the harvest in the regency.[83] Perhaps because the Bacris would be central to this transaction, Napoleon designated them his exclusive suppliers. On December 23, 1800, the first consul wrote to Talleyrand, setting out in some detail what his armies required: two million bottles of wine, brandy, and liquors, sheets, medicines, and oil; on their return, their ships were to carry rice, coffee, indigo, and sugar. "Several people," he noted, "are offering to take on this venture, but I prefer the House of Bacri, if it is available."[84] Napoleon may have been choosing to give the right impression to the dey, as opposed to selecting the best business. A month later he ordered Talleyrand "to present this Jew to me in my apartment," and that this should be understood as a mark of his consideration for the dey.[85] "This Jew" was Jacob Bacri.[86] If Napoleon wished to impress Mustapha, it was because he understood how closely the Bacris were linked with the Algerian ruler. To a significant extent, their business dealings were his; the debt that France owed to them was also, in part, owed to him. When Napoleon was sending instructions to Talleyrand, the Bacris were in debt to the regency for the sum of approximately 300,000 francs. This is also, perhaps, why article 13 of the eventual peace treaty stated that "his Excellency the dey promises to have all sums that might be owing to French citizens by his subjects reimbursed, just as citizen Dubois-Thainville makes the commitment, in the name of his government, to have all those [debts] that might be legally claimed by Algerian subjects settled."[87] Thainville

83. AMAE 8CCC/35, p. 96, 9 vendémiaire an 8 (October 1, 1800), Talleyrand to Dubois-Thainville.

84. Napoleon to Talleyrand [letter 5241], December 23, 1800, in *Correspondance de Napoléon Ier*, vol. 6, *1799–1801*, 544. Documents from the sequestration of Jacob Bacri's boats in Marseilles, at the time of the outbreak of war, demonstrate that the Bacris did, indeed, meet Napoleon's request. Seven boats were bound for Malta. Their cargo included wine, salted meat, brandy, vinegar, haricot beans, wood for burning, and paper (Hildesheimer, "Grandeur et décadence," 398). It is ironic that these deliveries would have been held up by order of Napoleon himself.

85. Napoleon to Talleyrand [letter 5324], January 26, 1801, in *Correspondance de Napoléon Ier*, vol. 6, 589.

86. See Deval's *Mémoire*. The same story is told in the *Rapport*, although "juif" is changed to "négociant," or merchant.

87. *Traité de paix entre la Régence d'Alger et la France, le 17 décembre 1801*, reproduced in Laborde, *Au Roi et aux chambres*, v.

promised, in the name of his government, that as soon as political and commercial relations had been re-established, the government's first priority would be to set dates for resurrection of those payments "interrupted by the rupture."[88] This was an extraordinary acknowledgement of liability, in an age when treaties between the Barbary States and those of Europe were overwhelmingly dictated by the latter's self-interest.[89]

In its willingness to accommodate the Bacri debt, and as a result of the success of its approach in restoring peace, France was able to build a narrative of successful imperialism. Through clever diplomacy, the French had managed not only to establish good relations with Algiers, but also to gain some control over trade. They were helped in this by the contrast in Britain's approach, and Falcon's consequent repeated failures to meet Whitehall's requirements. Thainville took great delight in reporting each of his British counterpart's humiliations. Once Thainville had settled in the regency, he discovered that just a few days after Falcon's arrival, he had made proposals to Mustapha. These were met with rejection, and Falcon promptly boarded a boat and departed. "They threaten to send a new agent," Thainville reported to Talleyrand; "I await him with confidence." After all, there was general indignation in Algiers at the tyranny of the English, and Thainville was doing all he could to ensure that these feelings were not left to die down.[90] Barely two weeks later, Thainville, not bothering to disguise his message in code on this occasion, returned once again to the events around Falcon's arrival in the regency, reporting that the English had "failed ignominiously." Falcon had demanded the return of 200 Maltese, Neapolitan, and Mahonese slaves, who at the time of their seizure had been holding English passports. "With all English haughtiness," Thainville remarked, the English consul had even stated that the immediate release of these men was a condition of his remaining in the regency. In an uncharacteristically short phrase, Thainville reported, "The dey refused everything, and Mr. Falcon immediately sailed away." But the British consul's absence would be only brief;

88. AMAE 8CCC/44, p. 89, October 1818, Pierre Deval, *Mémoire analytique*.

89. Pennell, "Treaty Law," 238. In his broad survey of treaties, Pennell found that "questions of finance" only became important from the middle of the nineteenth century.

90. AMAE 8CCC/35, p. 38, 13 thermidor an 8 (August 1, 1800), Thainville to Talleyrand.

Falcon returned soon after. While the British consul had been with Lord Admiral Keith, Thainville had arrived in Algiers, and was "received with distinction," negotiating the armistice and the manumission of slaves. "Every day," in the regency, "the French nation" regained the consideration appropriate to its power. Shortly after his return, Falcon presented himself at the palace. This time, "he was all respectfulness," presenting "a very friendly epistle" from Keith. But, Thainville reported, Falcon was met with a cold reception, and, Thainville went on, rising to a crescendo of underlining, "<u>this envoy from a nation that calls itself dominant on seas, honorably transported here on a warship, was infinitely smaller than the republic's agent, obscurely thrown onto these shores with the sense of his dignity and reason as his only weapon.</u>" Falcon left the palace and went to visit Joseph and Naphtali, "begging" them to forget any bad feeling that had existed between them.[91] Thainville made good use of the easy contrast: as he reported to Talleyrand, his situation, on the other hand, only continued to improve.[92]

Mustapha was still trying to recover a packet that had been captured by an English privateer and declared a valid prize in Mahon. The dey, Falcon reported, continued to insist on its return, and claimed that it belonged to him, even though an "astonished" Falcon could not understand why "His Highness should claim as his property a vessel belonging to the Jews and employed by them solely for the purpose of carrying on a traitorous correspondence with the enemies of His Majesty, the Grand Seignior and the regency, and that had been protected by a French privateer." But Mustapha maintained a stubborn refusal to supply the English until its return. Falcon was keen for Lord Admiral Keith to adopt "those measures that are necessary to expel the Jews Busnach and Bacri from this country." They alone were "the cause of every dispute."[93] But, in the end, Falcon was forced to concede. In August, he wrote to L. General Fox, at Mahon, who had the offending vessel liberated and returned to Algiers, where it arrived on September 3. With

---

91. AMAE 8CCC/35, p. 85, 19 fructidor an 8 (September 6, 1800), Thainville to Talleyrand.

92. AMAE 8CCC/35, p. 92, 3 vendémiaire an 8 (September 25, 1800), Thainville to Talleyrand.

93. TNA FO 3/9, p. 69, July 19, 1801, Falcon to Portland.

the peace treaty recently signed, a happy and relaxed Thainville mused that the lower the English stooped, the more they lost influence: they brought the Bacri and Busnach ship reclaimed by Mustapha into port, "richly loaded for the Jews' account."[94] This was the price of their inability to bend to pragmatism. In November, Falcon wrote to Keith, complaining, as was increasingly his wont. On this occasion, his problem was that Naphtali was prejudicing Mustapha against the British, for their seizure of Malta. Mustapha was threatening to instruct his cruisers to pursue and capture Maltese ships.

The British response to news of the French peace only served to deepen the hole they had dug for themselves. On learning of the treaty, an outraged Lord Admiral Keith had a long letter delivered to Mustapha. It was not without surprise, Keith stated, that he had learned that "an ambassador of the French nation, the greatest enemy of the Muslims, was showered with consideration and with gifts on his arrival here, and even managed to sign an indefinite peace with this regency." Thainville, who had obtained a copy of the letter, reported to Talleyrand that Lord Admiral Keith wanted the dey to "take up arms against us again" and was demanding the French consul's immediate expulsion from Algiers, making this a condition for the return of the captured boat sitting in the docks at Mahon. If previously the English had operated against Thainville secretly, now they had "taken off their mask," attacking him openly. Thainville reported that he had visited Bacri and Busnach, as he often did, to discuss events. He found them, he noted, very worried. But he, as he reported to his minister, felt only satisfaction. Keith's actions were nothing less than "pitiful." In sending his agent with a letter, Keith had caused offence not to France, but to the regency. "According to Lord Admiral Keith, the dey of Algiers owes him an account of all his actions; he no longer has the right, without his permission, to receive the agent of any power, and from now on this regency is to be governed by agents from London."[95] Keith continued to make threats. In late August, the admiral wrote to Mustapha

94. AMAE 8CCC/35, p. 112, 11 vendémiaire an 8 (October 3, 1800), Thainville to Talleyrand.

95. AMAE 8CCC/35, p. 68, 4 fructidor an 8 (August 22, 1800), Thainville to Talleyrand.

to announce that he would be departing from Mahon, travelling with a squadron, to Algiers, in the hope that he and the dey would get along better face-to-face than they had done in correspondence. Thainville, who had seen the letter, reported in code that Mustapha "immediately ordered defense preparations."[96] Mustapha's own diplomacy was the last straw for Keith. The dey had pressured Tunis into signing a truce with France,[97] and in response, Keith went to the sultan. Algiers was a state subject to Ottoman imperialism, and this fact was Britain's trump card. A second *firman* was sent to Mustapha, and he was obliged to declare war on France once again. On January 30, Thainville left the consulate, at the head of all the French in the regency, and set sail for Alicante, where they arrived the following morning. His only choice "in this difficult situation," as he wrote to Talleyrand, "was to allow myself to be shamefully expelled from Africa, or to use all means to incite the Algerian government to a just resistance."[98] Mustapha released all those taken captive under British colors or protection, along with their ships. And Falcon, to his delight, was suddenly able to access a new shipment of supplies for Minorca.[99] Thainville, in comfortable exile in Spain, had time for reflection, and, perhaps, for gaining some perspective on his situation. At the very end of a characteristically long letter, he explained to Talleyrand that the Franco-British rivalry in which he was so deeply involved, in fact contributed to the regency's power.[100]

In the regency, the war played out through diplomacy. Each of the two powers, through their respective representatives, needed precedence and the access to grain that it brought. They needed, too, to prevent the other from gaining this access. France, prepared to make concessions to Mustapha on the subject of the money owed to the Bacris, was more successful in the regency than Britain. Ultimately it was Britain that proved more adept at playing the game

96. AMAE 8CCC/35, p. 76, 10 fructidor an 8 (August 28, 1800), Thainville to Talleyrand.

97. Moalla, *The Regency of Tunis and the Ottoman Porte, 1777–1814*, 61.

98. AMAE 8CCC/35, p. 85, 19 fructidor an 8 (September 6, 1800), Thainville to Talleyrand.

99. TNA FO 3/9, p. 2, January 30, 1801, Falcon to Portland.

100. AMAE 8CCC/35, p. 85, 19 fructidor an 8 (September 6, 1800), Thainville to Talleyrand.

of imperialism, drawing on the regency's indebtedness to the Porte. Initially, however, Britain's inability (or unwillingness) to recognize the different way the regency functioned, had led to failure. But while the Bacris were able to place themselves at the center of diplomacy in the regency, in a parallel to Britain, their inability to recognize the different way France functioned as a regime meant that they were forced to endure the humiliation and losses brought about by sequestration.

By the time of Thainville's exile, the war had been going on for almost a decade. The rivalry was exhausting for all involved, and both Britain and France were keen to find a peaceful settlement. A preliminary treaty was signed on September 30, 1801. Six months later, in late March, Joseph Bonaparte and the Marquis Cornwallis met in Amiens to sign a conclusive peace, which, as it transpired, turned out to be more of a truce; barely fourteen months later, in May 1803, the peace was broken. The peace had always been an uneasy one: Britain had only agreed to it because it had lost its continental allies and faced France alone. France flouted its obligations under the treaty: the promise to evacuate Holland was not fulfilled, and in 1803, French forces entered Switzerland. As soon as Britain was able to recruit a new continental ally, the resumption of hostilities was inevitable. The new coalition, including Russia and Austria, set as one of its goals the expulsion of France from the eastern Mediterranean.[101] What were the echoes of these events in Algiers? With the peace of Amiens, shipping from North Africa was quickly reestablished. The need for wheat could now be met without the danger of ships being captured. But the re-declaration of war brought much of Europe into the conflict, and shipping once again became a problem.[102] The fortunes of the Bacris were, of course, closely linked to the state of international diplomacy. But their good fortune depended, also, on the stability of the regime they had managed to establish in Algiers itself. And here, their good fortune was shortly to come to an end.

101. See Lyons, *Napoleon Bonaparte and the Legacy of the French Revolution*, 204.
102. Panzac, *Les Corsaires barbaresques*, 137.

CHAPTER THREE

"Assassination of the King of the Jews" (Long Live the King)

NAPHTALI BUSNACH WAS assassinated on June 28, 1805. It was a Friday. At seven in the morning, Naphtali was sitting in the morning sun, near the palace. A janissary by the name of Yahia approached. The two men knew one another; just a few days before, Yahia had gone to see Naphtali, looking for work. Naphtali had sent him away, and now Yahia returned, seeking revenge. Approaching the unsuspecting Busnach, Yahia shot him, three times. Mortally wounded, Naphtali was able to make his way home, where he died shortly after midday, surrounded by his family. That same afternoon, his corpse was taken to the Jewish cemetery of Ayoun Skakna (Hot Springs), which stood on land that Naphtali himself had purchased. The community buried him quickly, almost furtively. Only eight people were present to see the head of the community, the most powerful Jew in Algiers, committed to his final place of rest.

The assassinations of Naphtali and of Joseph's son, David, in 1805 and 1811, respectively, were catastrophic events in the lives of the Bacris. In the eyes of the French, British, and US consuls, everything revolved around Naphtali. His unprecedented influence over the Dey Mustapha determined their ability to fulfill instructions.[1] Consuls anticipated difficulty and understood successes—particularly that of their competitors—through the lens of their conviction that the Bacris enjoyed inordinate power in the regency. The early nineteenth century was a period of intense contest between France and Britain, with the third, fourth, and fifth coalitions of the Napoleonic Wars fighting across central Europe and in the Iberian Peninsula. Competition between consuls in the regency was a reflection of these wars. France and Britain and their allies competed for greater power and influence, as well as to service the need for supplies. The French and British powers were convinced that Bacris determined the direction taken by the imperial contest as it played out in the regency. It was their firmly held view that not only did the Bacris block them for their own advantage, but also that they worked hand in glove with the imperial competitor. What French and British consuls were able to achieve depended entirely—so they believed—on the Bacris. What happened to the consuls' relationships with the Bacris when Naphtali, and then David, were brutally and suddenly murdered? Did their perception of the contest change? The assassinations, and consuls' reactions to the same, allow us to see how they understood their situation—and the centrality of the Bacris—in the diplomatic contest in Algiers.

At the turn of the nineteenth century, Naphtali Busnach was a figure of great interest and legend. In Britain, his assassination was reported in the preeminent London newspaper, the *Times*, and in France, in the *Journal de l'Empire*, previously the *Journal des débats*, which was one of just four political newspapers under Napoleon.[2] Contained within these accounts of his death are many of the tropes that would come to define Naphtali Busnach. He exercised power to a degree never before seen. With that power came arrogance and insolence. No other figure had as much influence over the dey, Mustapha Pasha. Busnach had managed to satisfy all of Mustapha's fantasies of power and wealth. The *Journal de l'Empire* reported that Naphtali "dealt directly with representatives of different powers and would not allow anyone to approach

---

1. Touati, *Le Commerce du blé*, 354.

2. "French and Dutch Papers," *The Times*, September 17, 1805; "Nouvelles étrangères," *Journal de l'Empire*, July 25, 1805.

the prince whom he circumvented day and night through his accomplices."

> Busnach would mete out posts—and he would elect and depose at will the beys or governors of the provinces, with whom he maintained private correspondence. He would determine the sums they were to deliver to the dey, and he held the keys to the treasury. He had taken control of all trade and eliminated all competition. He commanded the navy of Algiers and those of the other ports of the regency. Corsairs would only put to sea at his command and they would set their course in accordance with the information he received from Europe, where he had numerous correspondents. He would seize all the takings before they were put up for public sale. In a word, he had managed to break all the time-honored customs, which here are held as sacred law. This form of behavior was reinforced by insolence combined with a great deal of ignominy, though also with uncommon courage.[3]

A very different Naphtali to the one described in the *Journal* was commemorated by his family on his gravestone. Busnach's gravestone was typical: a marble block, rounded at the top, and measuring one meter wide, and half a meter in height. Inscriptions in Hebrew were carved into each side, displaying Busnach's name and titles, laudatory epithets, and the funerary acronym. According to common practice, a lamentation was inscribed on one large face of the stone.[4] "Oh my friends," it began,

> My intercessors before God
> My eyes stream and my back is burned by the fire
> How could I see a prince, a lord
> End, dreading the vicissitudes of time?
> [. . .]
> Alas! The sapphires are crushed on the earth!
> Ah! The generous are taken to the tomb!

3. "Nouvelles étrangères: Afrique," *Le Journal de l'Empire*, July 25, 1805, translated and reproduced in Fenton and Littman, *Exile in the Maghreb*, 103.

4. Isaac Bloch, chief rabbi of Algiers in the late nineteenth century, sought to recover the history of Algerian Jewry by transcribing inscriptions on gravestones, and searching for biographical details of their subjects. His *Inscriptions tumulaires des anciens cimetières israélites d'Alger* remains an important source.

Alas! The compassionate lie in the dust!
I mean he whose name was Naphtali.
Justice and charity shone forth from him
He belonged to the Busnach family
The best among the distinguished sons of Zion
[. . .] He has taken his place among the pure who shelter in the tent of
the Eternal.[5]

Attempts had been made on Busnach's life before. On September 18, 1801, eight militia infiltrated the palace while Mustapha was at the mosque. They promised a reward of one thousand sequins for whoever could bring the heads of the dey, the prime minister, and Busnach. Their attempt failed. A little over two years later, on January 27, 1804, Busnach was attacked while sitting outside in the street, in the very same place where Yahia was to find him. He was stabbed, but the knife-wielding janissary missed his mark: Busnach sustained only a wound to his hand. The following day, another janissary sought to finish what his colleague had begun: heavily armed, he broke into Busnach's house, but was caught almost immediately by the patrol that Mustapha had provided for his protection. Busnach was no stranger to violent death. In addition to these threats to his own life, his brother Benjamin had been murdered in the streets of Algiers by a janissary in 1792. In hindsight, therefore, it was easy to read these events as the buildup to an inevitable climax, as Thainville would do. By 1805, as the French consul in Algiers would have it, the great "mass of hatred that had gathered on Busnach's shoulders" made his death as certain as "a change of government was inevitable."[6] It is possible that Thainville was referring to the effect of the catastrophic harvests that had begun in 1803. Since 1798, Joseph and Naphtali and their families had enjoyed an effective quasi-monopoly over the wheat trade, and under their authority, wheat prices had risen dramatically. But from 1804, the effect of the drought was aggravated by an invasion of crickets, and unrest in the Algerian hinterland.[7] The shortages became a veritable famine, as wheat prices increased

5. Bloch, *Inscriptions tumulaires*, 94.
6. AMAE 8CCC/37, p. 217, 5 thermidor, an 13 (July 24, 1805), Thainville to Talleyrand. This was originally written in code.
7. Touati, *Le Commerce du blé*, 375.

tenfold, meaning that a construction worker would have to work fifty-six days to buy a measure of grain.[8] Busnach had profited disproportionately from his control over the trade, and he may well have become a figure of hatred. Naphtali was powerful, but he was also vulnerable to popular opinion.[9]

In 1805, Naphtali Busnach was buried quickly, ostensibly because no burials could take place on the Jewish Sabbath, which would begin at sunset. But Naphtali's legacy loomed larger than life over the regency, and his death marked a beginning, rather than an end. Janissaries, excited and emboldened by Busnach's death, and still outraged at the idea of Naphtali's influence over Mustapha, marched to the palace and demanded the right to pillage the Jewish community. Mustapha, fearful for his own life, allowed them three hours. The next day, on the Sabbath, the attack began. In typically hyperbolic language, Thainville described how "ferocious soldiers burst from their barracks."[10] They were armed with yataghans (long daggers with double-curved blades) and pistols. Encouraged by the local population, small groups of janissaries roamed the streets of Algiers. They found very few Jews, so the janissaries turned their attention to the Sarfati synagogue. They forced their way into that sacred space, and "stupefied" Jews were hacked to death as they prayed.[11] An anonymous *Elégie* on the massacre describes in detail how upstanding and beloved members of the community were "sliced up like onions" and left to lie dying in the synagogue in pools of their own blood.[12] Other janissaries, waiting at the synagogue entrance, attacked and killed fourteen men as they fled. They ripped the Torah scrolls to shreds. The violence then spread to surrounding synagogues. Jews were killed as they made their way home from prayers, and others were murdered in front of their wives and children, as janissaries broke into Jewish homes. Rapidly, murder became pillage. First Busnach's home and warehouses, and then all Jewish homes, were invaded, as janissaries were joined by the general population. Two

8. Touati, *Le Commerce du blé*, 390. McDougall, *A History of Algeria*, 46.

9. Schroeter, *The Sultan's Jew*, 2.

10. AMAE 8CCC/37, p. 215, 5 thermidor, an 13 (July 24, 1805), Thainville to Talleyrand.

11. Anon., *Elégie sur le sac d'Alger*, in Bloch, *Inscriptions tumulaires*, 139. An English translation of the elegy is also available in Fenton and Littman, *Exile in the Maghreb*, 106–13.

12. *Elégie sur le sac d'Alger*, in Bloch, *Inscriptions tumulaires*, 134.

hundred Jews sought refuge in Thainville's house, protected by the French flag, while looters emptied their homes of all valuables, filling the streets with their furniture and belongings. They tore items of jewelry from the bodies of the women wearing them, and in less than three hours, "all the Jewish homes had only their four walls left."[13]

With Jewish homes thoroughly ransacked, the violence then ceased as easily as it had begun. The *Elégie* laid the fault at Busnach's door: "Our leaders were the cause of our misfortune. [. . .] Naphtali was the beginning of our ruin."[14] It quickly became clear to all that while Busnach's warehouses had indeed been emptied, the Jewish community's poor had suffered most. That is not to say, however, that all of the well-to-do were spared. Elijah Bedjaia, an associate of the Bacris, was ruined when his home and warehouse were pillaged. Israel Sasportis, France's official commercial agent, described as "a trustworthy man, known for his integrity," lost his life in the violence.[15] But the women in the Busnach family had escaped their home through a low window, and were taken on board a Swedish ship anchored in the port. The Bacris took shelter in the home of a friendly non-Jewish neighbor. The Spanish consul claimed credit for this act of mercy. He organized for their home to be guarded, thereby protecting the Bacris' belongings from pillage. Thainville, however, told a different story, asserting that Joseph Bacri's house was spared because the Dey Mustapha had a vested interest in ensuring that the Bacris would be in a position to repay the moneys they owed to the regency. According to this narrative, Joseph was saved by his business partner, not out of any sense of attachment, but rather, out of greed. From Marseilles, Jacob Bacri, safe but anxious, wrote to his agent in Barcelona that events in Algiers might have cost them money, but given the circumstances, they should be happy to be "quits for a pecuniary sacrifice."[16] Jacob might also have been relieved that, unlike most of the Jewish community, his family could afford such a sacrifice. In the aftermath of the "general effervescence," some of the

13. AMAE 8CCC/37, p. 215, 5 thermidor, an 13 (July 24, 1805), Thainville to Talleyrand.

14. *Elégie sur le sac d'Alger*, in Bloch, *Inscriptions tumulaires*, 133.

15. AMAE 8CCC/39, p. 357, September 9, 1809, Thainville to Jean-Baptiste Nompère de Champagny, Ministre des relations extérieures.

16. ADBR 39 E 21, p. 183, 23 brumaire, an 14 (November 14, 1805), Jacob Bacri to Arabet, Gautier, Manning et Compagnie.

goods stolen from the poorest of the community were returned,[17] and the streets were quickly cleared. Christian slaves carried bodies to the Jewish cemetery outside the gate, where they were burned. The *Elégie* placed the number of dead at forty-two.

Thainville reported on the proceedings with horror and sympathy. In stark contrast, British consul Richard Cartwright, in Algiers since January 1805, was able to find a silver lining in the clouds that had gathered over Algiers. With Naphtali Busnach's death, French interest in that part of the world had "received a mortal stroke," and this could only be "highly advantageous to that of His Majesty and His dominions."[18] Cartwright certainly believed that the malign power affecting British interests in the regency was vested entirely in Naphtali. As the Jews of Algiers were being killed and pillaged, the British consul was busy making it known that he had found weapons and French cockades in Jewish homes (something he also reported to his minister, secretary of state for war and the colonies, the Earl of Camden). For Thainville, these were "unfortunate Jews" experiencing a "dreadful pillage," a level of sympathy never evinced by Cartwright. But then, perhaps Thainville felt bad for Algiers' Jews because they were Cartwright's victims too. Cartwright, or so Thainville claimed, first gave Yahia, Busnach's killer, asylum in his consulate, and then organized for him to board a vessel, in plain view of the public, bound for Gibraltar.[19] Both the Bacris and the British were equally insupportable. "It is not supposed that the death of Busnach was caused by the English," Thainville wrote, "to whom he had been very serviceable, even against the opinion of the dey, in the last settlement which they made here; but wherever an agent of the Government of London is to be found, he will be always ready to receive and protect even the murderer of the person who has served him."[20] Thainville's allegations were widely repeated, including in the pages of the *Times*, but their veracity has never been established. Cartwright himself did tell his minister, however, that he had been forewarned of what would

17. Bloch, *Inscriptions tumulaires*, 101.

18. TNA FO 3/10, p. 132, July 3, 1805, Cartwright to Earl Camden, Secretary of State for War and the Colonies.

19. AMAE 8CCC/37, pp. 260–61, 27 vendémiaire an 14 (October 19, 1805), Thainville to Talleyrand. See also *The Times*, September 17, 1805, 2, col. A.

20. AMAE 8CCC/37, p. 217, 5 thermidor, an 13 (July 24, 1805), Thainville to Talleyrand.

happen. On the Friday evening, the day preceding the attack, he received a message from Isaac Bensamon, Britain's commercial agent and sometime fill-in consul, who had been "apprised," by "a friendly Moor," of what was to take place. (Bensamon wrote to beg that he might have Cartwright's badge as protection.)[21] This was news that Cartwright, notably, failed to pass on.

In the wake of the massacre, the janissaries demanded that only those Jews who practiced a trade should be allowed to remain. Mustapha gave the order for Jews to leave Algiers, and hundreds fled the city. On July 1, a French boat carried one hundred people to Tunis. Nine days later, two hundred people boarded a Ragusan vessel to Livorno. Among them were the relatives of Naphtali Busnach, and most of the Bacri family. Joseph Bacri and his son, David, as well as Michel Busnach, the brother of Naphtali, remained in Algiers on Mustapha's orders. They were to square the family's accounts with the regency. Joseph, who had shown great courage in remaining alone in his home during the massacre, was named head of the Jewish community—*muqaddam*—by Mustapha, in Busnach's place. David carried on Naphtali's work. Indeed, it seemed to Thainville that they had forgotten the recent events and managed to maintain their power and influence. Had Naphtali's death changed nothing? In July, Thainville was negotiating with David for the payment of funds that the Bacris owed to France's African Company from the time of the war. David promised to furnish accounts once calm had been reestablished. But calm was to be some time coming.

Despite the apparent continuity, Naphtali's death had changed the situation. If Naphtali Busnach had been the "soul" of the regime, then his death made the downfall of Mustapha's government certain. The regime was, in the eyes of the angry militia, "indelibly stained with Judaism," or so Thainville explained, and nothing could save it.[22] On August 31, a deputation of janissaries made its way to the palace, to signal to the dey and prime minister that they must leave. Both men tried to reach sanctuary in a marabout, or holy shrine. The prime minister, elderly and slow, was killed by a patrol close to the palace.

21. TNA FO 3/10, p. 132, July 3, 1805, Cartwright to Camden.
22. AMAE 8CCC/37, p. 245, 16 fructidor an 13 (September 3, 1805), Thainville to Talleyrand.

Mustapha managed to reach a shrine, but found it locked, and fell victim to another patrol. The bodies of the two men, stripped of clothing, were left to the mercy of the crowd, a populace, in Thainville's estimation, that was "the most barbaric in the world."[23] The new dey, Ahmed Pasha, the former chief scribe who had been pushed out by Busnach, was immediately placed on the throne. Thainville found Ahmed to be "as well informed and affable as his predecessor was ignorant and coarse."[24] He described how the janissaries surrounded their new leader, bowing and kissing his hand. Then the speaker of the barracks addressed him:

> We establish you our ruler. You will walk in the footsteps of the illustrious Barbarossa. You will live modestly, as he did. Your predecessor, governed by miserable Jews, ruined and debased the state through mad spending and extravagant building. You will abstain from taking counsel from any Jew, and you will only allow the head of the Jewish nation to enter the palace, so that he can pay the tributes owed.[25]

Ahmed Pasha took his oath seriously. And in his eyes, Joseph and David Bacri stood in for Naphtali. Having lost his post as chief scribe because of Busnach, and now in power, he did not deal with the Bacris affably. He demanded the immediate payment of outstanding accounts, amounting to some two million francs. All of Naphtali's assets were seized. Busnach ships were claimed by the regency as they arrived into port. Many of the vessels were bought by David Duran, the business rival and great enemy of the Bacris. On September 10, David and Joseph were told that not only were they to pay Naphtali's debts to the treasury, but that their own lives were now valued at four million francs. When they refused to pay, they were arrested, together with their friends, the brothers Moses and Judah Amar, and thrown in prison. This was tantamount to a death sentence, and indeed, Joseph, David, and the Amars would have been executed but for the intervention of several consuls. The

---

23. AMAE 8CCC/37, p. 246, 16 fructidor an 13 (September 3, 1805), Thainville to Talleyrand.

24. AMAE 8CCC/37, p. 247, 16 fructidor an 13 (September 3, 1805), Thainville to Talleyrand.

25. AMAE 8CCC/37, p. 246, 16 fructidor an 13 (September 3, 1805), Thainville to Talleyrand.

four men were held in detention for ten days, chained together in pairs, their days spent laboring alongside the regency's most unfortunate slaves. During this time, their friends among the consuls were persuading Ahmed to agree to an arrangement that would save the Bacris' lives. This was the reward brought by personal relations, by the fact that even though they might feel ambivalent toward the Bacris at best, consuls also felt that they knew them and needed them. Under the terms of the agreement reached, the Bacris, father and son, would be able to pay the four million francs Ahmed Pasha demanded, in twice monthly advances of 100,000 francs. They were released from prison on September 20, but were obliged to reside in the home of their adversary David Duran, most probably an experience calculated to be humiliating, until the first payment was made on October 28. While his enemies were in prison, Duran had become head of the Jewish community and commercial agent to the dey. Duran's complicity in the downfall of the Busnachs and Bacris is suggested by some sources. For instance, according to *The Book of Friendship of Nations*, a source on which nineteenth-century rabbi Isaac Bloch draws, Duran was no stranger to the disaster that befell the Busnachs and Bacris.[26] Duran and his advisors had apparently sworn to destroy the house of Bacri, in competition with his own.

If Bloch's sources, lost to time, were indeed correct, Duran underestimated the Bacris. Once the first payment had been made, Joseph and David, along with Moses and Judah Amar, were able to go home. Joseph and David resumed their activities, Joseph as agent for Spain, David as agent for Sweden and the United States.[27] Tobias Lear, best known as George Washington's private secretary, was US consul in Algiers from 1803 until his disgrace and expulsion in 1812. Lear dealt directly with David Bacri, borrowing cash and purchasing luxury items. On June 13, 1805, shortly before Naphtali's assassination, and on a day Lear noted in his diary as being one of fair weather and a strong wind, he bought a diamond ring from David, along with cloth and caftan, as a gift to Mustapha on

26. *Sefer Hesed Leumim*, or *The Book of Friendship of Nations*, is, according to Bloch, signed by members of the Jewish community of Algiers: Elie Cohen Solal, Baruch Tubiana, Abraham de Salomon Mesguiche and Sadia Kadjidj. This book no longer exists.

27. Bloch, *Inscriptions tumulaires*, 103–4.

the occasion of the circumcision of his son.[28] But Lear did not see himself as taking part in the imperial contest that so occupied France and Britain. He was an appreciably more clear-sighted observer of events. Lear saw his transactions with David as a necessary evil, a local custom to be submitted to, even if his judgement condemned it.[29] He experimented with diplomacy in the regency, seeking to establish what sort of relations might best position the United States. On one occasion, Lear described to James Madison how David Bacri came to his house, to inform Lear that the dey wished to purchase one of the watches he had recently received from Livorno.

> How the dey could know I had watches was mysterious to me, unless he was informed by the Jews, who by their correspondence with Leghorn [Livorno], where a brother of Bacri and one of Busnach is established, and are very rich, had sent information to their brothers here [. . .] as it is well known that not an article is sent to this place from any part of the Mediterranean but what is known to this House, through their correspondents.[30]

Lear chose to make a gift of a watch, all the more so because it was Ramadan, and it would be "impolitic" for a Christian to irritate the dey. Thus he sent one with the dragoman with his best respects, requesting that the dey accept it, and apologizing that he "had not one more worthy his acceptance." The dragoman returned with "many expressions of thanks, and promises of remembrance from the dey. I shall see," Lear mused, "how this experiment operates."[31]

The Bacris missed their third payment, and as a result, in early May 1806, David Bacri and Moses Amar found themselves once again in prison. But, claiming to be short of funds, the Bacris persuaded Ahmed to recover the amount immediately owing from their debtors, and to push back indefinitely the final deadline for payment of the remainder. This was a striking victory for father and son. A second one, of even greater significance, was still to come. Drawing once

---

28. NARA M23, roll 8, vol. 7, part 1, June 13, 1805.

29. NARA M23, roll 9, vol. 7, part 2, p. 405, September 15, 1807, Lear to Secretary of State Madison.

30. Tobias Lear Papers, January 8, 1804, box 1, pp. 2–3, Clements Library, University of Michigan, Lear to Madison.

31. Tobias Lear Papers, January 8, 1804, box 1, pp. 2–3, Clements Library, University of Michigan, Lear to Madison.

again most probably on the elusive *Book of Friendship of Nations*, Bloch claims that Duran, sworn rival of the Bacri and Busnach families, maintained a rule of terror over the Jewish community. While they were free, Joseph and David had persuaded the community to make a complaint against Duran to the Dey Ahmed. Whether this swayed the dey we cannot know. What is certain, however, is that on July 20, 1806, Duran lost his title, and he was replaced by his friend, Ben Tibi. But the Bacris were not done yet. Their "underground machinations" continued for some months, until finally, on November 1, David Bacri was named head of the Jewish community in Algiers. This role, which they could use to build economic power, was pivotal. On this occasion, the four-million-franc debt evaporated, allowing the Bacris to get on with doing business.[32]

Things might have been going well for the Bacris, but the same could not be said for Thainville. The contest with the British was becoming more intense. Initially, when Ahmed Pasha came to the throne, relations started on a good footing for the French consul. When the ceremonial artillery rounds announced Ahmed's ascension to the throne, Thainville made his way to the palace to compliment the new dey. There, he found Cartwright sitting waiting by the door, as everyone else rushed past him; a situation that Thainville judged unbefitting of the dignity of the British consul's position. For his part, the French consul waited for no one; ploughing forward, he split the crowd, much like Moses did the Red Sea, his dragoman walking ahead to clear his path. Cartwright followed him into the palace, and, as soon as both men crossed the threshold, the British consul set off, running like a madman to beat Thainville to the throne. Unfortunately for Cartwright, "his legs were not able to meet the standard set by his desires." For, as Thainville went on, for Talleyrand's benefit, "I had already taken the hand of the prince and given the ritual compliment, which is very short, when Cartwright brusquely seized the other. The dey held my dragoman back to ask the reason for the English agent's haste, which made everyone laugh."[33] Soon enough, however, the balance shifted, and it was

32. Bloch, *Inscriptions tumulaires*, 116. Bloch claims to have gleaned most of these details from correspondence registered in the Spanish consulate.

33. AMAE 8CCC/37, p. 251, 29 fructidor an 13 (September 16, 1805), Thainville to Talleyrand.

the British consul who enjoyed the dey's favor. In this new regime, Cartwright found a new, appreciative audience. Both Ahmed Pasha and his son-in-law, the Aga, were "personal acquaintances," Cartwright's "well-wishers," "most pronounced friends of the British nation," and all in all "the most desirable men for such situations"— words of striking effusiveness from a man who wrote very few letters during his brief post. Cartwright's new friends had, he went on,

> publicly declared they desire to have no other friends than the English, have voluntarily given the wheat trade of this country and have even refused permission to the French consul to introduce a single merchant either here or at Oran; telling him he would have English only.[34]

Key to his success, "thank God," as he wrote to his minister, was that "the Jewish influence was now quite at an end."[35] On his initial appointment, according to Thainville, Cartwright had paid court to Bacri and Busnach. The latter, who shortly before his death had become "the declared enemy of France," extolled Cartwright's virtues to those in power, allowing the British consul to execute his instructions, "to damage France in every way possible," or so Thainville reported miserably.[36] Yet from Cartwright's perspective, Naphtali's power had been malign, and with his death, British fortunes in the regency could rise. The conviction held by consuls that the Bacris always worked against their respective power, and for the benefit of the competitor, remained an enduring constant across consulships.

Cartwright went daily to the new heads of the regency to "grovel" before them. A jealous Thainville noted that he told them, constantly, that they had no truer friends than the British.[37] Lear wrote, more dispassionately, that the British were in good favor in the regency. They seemed, he reflected, "to have pocketed the repeated insults which they have received from time to time, and have made large presents to secure their favorable reception here." They had promised to protect the regency against France, from which, he felt, they had "much to apprehend." Perhaps they had

---

34. TNA FO 3/10, pp. 137–38, September 11, 1805, Cartwright to Camden.

35. TNA FO 3/10, p. 138, September 11, 1805, Cartwright to Camden.

36. AMAE 8CCC/37, p. 260, 27 vendémiaire, an 14 (October 19, 1805), Thainville to Talleyrand.

37. AMAE 8CCC/37, p. 249, 16 fructidor an 13 (September 3, 1805), Thainville to Talleyrand.

learned from their previous failures. Thainville, on the other hand, was "in continual difficulties."[38] The dey had given the concessions and the rights to coral fishing to the British, who had paid forty thousand dollars for these privileges, he reported. But this would bring them nothing, as Lear detailed: "the Jews" took "the whole cream of the trade," and through them, it would go to the French.[39]

Even when things appeared to be going well, circumstances could change and personal relationships could turn sour. In this period of great uncertainty and fickle fortunes, Cartwright's star shone brightly, but briefly. In early 1806, Lear noted to James Madison that the British consul had "presumed too much on his influence," conversing too freely in Turkish, and rendering himself "very obnoxious to the dey and regency." This was causing new difficulties for Britain in the regency, and the dey was demanding a new consul.[40] Cartwright's stay in Algiers lasted barely more than a year; arriving in January 1805, he departed again, a bitter man, in February 1806, a month after Lear's letter. In late 1805, Cartwright had written to Camden. For the last twenty years, he wrote, exaggerating somewhat, Algiers had been governed by "a wealthy Jew merchant whose influence invariably favored the views of our enemies." But things had now gone from bad to worse. As it turned out, Busnach had only been the ostensible Jew ruler. Following his disappearance, now the real one had gained power. The Bacris' local knowledge, combined with

> their great command of capital shortly set them free, when, soon after their most powerful enemies (the friends of Great Britain) were either strangled, banished or sent out of the capital and they are become more powerful than heretofore as they themselves foretold would be the case when groaning under heavy chains in a horrid dungeon. And the tables now has [sic] completely turned against the British.[41]

What he experienced in Algiers, Cartwright wrote, had been literally "a summary of all the horrors and indignities that have been offered to the British nation for the last thirty years."[42]

38. NARA M23, roll 9, vol. 7, part 2, p. 304, November 8, 1807, Lear to Madison.
39. NARA M23, roll 9, vol. 7, part 2, p. 414, April 6, 1807, Lear to Madison.
40. NARA M23, roll 9, vol. 7, part 2, p. 383, January 5, 1806, Lear to Madison.
41. TNA FO 3/10, p. 143, December 5, 1805, Cartwright to Camden.
42. Cited in Playfair, *The Scourge of Christendom*, 237–38.

But Cartwright, Thainville, and the other consuls misunderstood the Bacris and Busnachs. Perhaps they were, indeed, powerful. Perhaps they did, in fact, play politics, befriending and enabling, or cutting out one or the other power. Indeed, on one occasion, the Bacris offered Thainville to send the foodstuffs desperately needed in Marseilles, if the French government would deliver them from certain hindrances placed in their way by the "government of London."[43] But this was not, as the consuls read it, for the sake of the conflict. The Bacris did play on the rivalry when it suited them, but they did not see themselves as parties in it. Everything they did was entirely for their own sakes, or, more accurately, for the sake of their business. What the Bacris coveted was the post of *muqaddam*, or head of the Jewish community. The bitter and violent rivalry with the Durans and their associates makes clear just how desirable the post was. But for Cartwright and Thainville, the two families' power lay in politics: first, in their ability to gain influence over the dey and the elite of the regency, and then, in the cavalier way they played with the same. For these consuls, the Bacris' Jewishness lent itself to ideas of them as avaricious and duplicitous. Just like his competitor, Thainville, Cartwright saw Bacris at the center of events, particularly when the course of these did not turn in his favor. The British and French consuls' astonishment and dismay in the face of the families' ability to recover reveals this gap in understanding and expectation. As long as the Bacris had a *muqaddam*, they could carry on: their actions were invested in the position, not in the person occupying it. When he became *muqaddam* in 1806, David did not seek to follow the example of his cousin Naphtali in gaining influence over the dey. Despite this, he did continue his cousin's practice—as well as that of his father, Joseph—of bringing the dey and the ruling elite into his business ventures so that they might also profit from his activities. David managed to rebuild and surpass the family's previous great wealth.

Physically, David Bacri was striking: handsome, with a noble carriage, he was powerful and athletic. So struck by his good looks was Elizabeth, the daughter of new British consul Henry Stanyford Blanckley, that the young girl dreamt of him day and night, long after

43. AMAE 8CCC/39, p. 171, July 23, 1808, Thainville to Champagny.

his death. "You could not mistake his being a son of Israel," she wrote, "for the peculiar characteristics of his race were strongly engraved upon his handsome, noble features; but he fully realized one's personification of a descendant of the princes of the house of Judah, and his dignified and highly refined address was in perfect keeping with his appearance."[44] As a businessman, David Bacri took the family to new heights. Over the course of five years as head of the Jewish community, years of bitter enmity with the Durans, continued corsairing and slavery, sporadic violence, and a procession of changing deys, each one requiring a new negotiation, David amassed what was, by all accounts, an enormous fortune. Witnesses reported his wealth to be "incalculable."[45] Lear noted that David was the only man in Algiers who could command large sums of cash at little notice.[46] British correspondence claimed that David Bacri had loaned money privately and directly to Napoleon himself.[47]

David traded in all that crossed the Mediterranean; buying, selling, and transporting much-desired soda ash (used in dyeing processes), as well as sulfur, sumac, cotton, olive oil, salted tuna, sugar, cocoa, cinnamon, indigo, leathers from America, and cork. Much of this came in the cargoes of captured ships, and he would buy both vessel and cargo. David acquired several boats in this manner. On one occasion, one of David's vessels was used to transport a lion, a gift from the dey to Napoleon. For a while, David bought mostly British boats, captured and brought to Algiers by the French corsair Captain Bavastro, and his crew on the *Intrepid*. In 1809, he bought no less than five British and Spanish boats, caught by corsairs. This was a great boon to the regency, which could lessen its reliance on European powers for ships to carry precious gifts and emissaries.[48] Some of David's boats had Jewish names: the *Moses* carried out a good trade for him, as did the *Aziza*. Another of his boats was *The Three Brothers*. Did David choose the name? If so, to which of the

44. Broughton, *Six Years Residence in Algiers*, 205. Henry Blanckley had previously served in the American War of Independence, and at the siege of Gibraltar, after which he was appointed consul for the Balearic Islands, a post he occupied for nineteen years.

45. Broughton, *Six Years Residence in Algiers*, 206.

46. NARA M23, roll 9, p. 316, December 31, 1807, Lear to Madison.

47. Broughton, *Six Years Residence in Algiers*, 206. This claim was also recorded in Barnard, *Travels in Algeirs* [sic], 41.

48. Haddey, *Le Livre d'or des israélites algériens*, 69–70.

three brothers might it have referred? Mordecai had died a decade before. Abraham, Salomon, and David's own father Joseph were closest in business. Could it have been that the rift between the three and their younger brother Jacob had already begun to open?

David's purchases of these captured boats and their cargo were made in the face of repeated threats from the British. Yet while diplomacy played out on one level, on another, Algiers was like a village. Prominent Jews and Europeans could not help but rub shoulders. David Bacri, for instance, was a visitor to the Blanckleys' home on occasions of ceremony. In November 1807, the Dey Ahmed was deposed and the Jewish community believed another attack was imminent. David chose to seek refuge in the British consulate. Mrs. Blanckley reported finding "many Jews and their families" who had taken sanctuary in their town house. Among their number she noted "even Bacri," whom she described as "the great French adherent."[49] But even the French could be friendly. After all, the expatriate community was small, and all shared the common experience of isolation.[50] In early 1809, Mrs. Blanckley recorded in her diary that "the French Consul, his lady, with little Irène, and the rest of the French attachés," had all come to breakfast at the English consulate and had stayed until two o'clock.[51]

The easy social life that Thainville, Blanckley, and their families enjoyed, suggests that the professions of great enmity that run throughout their official correspondence may have been performance, to an extent. The consuls were telling their superiors what their role required, and what the state of war demanded of them. But fellow consuls, officially at war, could also put antagonisms to one side, and meet on the common ground of a shared understanding of the requirements of national dignity, in what all consuls felt to be the most undignified of countries. In March 1808, Lear reported to James Madison that the Danish consul had been arrested and imprisoned because his country had not paid the annuities. Lear met with the French and Swedish consuls, securing their agreement to send for the others the following morning, to organize the liberation of

49. Broughton, *Six Years Residence in Algiers*, 110.
50. See Richard Pennell's work on the sociability of consuls, in "Treaty Law," 240.
51. Broughton, *Six Years Residence in Algiers*, 127.

the unfortunate Dane. At noon the following day, they proceeded as a group to the palace, and interceded on the Danish consul's behalf. The dey agreed to release him. Following this incident of imprisonment—a "barbarous outrage"—the consuls all agreed to enter into a compact, and in mid-April, they issued a joint statement, which all of them signed, each retaining a copy.[52] These diplomatic efforts had, apparently, little effect. In May 1808, Fraissinet, the now-elderly French merchant and Dutch consul was, in turn, imprisoned for the non-arrival of the biennial present. Blanckley, the British consul, accompanied Thainville to his audience with the dey to demand the man's release. As they left the palace, Blanckley, also elderly and frail, asked Thainville's permission to take his arm. "Let us prove to the barbarians," Blanckley stated, "that although we are at war, we will always be united when it is a question of supporting the rights and the dignity of the European name." Unable to resist scoring points, Thainville responded that Blanckley would "always find such sentiments in French agents." Both men shared a common conception of honor.[53] All consuls, it would seem, shared an understanding of what nations were, and how their own nation must be represented and perceived. It was when this, in particular, was attacked that the threat to national sovereignty, far from the metropole, overrode national contest or enmity. For both Thainville and Blanckley, as for so many others, it was the Bacris who best exemplified this lack of respect for national dignity, and the many outrages of which they were the source came down to this.

Unlike his father and brother-in-law, David did not pursue a life of politics and diplomacy. His was, perhaps, a different dey—or deys—and he did not seek to control the rulers who now replaced one another, often in rapid succession, in the way that Naphtali reportedly had done. Perhaps David felt that his uncle's example served as a lesson. Lear thought that the family would not display their influence so openly as before.[54] Nonetheless, such was the state of affairs in Algiers that David did need to establish and maintain powerful friends. He brought the dey and his ministers in on

52. NARA M23, roll 10, vol. 8, n.p., March 28, 1808, Lear to Madison.
53. AMAE 8CCC/39, p. 133, May 20, 1808, Thainville to Champagny.
54. NARA M23, roll 9, p. 358, January 5, 1806, Lear to Madison.

his business dealings. As Blanckley noted to Admiral Lord Collingwood, Commander in Chief of the British fleet in the Mediterranean, unless David had "interest about the palace," he was unable to
maintain what Blanckley called his "illicit commerce, which he does
by promise of a certain portion of profits gained."[55] This served as
a guarantee: if one of David's boats was captured by a corsair, and
a powerful member of the regency elite had an interest in its cargo,
then that person would do David's work in insisting on the boat's
return. This theory would be tested by actual events, as one of David's
boats was captured by an English corsair and taken to Malta. The
boat at the time was flying the Algerian flag, and its papers were
all in order, making the capture illegal, by maritime law. When the
same English corsair casually moored his boat at Algiers, the dey
immediately placed an embargo on it. Advised, allegedly, by David,
the dey informed Blanckley that he must cease all communication
with the elite of the regency as long as the Bacris' polacca had not
been reinstated. The captured boat was promptly returned.[56] Then in
August 1808, another Bacri boat, *The Three Brothers*, was captured by
a Spanish corsair and taken to the Port of Roses, in Catalonia, where
the crew and passengers were all imprisoned. But several ministers of
the regency had invested in this particular voyage—another example
of the practice of mutual enrichment practiced by the Bacris and the
regency's elite. The Spanish consul immediately forwarded the dey's
claim to the Spanish foreign minister, who had the boat released.[57]
Joseph was, of course, Spain's commercial agent in Algiers, and the
Bacris had a good relationship with the power that was, historically,
the great enemy of the Jews. The Bacris lent a great deal of money
to Spaniards in Algiers. In 1809, this amounted to 55,783 piasters,
including money lent to the Holy Father Joseph Novela, who administered the Royal Spanish Hospital, totaling 25,030 piasters. (These
accounts would be settled in 1814.)[58]

Relations were less friendly with Britain, and David had more
than one confrontation with its government. The British did not like

55. TNA FO 3/11, p. 276, August 18, 1809, Blanckley to Baron Collingwood, Commander
in Chief of the Mediterranean Fleet.
56. Bloch, *Inscriptions tumulaires*, 114.
57. Bloch, *Inscriptions tumulaires*, 114–15.
58. Bloch, *Inscriptions tumulaires*, 114.

watching their ships pass into the hands of the Bacris. More serious, however, for the British at least, was the way the Bacris were able to interrupt their enjoyment of the trade concessions stolen by Blanckley during the period of coolness in Franco-Algerian relations. British usurpation of the concessions was a serious blow to the special historic relationship with the regency so valued by France. Among the concessions afforded in 1807 were permission to engage in coral fishing, but also exclusive trade from Bona, as well as the right to occupy La Calle. Blanckley agreed to pay an annual rate of fifty thousand hard dollars in exchange for these monopolies, as well as "for the complete overthrow of the French interest" in Algiers.[59] But their enjoyment of the coup and the benefits it brought was over before it had begun. In 1807, having gained the confidence of the Dey Ahmed Pasha, David obtained the monopoly over trade from Bougie for the family. Lear observed that Britain's money would bring them nothing—a prediction that would turn out to be correct. As early as March 1807, Thainville, who had "been able to procure" a copy of the deed passed between Algiers and Britain that granted La Calle, Bona, and the coral fishery to the latter, noted to Talleyrand that Collo (on the Mediterranean coast, to the east of Algiers) had been taken away from the British, and conceded to David Bacri.[60] The Bacris' efforts destroyed trade from Bona, which had been the main objective of the concessions for the British. They were forced to give up the concessions, and to allow them to return to French control.

The Bacris, it would seem, found a way to achieve their aims, "playing," as Lear saw it, with Franco-British rivalry. By July, Blanckley was reporting to Whitehall that there had been a backlash against his undertakings: Thainville was trying to undermine Blanckley's influence with the Dey Ahmed by means of "their agents (the Jews)."[61] Thainville would have hotly disputed the idea that he had any agents working for him in any way. He did know that Blanckley was in the process of negotiating with Ahmed to take over the concessions and the rights to coral fishing from France. He was,

59. TNA FO 3/11, p. 1, February 9, 1807, Blanckley to William Windham, Secretary for War and the Colonies.

60. AMAE 8CCC/38, p. 213, March 27, 1807, Thainville to Talleyrand.

61. TNA FO 3/11, p. 29, July 26, 1807, Blanckley to Viscount Castlereagh, Secretary of State for War and the Colonies.

predictably, filled with the fire of moral outrage, all the more so when, early in 1807, the message came from Ahmed that Thainville was to move all of France's property from the warehouses in Bona, and to be sure to remember to hand over the keys. Early in 1808, when it had appeared that Thainville might yet bask in good favor, Lear had written to Madison that if France and the regency were to reconcile, there would probably be "a difference with the other great power."[62] In November, he noted that the British were "in high favor." But, he observed, "these people" understood "the game they have to play between Britain and France too well to give themselves entirely up to one or the other, unless pushed thereto by the conduct of one or the other towards them."[63] The Bacris may not have seen themselves as players in the conflict, but this does not mean that they did not understand it. And, as Lear suggested, and as they themselves demonstrated, in the regency they were able to exploit Franco-British enmity to their own ends.

Throughout these dealings, the Bacris' closest and most complex relationship was, still, with France. It was a relationship of mutual need: the Bacris needed to be on good terms with France so that they might pursue repayment of the considerable debt owed them. Where France was concerned, part of the money they owed to the Bacris was actually money belonging to the dey, and so they needed the Bacris for the maintenance of good terms with the regency. On more than one occasion, David and Joseph stepped in to save Thainville from difficulty. In mid-1807, Thainville reported, in code, that the captain of a Spanish ship coming from Marseilles had announced Napoleon's death. On receiving this news, the Algerians were said to have made a display of "the most horrible joy." In response, Thainville had a letter circulated to correct the dreadful and malicious misinformation, and this was seconded by "Mr Bacri," who, summoned to the palace, confirmed the French consul's version of events.[64] Late in 1808, Thainville's relationship with the Dey Ahmed was breaking down. The French consul had negotiated the release of 106 Genoese prisoners. Ahmed agreed to their release on the basis that, in exchange, some Algerian subjects who had

62. NARA M23, roll 10, vol. 8, n.p., January 4, 1808, Lear to Madison.
63. NARA M23, roll 10, vol. 8, n.p., November 1810, Lear to Secretary of State Robert Smith.
64. AMAE 8CCC/38, p. 231, May 28, 1807, Thainville to Talleyrand.

been enslaved in Portugal would be liberated. As well as this, the dey insisted on the standard consular presents. These were, after all, markers of a personal and equal relationship. It was why, for example, Napoleon was sent a lion. But France, very much occupied with fighting Britain in northern Europe, was consistently failing to fulfill these undertakings. Tired of waiting, Ahmed granted Thainville just forty-eight hours to produce the presents, or, as the consul reported, he was to be chained to a cart, carrying stones from the mountains. It was the Bacris who "stopped [the dey's] intentions."[65] Bacris also supplied the boats for the transport of the freed French slaves, though not without making Thainville wait—French passengers could not be allowed to compromise the safety of cargoes.[66] If they were helping France, this was because of the debt, rather than any desire to favor the French, and this assistance could not be allowed to get in the way of business.

From the perspective of Western powers other than Napoleonic France, the giving of gifts was a necessary evil. State-to-state diplomacy between European and Barbary States was a system based on the idea of gifts. Gifts were both personal and diplomatic: they created ties and obligations between states. They established personal relationships. In exchange for presents from a Christian ruler, Maghrebi deys and beys would respect that power's ships and give them access to exports.[67] Gifts were expected "when a new consul arrived, at the conclusion of treaties and also upon their renewal after the enthronement of a king or accession of a new dey."[68] It was expected in Algiers that consuls would not only offer gifts to the dey, but to his extended family and his court, as well. For a consul, a successful gift giving would establish good relations with the regency's elite, and open access to spheres of influence. Each consul had a particular friend among the dey's ministers, who would often intercede on their behalf. Gift-giving worked both ways: deys expected gifts, but they also offered them in return. It was common for one of the regency's elite to offer the gift of a horse to the consul, and to send wild animals, specifically for the king, or for Napoleon,

65. AMAE 8CCC/39, p. 203, November 17, 1808, Thainville to Champagny.
66. AMAE 8CCC/39, p. 208, November 17, 1808, Thainville to Champagny.
67. Windler, "Tributes and Presents in Franco-Tunisian Diplomacy," 172.
68. Windler, "Tributes and Presents in Franco-Tunisian Diplomacy," 175–76.

when he ruled. In the eyes of successive deys, the giving of gifts marked parity and equality in the relationship between states. The dey, who saw diplomacy with the Western states as dealings between equals, would request the same of France and Britain that was expected of him. In 1821, for example, Hussein requested permission for an Algerian frigate to be repaired and rebuilt as needed in the French port of Toulon, "as a token of the friendship and good terms that exist between the two governments."[69]

British consul Charles Logie claimed that the practice of exchanging gifts had begun in Algiers after the Spanish peace. In order to obtain peace, in 1793, Spain had offered "money and the most costly jewels, and every rich article that can be found or they point out, ships of war and store ships to carry their ambassadors and presents, constructors to build their cruisers, in short everything the Spanish court can trace they wish to have or ask for." In fact, Logie pointed out, all the courts—excepting Britain—gave expensive, luxury gifts as a yearly tribute "to more than a hundred people down to the dey's barber," as well as consular presents every second year "and for making their peace from millions down to upward of a hundred thousand sequins in money."[70] When tributes were not forthcoming, the dey would encourage them. In 1799, Mustafa summoned the Dutch consul, a Frenchman named Fraissinet, "to explain to him that the Netherlands were neglecting their friendship." Its reinvigoration required investment on the part of the Netherlands (then the Batavian Republic), including the payment of 157,300 florins promised by the previous consul, and a "big present" to mark the renewal of peace following Mustapha's ascension to power.[71] (The practice continued: in 1807, Austria agreed to pay fifty thousand Spanish piasters, while the Netherlands paid forty thousand, Spain twelve thousand, and Britain ten thousand.) After Fraissinet agreed to pay fifty thousand florins every two months, Naphtali offered to advance the sums for a commission of two percent. Among the booty captured by corsairing was specie, and the Bacris made use of the largesse to advance cash when consuls needed it.

69. AMAE 8CCC/45, p. 387, November 10, 1821, Deval to Etienne-Denis Pasquier, Ministre des affaires étrangères.

70. TNA FO 3/7, p. 129, November 6, 1793, Logie to Dundas.

71. Van Krieken, *Corsaires et marchands*, 125.

But deys did not always live long enough to enjoy their largesse. There was no certainty or security in the position of dey, as Musta-pha's brutal end illustrated. While in neighboring regencies, local elites emerged to form dynasties, in Algiers, the continued refresh-ing of elites from the Turkish center meant that the dey, his min-isters, and janissaries had a significantly stronger Turkish charac-ter than elsewhere.[72] Deys were at the mercy of their janissaries. On November 7, 1808, Ahmed was killed by his janissaries, who expressed their rage by carrying his head triumphantly through the city and throwing his mutilated body outside the city gates. He was replaced by Ali Khodja, a poor and highly devout man, whose period of rule would be brief. Ali Khodja was murdered on March 4, 1809, strangled by his own militia.

Thainville was saved from having to produce the expected gifts, in a sense, by Ali Khodja's death. But then Hadj Ali came to power, and the new ruler chose to maintain the regency's demands on France, both for presents and for the liberation of Algerian slaves in Portugal. The demands continued even as the dey changed. The breakdown in relations between the regency and France's repre-sentative meant that Thainville, who had been granted leave by his own government, was not, in fact, permitted to leave Algiers. Once again, it took the intervention of David Bacri to secure an outcome favorable to the French. As Thainville later reported from the rela-tive comfort of quarantine in Marseilles, Hadj Ali eventually agreed to allow the French consul to depart. France, in turn, was given six months to return the enslaved Algerians, or pay an indemnity of 32,000 piasters. It was David who provided the funds, together with the Swedish consul, Norderling, who stood as guarantor, thus lib-erating boats, loaded and ready to sail, trapped in the port. Once again, business took precedence and dictated the Bacris' actions. In June 1809, after almost nine years in Algiers, Thainville was able to return to France for six months' leave. Setting sail on June 21, he was accompanied on his way to the marina "by all the consuls and a great throng of Europeans."[73] Thainville loved nothing more than a great

---

72. Shuval, "The Ottoman Algerian Elite and its Ideology," 326.
73. AMAE 8CCC/39, pp. 300–301, July 2, 1809, Thainville to Champagny.

send-off. The vice-consul, Alexandre Raguenau de la Chesnaye, was to represent France in his absence.

By the time Thainville departed, David's business dealings had extended to all the main ports of Algiers. Thainville might write to the interim consul in Algiers that "the Jews" were not as powerful as they had been, but this was the observation of a rather overbearing consul on leave indulging in a little wishful thinking.[74] In the eyes of the French still in Algiers, the Bacris maintained enough influence to frustrate French designs in the regency. In the port of Oran, France's vice-consul, Negrotto, had been expelled, and the cargoes of captured ships brought to that city had been placed in warehouses. One of these cargoes was of considerable value. Keen to find a way to buy it, the Bacris persuaded the naval minister to agree to sell it by public auction. But the acting French consul, Ferrier, refused to allow the auction to go ahead. In response, the Jews "rushed to tell the English consul." Blanckley was quick to intervene against Ferrier, and thus "to destroy the beginnings of favorable relations [between France and the regency] which could have undermined the favor he enjoys, in the greatest degree and without obstacles, since Mr. Raguenau's departure."[75] (Raguenau had been forcibly expelled from the regency in April 1810, following a misunderstanding over a captured boat.) Not that Blanckley felt any sense of collaboration with the Bacris. During one audience with the dey, he had complained that "the French and the Jews would do all in their power to involve us in disputes." He was happy to be able to report to Admiral Lord Collingwood, commander in chief of the Mediterranean fleet, that the dey assured him he would not allow this to happen.[76]

In 1811, disaster was to strike the Bacris for a second time. On February 4, David Bacri was called to the palace. Blanckley's wife, apparently well-informed, described events. At first, she wrote, he was "received with apparent courtesy,"

> indeed the Dey was almost unusually gracious during the whole time of the audience, conversing on the most indifferent topics; and it was

74. AMAE 8CCC/40, p. 100, August 9, 1810, Thainville to Raguenau.
75. AMAE 8CCC/40, p. 161, February 16, 1811, Ferrier to Champagny.
76. TNA FO 3/11, p. 284, September 8, 1809, Blanckley to Collingwood.

only on the unfortunate victim's leaving the barbarous Presence, that he had even a suspicion of the dreadful fate to which the smiling tyrant had doomed him. As he descended into the skiffa of the palace, two of the chaousses [sic] seized him, whilst a third, wielding a sabre, but too evidently informed him of the sentence that had been passed upon him.[77]

Almost six years after his cousin Naphtali was gunned down in the street, David too was murdered, beheaded at the door to the palace. But while no one was in any doubt as to the reasons behind Naphtali's assassination, theories abounded regarding the cause of David's sudden, violent death. For the Blanckleys, the fact that David's "enormous treasures" were confiscated by the dey immediately afterwards "left no room for hesitation on the subject." Hadj Ali coveted David's wealth, thought to be "incalculable."[78] The Spanish understood events differently. Their vice-consul in Oran told his foreign minister in Madrid, Don Eusebio de Bardaxi y Azara, that "apparently," Napoleon had "named the said Jew his consul general in Algiers, with the power to bestow power upon others, as well as to remove it, and that Bacri was involved in intrigues against the English nation." Despite this being nothing more than an unconfirmed rumor, Mr. Higuero, the Spanish functionary, felt entitled to add that David had "paid the deserved price for his *francisation*." This was, Higuero said, a "just justice."[79] Sophia Barnard, in Algiers for three months with her merchant husband, shared the Spanish vice-consul's assessment and perspective, confirming for the readers of her *Travels in Algeirs* [sic] that David had indeed been conducting business with Napoleon. The two men had "long carried on a secret correspondence." David had supplied Napoleon with funds to provision his armies in Spain and Portugal. David's execution, Barnard concluded, was a punishment for this collusion, and it was merited.[80] It is striking that these two commentators both channeled their own enmity through David. Others had different interpretations of

---

77. Broughton, *Six Years Residence in Algiers*, 204. "Chaousses"—i.e., *chaouches*—translates loosely here to sergeants.

78. Broughton, *Six Years Residence in Algiers*, 206.

79. Bloch, *Inscriptions tumulaires*, 116–17.

80. Barnard, *Travels in Algeirs*. The list of punishments is detailed on pages 66–67.

the event. Mordecai Noah, the high-profile American Jew who had a very short-lived diplomatic career in the Ottoman Empire, claimed that David lost his head because he had loaned money to the Spanish consul even though the dey had ordered him not to. Hadj Ali had had David's letters intercepted, and David's death warrant was signed.[81] If Noah's interpretation was correct, it is possible that the Spanish consul was seeking to deflect blame.

There was another, further, theory behind David's death, and once again, the clear-sighted Lear saw it. This one involved the ongoing enmity between Bacris and Durans. A few days after David's death, he noted, Joseph had been authorized to take charge of his affairs and carry them on as usual. Lear concluded from this that the cause of David's execution must have been "entirely personal."[82] "Local wisdom," too, "remembered libelous denunciations made against David, of blame for misappropriations, of which he was supposedly guilty, in the management of the Jewish community's fund."[83] A version of Lear's theory would be republished decades later by Bloch, after France colonized Algeria. In early 1811, so the report went, Hadj Ali had become fearful, and was finding conspiracies all around. "He condemned people to death without regard for their position or dignity," and David Bacri was one such victim. This was an execution committed on the basis of unproven suspicions: another Jew, "his enemy, falsely accused him of having complained to the Porte [the central Ottoman government] against him."[84] Bloch was certain: David Bacri had an enemy, and that enemy was none other than David Duran. David's tombstone and epitaph, clearly modelled on Naphtali's, found space to detail his betrayal.

> Leave me, my brothers, I weep in my great distress
> My heart and my back are burned by the fire.
>
> How could I see a prince, a lord
> End, dreading the vicissitudes of time?
> After it nourished him with all delights,

81. Noah, *Travels in England, France, Spain, and the Barbary States*, 426.

82. NARA M23, roll 10, vol. 8, n.p., April 22, 1811, Lear to Secretary of State James Monroe. Original emphasis.

83. Bloch, *Inscriptions tumulaires*, 116.

84. *Tableau de la situation des établissements français dans l'Algérie, 1844–1845*, 567.

It deals him a blow with its ardent flame, and he perishes
An old enemy

For nothing, without any crime from him
Set an ambush and struck, like a snake
With the poison on his tongue, he burnt and consumed him

This was an epitaph bristling with fury. Perhaps it was the work of Joseph, mourning the loss of his beautiful son. In a rage of vengeance, the epitaph went on:

God is vengeful: he demanded his blood in return
And the enemy's head was cut off. His neck was broken
Like that of a cow, stoned to death, like the scapegoat
His horn was brought down to the level of his hoof
His supporters were dispersed, like thorns, cut off
Like a thorn lost in a deserted land
[. . .]

And it concluded, in grief:

His name was David, his face was handsome
In him, justice and charity shone forth
He was a priest of the Most High, pleasant plant
The best among the distinguished sons of Zion
[. . .] He took his place among the pure in the tent of the Eternal[85]

On his way back to Algiers, Thainville had informed his minister, now the Duc de Cadore, that he had received news from the Bacris in Livorno of David's death. Sensing worse to come, he told the minister that the murder appeared to be "a prelude to new unrest in Algiers."[86] In Algiers, too, members of the Jewish community panicked. Ten days after David was killed, Jacob presented himself at the door of the British consulate. In hiding for some time "in some less secure place," Mrs. Blanckley reported, Jacob now came to the British consul's town house, begging for protection. With sanctuary granted, he asked for secrecy, choosing to occupy a room in a

85. Bloch, *Inscriptions tumulaires*, 110.
86. AMAE 8CCC/40, p. 188, April 14, 1811, Thainville to Champagny.

little-used part of the house.[87] The memory of the events surrounding Naphtali's killing was clearly still fresh in Jacob's mind.

These suspicions of further unrest to come following David's assassination proved well founded, but the ensuing violent events did not take the same form they had in 1805. In the wake of David's death, and in what was becoming a pattern, David Duran was once again named head of the Jewish community in place of his recently executed enemy. But just nine months after David Bacri's death, on October 18, 1811, David Duran, too, was beheaded on the dey's orders. The previous evening Duran had gone to the palace, taking a gift of cakes and other delicacies to present to the dey for Ramadan. While there, or so Lear reported, Duran "made some complaints against Joseph [. . .] when the dey became angry, and told him that by the intrigues of himself and others, Bacri had been executed, and that he should follow him." Without further ado, Duran was taken to the palace gate, and decapitated, his body left there to be seen by all who entered.[88] On this occasion, it was Joseph who instigated the terror. Appointed head of the Jewish community following Duran's death, Joseph now took his revenge on those who had, as he saw it, engineered David's downfall. (Joseph was all the more bitter, perhaps, because his other son, David's brother Nathan, was a ne'er-do-well, and Joseph had cut him out of the family business.)[89] In early November, Joseph's storehouses were burnt down. Ben Tibi, Duran's associate, was accused, and immediately beheaded. The dey ordered all members of the Ben Tibi family to leave Algiers and had them taken to the Levant. In Broughton's *Six Years Residence in Algiers*, Mrs. Blanckley paints a picture of Ben Tibi's wretched widow and children being forced out of their home.[90] Joseph's vengeful wrath became legend. When Rabbi Isaac Aboulker went to the dey to complain on behalf of members of the community about Joseph's "exactions," Joseph, so popular wisdom had it, turned the accusation on the hapless rabbi, who was executed.[91]

87. Broughton, *Six Years Residence in Algiers*, 206.

88. NARA M23, roll 10, n.p., October 20, 1811, Lear to Monroe.

89. Archives nationales (AN) (Pierrefitte) F/7/6537, "Notes sur la famille Bacri d'Alger, de Livourne, de Marseille et ses cointéressés."

90. Broughton, *Six Years Residence in Algiers*, 234–36.

91. The story is told in Bloch, *Inscriptions tumulaires*, 126.

In June, back in Algiers for just over a month, Thainville wrote, in characteristically triumphal voice, that "the Jews' credit," so strong for the last twenty years, had now been "entirely wiped out."[92] Little did Thainville realize that in Jacob, the youngest Bacri brother, he had met his match. Thainville, by far the longest serving of all his contemporaries, simply would not understand the realities of the power dynamics in the regency. As long as there was a Bacri available and able to fill the post of *muqaddam*, the families could access the power that gave them license to break "time-honored customs," such as playing France and Britain to their advantage. By late October, an astonished Thainville was attributing Duran's death to "the Bacri Jews' intrigues," which now became more powerful every day. While Joseph was head of the Jewish nation, it was "the despicable Jacob" who governed the family and the business.[93] Having established himself in Marseilles around 1795, moving north to Paris shortly afterwards, Jacob's task had been to recover the money owed by France. He was unsuccessful and by 1811, Jacob had been back in Algiers for some time, possibly since 1808. Now he loomed large in Thainville's field of vision. Elizabeth Broughton, waxing lyrical on David's beauty and nobility, had wondered at Jacob's looks and carriage. She did not think David could have inherited his good looks, she mused, since his uncle Jacob "was of a far less aristocratic aspect."[94] For Thainville, Jacob was equally unattractive of character. Thainville could not bring himself to write about Jacob without appending an epithet to his name: when he was not despicable, he was villainous, or only too renowned. Jacob renewed the family's claims against France, and because of Jacob's closeness to the Dey Hadj Ali, Thainville's life became difficult, and he was increasingly hysterical. In late October, he reported that Hadj Ali was threatening to put him in chains if he did not address Jacob's claims. "I will remain resolute," a defiant Thainville wrote to his minister. "I will destroy the intrigue, and the intriguers, or I will leave my head here."[95] A month later he wrote to inform his new minister, the Duc de Bassano, that because of Jacob's

92. AMAE 8CCC/40, p. 210, June 7, 1811, Thainville to the Duc de Bassano, Ministre des relations extérieures.

93. AMAE 8CCC/40, p. 271, October 29, 1811, Thainville to Bassano.

94. Broughton, *Six Years Residence in Algiers*, 205.

95. AMAE 8CCC/40, p. 271, October 29, 1811, Thainville to Bassano.

claims on France, he was prevented from leaving Algiers. The dey continued to make threats. "Tomorrow," this letter concluded, at heights of rhetorical excess that only Thainville could reach, "I will probably be in prison. Long live the Emperor!"[96]

But Thainville was not alone in his displeasure; all sides found common cause in their disgruntlement with Jacob. With the death of Salomon, the brother in Livorno, and David gone, Jacob took on the running of the family business, together with his surviving older brother, Joseph. The remaining brothers continued to buy and sell boats and cargoes, and to ship goods, as David had done. In 1813, they were still buying captured boats, both Spanish and British, from French corsairs. The *Moses* was still taking goods around the Mediterranean in the Bacris' name, to Marseilles and Livorno. In the midst of a dragging, bitter war, the Bacris continued to show scant respect for the rules of conduct, dealing with France, but also, in 1811, calling on the British for help, when this suited them. At the same time, Blanckley complained that he was unable to buy much-needed corn, since grain had been "forestalled by the Jews."[97] Jacob did indeed cause trouble, seemingly for all around him. Thainville was sadly beleaguered, once again. Bassano, his minister, was on the road with Napoleon in eastern Europe, and mail, if it could pass at all, was slow. In May 1812, noting that he had not received any communication for some time, Thainville commented to Bassano that "I am as distant as if I were placed in India." Despite the absence of replies, Thainville nonetheless wrote regularly to his minister. Letters would pile up on his desk, awaiting a boat, when they would be sent, all at once. In his letters, he returned repeatedly to the subject of Jacob. It was because of Jacob's intrigues, Thainville reported himself telling them,

> That the good harmony that I had managed to reestablish between France and the regency had been disturbed again, that it was up to them to repair their insults towards His Majesty's agent, that the sums taken should especially be paid, and that then they would find me disposed to forget all the evils they had sought to do me.[98]

96. AMAE 8CCC/40, p. 280, November 21, 1811, Thainville to Bassano.

97. TNA FO 3/14, p. 30, February 10, 1812, Blanckley to Lord Liverpool, Secretary of State for War and the Colonies.

98. AMAE. 8CCC/40, p. 310, May 11, 1812, Thainville to Bassano.

Most especially, in order to achieve a rapprochement, the Bacris were to agree to provision France's armies in Spain. This they promised to do. But not quite three weeks later, on May 30, Thainville was obliged to observe that Jacob had recommenced his intrigues. "He had appeared to want to come closer to me," the increasingly lonely Thainville wrote, "but today he seems to be distancing himself."[99] Thainville struggled to reconcile his belief in the sanctity of national dignity and his perception of the remaining Bacris as not only powerful, but also hostile, and traitorous. Ultimately this affected the French consul's judgement.

By June 5, the situation was improving and Thainville was feeling confident again. After a long interview with Jacob and Joseph, he secured their commitment, once again, to send wheat to Spain. They had formally engaged to cease all intrigues against His Majesty's agent. Now, Thainville begged, if Napoleon could induce the Sultan to send a messenger to Algiers in support of the trade with France, "I will annihilate the Jews." As long as they retained some credit, France would never have a moment's tranquility. The idea of the appearance of the Sultan's messenger, moreover, made Jacob "tremble," and filled the British with dread.[100] On June 27, Thainville sent Bassano a coded message informing him that Jacob Bacri's good standing in the regency had dropped appreciably.[101] But this shift in Jacob's fortunes proved short-lived, as just a month later he persuaded Hadj Ali to declare war on the United States. Or so Thainville believed. On July 16, an American ship docked in the port, bringing the naval munitions that the United States had undertaken to supply annually to the regency as a payment for peace. Four days later, the goods were unloaded, and placed in the regency's warehouses at the marina. But the following day, without warning, Ali ordered the goods to be loaded back onto the ship. Lear received an order to pay money the United States owed the regency within four days, on pain of being placed in chains, and then to leave Algiers immediately. Over the following two days, Lear organized for the debt to be paid. Four days after the

99. AMAE 8CCC/40 30, p. 325, May 1812, Thainville to Bassano.
100. AMAE 8CCC/40, p. 342, June 5, 1812, Thainville to Bassano.
101. AMAE 8CCC/40, p. 344, June 27, 1812, Thainville to Bassano.

initial demand was made, however, on July 25, he was summoned to the port at six in the morning where he was told that the dey had declared war on the United States and was forcibly placed in a boat that then took him on board his ship. No explanation was given, but Thainville believed he understood what lay behind these events: the declaration of war on America was no less than "a new intrigue from the infamous Jacob Bacri." The "Bacri Jews," he went on, saw an opportunity to enrich themselves. They speculated on the bills that Lear had been obliged to supply them, and at a rate of exchange that yielded more than twenty-five percent profit. At the same time, the French consul claimed, they were speculating on the American captures that might be brought into port, and that, "through their intrigues," would be awarded to them. As mediators in brokering a US peace, they would also "make the Americans pay, dearly."[102] Thainville painted a picture of Bacris making money hand over fist.

Lear himself told a very different version of events. He explained to James Monroe that he had been expelled because

> After having concluded a truce with Portugal, and seeing Sicily under the protection of the British, [the dey] must make war upon some other nation, with or without a cause, in order to employ his cruisers, and that the extended and unprotected commerce of the U. States affords greater prospects of advantage from plunder and captures than he could expect from any other nation.[103]

Events had been put in train by the Dey Hadj Ali for his own purposes. True, Lear did borrow money from Jacob to secure his own departure. He reported as much to Monroe, in full detail and very matter-of-factly. But Lear saw no Bacris behind Hadj Ali. Even when, a month later, he had received news that—contrary to his predictions—no orders had in fact been given to detain US ships, he did not change his interpretation of events.[104] We cannot know which of the two men saw things correctly, or whether Thainville, driven to a point of conspiratorial belief from which he could not

102. AMAE 8CCC/40, pp. 354–55, July 27, 1812, Thainville to Bassano.
103. NARA M23, roll 10, July 29, 1812, Lear to Monroe.
104. NARA M23, roll 10, August 30, 1812, Lear to Monroe.

return, unconsciously invented facts to fit with his understanding. Jacob did lend funds to Lear at a rate of twenty-five percent, which Lear accepted without complaint. For Thainville, however, Jacob had gone beyond mere intervention in the war. According to the French consul, Jacob had set another war in train.

Bassano, holed up in Vilna with Napoleon's army, was having none of this. "You announce to me that the Jews' good standing has dropped appreciably," he wrote to Thainville. And yet at the same time, he pointed out, the French consul also attributed the declaration of war to "the intrigues of this Bacri." "This circumstance seems unlikely, to me." Rather, he instructed his consul, "It would be good to find out if this rupture could have happened at Britain's instigation."[105] Britain was Bassano's (and very likely his government's) preoccupation, when it came to Algiers. Late in 1811, he had told a mildly hysterical Thainville that his continued presence in Algiers was

> extremely useful for balance against English influence, which would otherwise push the regency to extremes which must be avoided, and to maintain our hope of the advantages that our relationship with this country present if you manage to re-establish our commerce.[106]

After all, if Hadj Ali was committing "excesses," and refusing to communicate directly with Thainville, then, as far as France's foreign minister was concerned, this was only because his ministers had been "corrupted by Britain, and by a few scoundrels like the Bacri Jews."[107] Thainville maintained a stubborn belief in Jacob's avarice and amorality. Lear's version of events suggests that Jacob was, perhaps, not quite so powerful, but Thainville was trapped by his prejudices and perceptions.

Had Bassano been in a position to ask the British, he would have found that they felt equally strongly about the Bacris. In May 1812, Blanckley had left Algiers, accompanied by his family, and was replaced by Hugh MacDonell. The new British consul decided early on that "those people," as he described them to Colonel Sir

---

105. AMAE 8CCC/40, p. 372, October 10, 1812, Bassano to Thainville.
106. AMAE 8CCC/40, p. 281, October 29, 1811, Bassano to Thainville.
107. AMAE 8CCC/40, p. 300, April 30, 1812, Bassano to Thainville.

Henry Bunbury, under-secretary of state for war and the colonies, had great influence in Algiers, and this was "incompatible with the prosperity of the British."[108] The Bacris were firmly in the French camp. Blanckley had purchased wheat from the Bacris. This was to be sent to Lisbon, but in transportation it was taken by a French corsair and carried into Malaga, where the cargo was sold. Sir Charles Stuart, then envoy extraordinary and minister plenipotentiary to Portugal, wrote to suggest, rather peremptorily, that the Bacris should cover the cost of the lost wheat. This, MacDonell complained to Bunbury, was "a construction their engagement would not bear out." They could not be expected "to take an active part or to side against the interest of France."[109]

For the Bacris, maneuvering and surviving through the interstices of national and imperial rivalries, the stakes could not have been higher, both in terms of the rewards for victory, and the penalties for failure. In their port city, capable of extraordinary violence, two heads of the family had come to a horrific, unpunished end. Yet even grieving and bitter, and they themselves often threatened, they persisted in their business. One "king" would be assassinated, only for another member of the Bacri family to take his place.

Over the course of more than a decade, members of the Bacri family managed to foil and interrupt the projects of both France and Britain in Algiers. Now, if Joseph was nominally "king," Jacob was his evil vizier, dealing and scheming, and seemingly uncontrollable. Both French and British consuls were unable or unwilling— or perhaps both—to understand the nature of politics and power relations in the regency, and thus of the Bacris' ability to maintain influence—of one Bacri to take the place of another. They did not see how the role of *muqaddam* allowed the Bacris to prosper within the structures of government in the regency.

The inability of consuls to discern this different framework speaks to their obsessions. They were representatives of their nation, needing to manifest its greatness in the establishment of relations of unequal power, and in the blocking of the imperial competitor. Through the contest, these two nations were busy defining

108. TNA FO 3/14, p. 115, July 4, 1812, MacDonell to Bunbury.
109. TNA FO 3/14, p. 151, November 1, 1812, MacDonell to Bunbury.

themselves. The insight of Sir Lewes Roberts, a ship's captain and merchant with the Levant Company in the seventeenth century, is instructive: "Imperial power was grounded first and before the use of any cannons or swords on *the mere knowledge of their nation abroad*."[110] As France and Britain competed in this far-off place, they came to know themselves as imperial powers. Yet in this contest of empire and diplomacy, the Bacris constantly thwarted the consuls' imperial plans, or so these men believed. Explanation for the failures of the British and French all came to be focused in various members of the extended Bacri family. Each consul was convinced that he needed to destroy the other's influence so as to access precious resources, but each was also limited by what they believed they could not achieve. Blanckley could not definitively claim the coveted concessions for Britain, and Cartwright quite simply failed to maintain good relations. Thainville, meanwhile, could not rein in Jacob. They reported their travails to their respective metropoles in some detail, so that the Bacris became known in Paris, London, and Madrid, as well as in Washington. Imperial projects for Algiers, conceived in the metropole, were adapted and reshaped at the periphery, where the Bacris were incorporated into the narrative of ambition and disappointment. But although the French consul enjoyed no success, France did have one means at their disposal by which the Bacris might be brought under control. This involved taking what the Bacris, apparently, valued most.

110. Cited in Zwierlein, *Imperial Unknowns*, 113.

CHAPTER FOUR

Difficult Relationships

RELATIONSHIPS BETWEEN CONSULS, the Bacris, and the regency were not always easy. Consuls encountered constant frustrations and difficulties. More often than not, members of the Bacri family were able to turn these difficulties to their financial advantage, being on hand to supply necessary specie, or diplomatic aid. But difficult relationships—both within the family, and in their most significant relationship in this story, between the Bacris, the regency, and France—also contributed to the Bacris' downfall.

The Bacris' relationship with France dated back to the beginning of the revolution, and was one in which all parties were particularly entangled. France and the Bacris mattered to one another. France had run up a huge debt for vast quantities of wheat supplied by the family, and this—in an increasingly familiar pattern—was owed not only to the Bacris, but also to the dey, their business partner. And France had a longstanding relationship with the regency more broadly. Right throughout the eighteenth century, the French regime had been the regency's best customer for raw produce. Since the seventeenth century, France had held concessions and had built a fortified trading post on the Algerian coast at La Calle (El Kala). The Bacris brought both regimes much closer, both because the debt complicated relations, and because members of the extended family established themselves in France and Livorno (which was shortly to become part of the French empire). In 1794, Jacob, the youngest of the brothers, moved to Marseilles, where he was joined by one of Naphtali's brothers, Michel. In 1787, Salomon, another of the Bacri brothers, moved to Livorno, and over the ensuing years he was joined by several members of the family.

These relationships were significant, but they were also complex, and, at times, difficult. Napoleon, deep in total war, consistently refused to acknowledge the Algerian convention of exchanging gifts, creating offense to the regency; and in Algiers, Thainville had not only to deal with an offended dey, but also with the Bacris, whom he had come to see as his implacable adversaries. The Bacris had managed to go on in the face of horrific violence. Now they, too, were beset by challenges, not only from within, but also from without. Their inability to trust one another was to test the family network severely, as members of the Bacri family committed financial fraud against one another. But when France attacked their business, this created a different sort of strain. The presence of Bacris on French soil made them pawns in a diplomatic game of repeated sequestrations, where in order to ensure the safety of French citizens and their property in Algiers, Bacris and their belongings would be held under guard. Under such difficult circumstances, all of these relationships began to break down.

As we saw in chapter 1, in 1794, the Bacris agreed to send Algerian wheat to a desperate, cash-strapped France on credit. The monies owed for this wheat remained unpaid until 1820, notwithstanding efforts by the brothers—particularly Jacob—over decades, to have France repay them. At times, France used the debt to tie the Bacris to them, inveigling them to provide services, or indeed, more wheat, on the promise of an impending repayment. It was this debt, and Jacob's failure to obtain the promised repayment, that lay behind the implosion of the family network. Even before the terrible events surrounding Naphtali's assassination, the two families had set in train what was to be a long, bitter process of rivalry and infighting. We are not party to the family dynamic, although both events and the correspondence allow for some conjecture. Whether Jacob took it upon himself to move to France or whether he was sent there by his brothers is unclear. They seem to have had little faith in his ability to carry out his allotted mission. Abraham sought and gained government permission to travel from London to Paris, in the midst of a war, to be with Jacob, perhaps to supervise the untrustworthy youngest brother closely. In Livorno, Salomon and Moses Busnach,

Naphtali's brother, actually agreed between themselves that they would not help Jacob or Michel Busnach when the two fell out, both deep in debt. In Algiers, Joseph and Naphtali went to some trouble to distance themselves from the two. His elder brothers' mistrust may have stemmed from Jacob's inability to properly understand his new context in France. Indeed, Jacob's incapacity to work across different state contexts was to have disastrous results. Across the events that play out in this chapter, including repeated sequestrations and the collapse of the family network, Jacob continued to use approaches that he took, fully formed, from the world he knew, but which had little or no effect in a place marked by very different systems of power.

In the regency, the French consul Thainville was doing much the same. He continued to insist that the Bacris conspired with Britain against France. But while the consul who had served in the regency since 1801, with a break of just six months, maintained his belief in conspiracy, events around him moved on, and relations—and his posting—began to sour. Thainville faced challenges in the regency; he was a servant to his regime, after all, and his regime was increasingly beleaguered. One after another, deys maintained their insistence that the wheat debt must be repaid, but no agreement came from France, busy fighting wars on all fronts. Not only did Napoleon refuse to consider making payments, the French leader also declined to send any customary gifts. For a regime that understood the offering of gifts to be intrinsic to relations and the acknowledgement of parity in status, this was insulting. It was Thainville who bore the brunt of regency outrage. But Thainville himself was also busy with outrage, directed particularly at the behavior of Jacob, once the youngest brother had reestablished himself in the regency. Thainville was ultimately to be consumed by the indignation that he had so carefully cultivated over the course of his posting. The final insult, in fourteen years of accumulated outrages committed against him and the emperor he so faithfully served, was to come on the occasion of his final departure, when he did not receive the dignified send-off he had always anticipated.

Throughout these difficult times, Thainville's dignity and security, and by extension, that of France, were repeatedly saved, as he saw it, by sequestration. Only the threat of having their livelihoods effectively blocked in France and Livorno prevented the Bacris from acting against him in Algiers, prejudicing—in his eyes—the dey against him. The repeated tit-for-tat sequestrations between France and the regency bound the two regimes together. The Bacris were always to be found at the center of these. The sequestrations form the backdrop to the history of entanglement, difficulty, and failure over this period.

Sequestration was a practice with a long precedent, both in law and in diplomacy, as well as according to *jus bello*, the laws of rightful war. In the Middle Ages, debtors unable to make necessary payments would see their goods seized in lieu. In times of war, it was a standard practice to expel enemy subjects and seize their wealth. In the diplomacy of the seventeenth century, sequestration was in common usage. Individuals who had experienced damages or losses at the hands of a foreign individual or power could seek recourse with their sovereign for justice. This would take the form of a reprisal, whereby they would compensate their loss legally, by seizing the belongings of compatriots of those who had done them wrong. This was an accepted procedure that was not understood as a declaration of war. It could, however, provoke an opposite, but equal action, and reprisals could escalate to the point of affecting diplomatic relations.[1]

Both regimes were users of the practice, as we saw in chapter 2, with the imprisonment of the unfortunate Moltedo after the Porte declared war on France, and France's responding imprisonment of Jacob in Paris. When, in the eyes of the French regime, the regency behaved in an unacceptable manner—declaring war, attacking French ships, refusing to allow a consul to leave, or insisting, violently, that a consul leave—then France responded by sequestering all Algerians to be found in France, together with their belongings. This was a way of ensuring the safety of French citizens in the regency. Members of the Bacri family were to find themselves the repeated targets of sequestration over the years to come. Sequestration was certainly an effective technique. The family suffered financially each time their warehouses were closed and their ships forced to remain in the harbor. The stress of repeated sequestrations may well have contributed to the public and spectacular collapse of the

1. Girard, "La Saisie des biens des Français en Espagne en 1625," 314–15.

family network. But the Bacris were also adept at creating their own suffering, in both their business and personal lives.

The first indication of trouble in the Bacri family came from Thainville, in Algiers. In October 1803, Thainville communicated some surprising news to Talleyrand. He had, he wrote, received a letter from Joseph and Naphtali, informing him that they had broken off all communication with their respective brothers (Jacob and Michel, both in France), and they wished for this information to be communicated to France, as a matter of urgency. In particular, the minister was not to pay Jacob or Michel any of the money owed by France to the Bacris. Two days later they came to the consulate, together with Jacob Marali and Isaac Abulker, two religious authorities whom Thainville described as "the highest judges of the Hebrew nation,"[2] to register an official declaration to the effect that they alone, together with Salomon Bacri and David Busnach in Livorno, constituted the House of Bacri Brothers and Busnach. Jacob and Michel had never been included in the company, could claim no interest in it, or demand anything from it, and if they had done business for the family, such as receiving and on-selling cargoes in Marseilles, they had been acting merely as brokers.[3]

In fact, for more than a year, both Thainville and Falcon had been reporting that Joseph and Naphtali had been grumbling about their relatives in Paris and Marseilles. In July 1802, Naphtali had complained to the French consul that Jacob and Michel had misled him, with troubling consequences for France: they had claimed that Napoleon would have the 200,000 piasters they were requesting repaid.[4] Thainville felt that Jacob and Michel did, indeed, mislead Naphtali, particularly where France was concerned: Busnach had no true idea of that nation's principles and its strength.[5] Falcon, too, was aware that all was not well. The Bacris might be "immensely

2. AMAE 8CCC/36, p. 437, 20 vendémiaire an 12 (October 13, 1803), Talleyrand to Thainville.

3. AMAE 8CCC/36, p. 440, 20 vendémiaire an 12 (October 13, 1803), "Extrait des Registres de la chancellerie du commissariat général des relations commerciales de la République française à Alger."

4. AMAE 8CCC/36, p. 165, 12 messidor an 10 (July 1, 1802), Talleyrand to Thainville.

5. AMAE 8CCC/36, p. 322, 3 pluviôse, an 11 (January 23, 1803), Talleyrand to Thainville.

rich," but the Paris branch constituted "a great drain upon them, being extremely dissipated."[6]

Jacob saw things somewhat differently from his brothers. In his business letters, he would refer to the Algiers branch, possessively, as "my Algiers house."[7] Whether or not the brothers worked in partnership, and who had the greatest authority, is difficult to tell. The business letters suggest that the Bacris had systems of cooperation in place. Algiers would inform Jacob of dispatches, and Jacob, and presumably his brother Salomon in Livorno, would feed information back regarding prices and demand. They shared funds, sending them where the exchange rate was the most advantageous.[8] They shared agents, too: some, such as Dié Brothers in Alicante, became trusted confidants and go-betweens for the brothers. By mid-1802, as Jacob's attempts to recover the debt continued to meet with failure, the brothers appear to have been working together, but also in opposition. Jacob, now clearly short of funds, was writing to the family's agents, instructing them to send any statements of payments due to the Bacris in Algiers. When three thousand pounds sterling came due to be paid to Joseph Benhacok, a London merchant with whom the family dealt, Jacob wrote to his intermediary in Lisbon, Gaetano Carminati, to forward the requirement for payment to his brother in Algiers. He wrote again six weeks later, "confirming the same arrangement, in case my aforementioned House has given you an opposing order." This would have been, as Jacob explained, "because they were counting on considerable sums being paid to me here."[9] This, of course, was the debt owed to the Bacris by France, which it was Jacob's job to collect.

But Jacob does not appear to have been a competent businessman. By the time he made this admission to Carminati, not only had Jacob's efforts not borne fruit, but his financial situation more generally had become alarming. In March 1803, he left Paris for Livorno, in the hope of persuading Salomon to help him pay his

6. TNA FO 3/9, p. 309, July 25, 1802, Falcon to Sir George Shee, Undersecretary of State for the Home Department.

7. ADBR 39 E 21, p. 52, 28 vendémiaire an 10, (October 20, 1801), Jacob Bacri to Bentaleb Raïs et Compagnie, Lisbon.

8. ADBR 39 E 21, p. 22, July 14, 1801, Jacob Bacri to Carminati.

9. ADBR 39 E 21, p. 125, July 21, 1802, Jacob Bacri to Carminati.

mounting debts. His brothers were not prepared to bail him out—weak bonds of trust, perhaps always present in the family network, were now becoming clear. When Joseph and Naphtali in Algiers went to Thainville in October, to distance themselves officially from their respective brothers, they would have known what was happening on the Mediterranean's northern shores. Jacob had left his nephew, Naphtali's brother Michel, in charge of the business in France, transferring the business and all associated assets to his name. He intended to forward funds to Michel, for the payment of outstanding debts. His stay in Livorno ultimately extended to a year. From there, he returned to Marseilles in February 1804.

1804 was to be a difficult year for Jacob. He arrived in Marseilles to find his business in a terrible mess. Jacob had been sending money from Italy, believing that this was being used to cover debts. These funds, however, were not used for their destined purpose and as the year unfolded, Jacob uncovered a web of betrayal. At first, he thought that some mistake must have been made. As he wrote in February to the family's notary in Paris, Charles Rault, he had sent enough money from Italy for his debts to be repaid, "due date by due date, recovery by recovery." He had, he reported, received only a vague note from Michel Busnach, requesting a great deal more money, but Jacob was waiting on an exact account of transactions. He trusted that Michel would send this shortly.[10] Letters from his brothers in Algiers had made it clear to him that they were "angry about all the things that had been done to him" (although they had also taken steps to distance themselves from him), and Jacob had resolved to remain wide awake to business possibilities.[11]

Just a few days later, he had a clearer idea of the state of finances, and he began to see evidence of Michel Busnach's deception. It was clear that Michel did not see himself as part of the broader extended Bacri family. Accounts had come due, and Busnach had only made partial payments into Jacob's account. Busnach had received payment from the Algiers house for luxury goods supplied—in this case, by a firm of Geneva watchmakers—but had failed to pass this on to the watchmakers, telling them, instead, that Jacob was liable to pay

---

10. ADBR 39 E 21, p. 139, 25 pluviôse an 12 (February 15, 1804), Jacob Bacri to Rault.
11. ADBR 39 E 21, p. 140, 25 pluviôse an 12 (February 15, 1804), Jacob Bacri to Rault.

them. Still, Jacob felt, he need only discuss the matter with Michel, and they could decide, together, on a course of action.[12] In March, Jacob was still waiting for the book of accounts to be returned to him. When he asked for it, he was told "that it was still in Paris, I wrote to Paris, they told me it isn't there, and I am being tossed back and forth from one day to the next."[13] The book of accounts had disappeared, and Jacob escalated matters. He had Jacob Gozlan, Busnach's partner in crime, summoned to appear before the commercial court in Marseilles, in the hope that Gozlan would be ordered to deliver the book in question. Jacob now began to understand: Michel Busnach, together with Jacob Gozlan, had been cheating him. Jacob was deep in debt, and with his book of accounts still missing, he had no precise idea of the state of his business. Over the weeks and months that followed, Jacob's letters laid out his discoveries. On one occasion, Michel and Gozlan added extra zeros to payments promised from Jacob's accounts, so that five thousand francs would become five hundred thousand.[14] On another, Michel used the money that Jacob was sending from Livorno to withdraw deposits that Jacob had made with a pawnbroker when he was in Paris and refused to return the goods in question.[15]

By April, Jacob was angry. He wrote to Michel Busnach, also in Marseilles. "I have nothing to say to you," he began, "regarding the letter you have just written to me today." If Michel had wished to write about a Mr. Ferroul, to whom the Bacris owed money, Jacob responded that he "didn't know, and didn't care" whether or not this gentleman was a creditor. "All I know," he wrote, furiously, "is that you owe me an account, is that Mr. Gozlan owes me an account, give me, each of you, your account, and then we will see if Mr. Ferroul is our creditor."[16] Later that month, he wrote to his longstanding agents in Alicante, Dié Brothers, that neither Michel Busnach, nor Jacob Gozlan, nor Charles Rault had any role as his proxy.[17] Jacob found

---

12. ADBR 39 E 21, p. 128, 30 pluviose an 12 (February 20, 1804), Jacob Bacri to Rault.

13. ADBR 39 E 21, p. 131, 17 ventose an 12 (March 8, 1804), Jacob Bacri to Argand, Paris.

14. ADBR 39 E 21, p. 135, 28 germinal an 12 (April 18, 1804), Jacob Bacri to Sabaton Costantini, Marseilles.

15. ADBR 39 E 21, p. 206, March 25, 1806, Jacob Bacri to Galliani, Paris.

16. ADBR 39 E 21, p. 134, 27 germinal an 12 (April 17, 1804), Jacob Bacri to Michel Busnach.

17. ADBR 39 E 21, p. 132, 5 germinal an 12 (March 26, 1804), Jacob Bacri to Dié Brothers.

himself in a difficult position. He was obliged to respond to unanticipated creditors, among them a Mr. Bresson in Paris, in complete ignorance of the state of affairs in Paris. In a letter to Bresson, he explained that while the latter might have sent an account, according to which Bacri owed him 2,063 francs, Bacri was unable to confirm or repay this amount until he could obtain "knowledge of the operations and accounts Mr. Busnach carried out" after his departure from Paris. Jacob asked Bresson that he "be more than persuaded" that he would "press Mr. Busnach" for details so that he might repay the sum that was owed.[18] Several such letters are recorded in the logbook. Among the longstanding clients with whom Jacob had to deal were Blanc-Mavit and Mathieu, watchmakers in Geneva, who were unhappy at the way they had been treated by Michel.[19]

Jacob continued trying to sort out the remaining mess. Over the next weeks, ostensibly as he was going through his old accounts, he wrote to follow up on old transactions and debts he thought might still be outstanding. Letter after letter in his business register tells the same story. On the hunt for funds, he wrote to the French consul in Tunis, Jacques Devoize, to notaries and merchants in Marseilles and Paris, to the family's agents in Barcelona and Genoa, and to Manuel de las Heras, the former Spanish ambassador in Algiers.[20] The extent of Jacob's desperate correspondence gives a sense of the breadth of his contacts and his business. He sought funds for debts, hopefully unpaid, from as far back as 1797. He was still chasing funds in early 1805. Jacob tried everything he thought might help, but he was out of his depth. He had been doing what he had always done, and it was proving ineffective. He had the tale of his misfortune written out in full to transmit to a lawyer, who might represent him. But Jacob also sought a wider audience for his sorry tale, circulating the narrative to anyone he felt might take an interest, or view his case with sympathy.

18. ADBR 39 E 21, p. 135, 29 germinal an 12 (April 19, 1804), Jacob Bacri to Bresson, Paris.

19. ADBR 39 E 21, p. 136, 29 germinal an 12 (April 19, 1804), Jacob Bacri to Blanc-Mavit et Mathieu, Geneva.

20. De las Heras was clearly an important and well-known figure to the Bacris. He was also a member of the Council of the Indies, or the *Consejo de Indias*, formed in the second decade of the sixteenth century. This was one of the councils that functioned as aids in government to the king, such as the councils of state, war, and treasure. The function of the Council of the Indies was to regulate relations and commerce between Spain and its colonies in the new world.

It went to Isaac Arbib, Salomon's business partner and family friend in Tuscany, as well to as other members of his family. It also went to the brothers' agents. In April, he sent his statement to his longtime agents in Alicante, Dié Brothers, "certain" that they would "take part in that which involves me." Jacob asked, also, that they forward it to his nephew Nathan, Joseph's son in Livorno, "without letting him know that I sent it to you."[21] In May, he wrote to a merchant friend in Livorno, asking him to read the statement, to "let me know your feelings," and, seemingly just in case Arbib had not yet read it, to pass it to "our friend Arbib, and if you had the chance to have a conversation with our brothers on this subject, I hope that you would be so good as to let them know your judgement which, I flatter myself, will not be at all unfavorable to me."[22]

In Algiers and Livorno, Jacob's brothers were cognizant of his situation, since letters travelled back and forth at a great rate. Yet they seem to have been barely sympathetic. Jacob was left to deal with the betrayal alone, while the Algiers branch carried on with core business, shipping grain, largely to Spain. While, on the one hand, Jacob was pursuing Busnach and Gozlan through the courts, holding off creditors, and trying to recover funds owing, on the other, the family was, clearly, still understood to be central figures in the supply of grain, and Jacob was obliged to continue as the French face of the family business and carry on trading in that capacity, while desperately seeking redress for the spectacular fraud committed against the same business in France.

In June, Jacob was informed that the family in Algiers had appointed Jacob Gozlan to mediate between him and Busnach. Very unhappy about this, Jacob nevertheless accepted the arrangement, telling Gozlan that "even though I dislike everything about your intermediary role, I will accept it, as I do not wish to frustrate the will of my House in Algiers." Clearly, by now, when it came to the family business, Jacob was not in charge. Nonetheless, he went on, and perhaps in a bid to recover some dignity, "I advise you that my support is only brief," and, he threatened, if Gozlan "continued to delay the final

21. ADBR 39 E 21, p. 139, 10 floréal an 12 (April 30, 1804), Jacob Bacri to Dié Brothers.
22. ADBR 39 E 21, pp. 140–41, 20 floréal an 12 (10 May 1804), Jacob Bacri to Loujean, Livorno.

settling of our accounts," Jacob would revoke Gozlan's status. Jacob invited Gozlan, once again, to testify before witnesses that Gozlan, alone, was responsible for the "ridiculous hindrances" that prevented the settling of accounts. At midday the following Sunday, Gozlan, together with Busnach, were to come to Jacob's home, to make a statement that could then be sent to Algiers.[23] Unsurprisingly, the invitation was not taken up. Just one month earlier, Jacob had written to Gozlan in Judeo-Arabic, a language in which he seems to have allowed emotion to guide his pen: "You say that if possible we should gather like brothers and finish our business, and whatever is difficult for us should be passed on to our people in Algeria. [. . .] I always thought that one day [Michel and I] would be able to awaken our souls from the trouble we are in at the moment."[24] Michel and Gozlan's failure to gather on this occasion must have dashed any hope Jacob had for an awakening. Worse was to come.

We can't know when the news of Naphtali's murder and the attack on the community first reached Jacob. It would have come to him as he was recovering after a coach accident. The first indication he gave of his knowledge in the correspondence was a scrawled note in the ledger, dated July 19, 1805, recording that he had written to Dié Brothers in Alicante to "let them know about the unhappy event that occurred in Algiers," and "to beg them to please let me know what they have been able to learn."[25] That same day, he wrote to Manuel de las Heras, telling him: "Doubtless, you will have learned in Paris the disastrous event that happened in Algiers, I dispense with giving you the distressing details, even though my family was preserved, it concerns me none the less greatly for the loss of our relative Neftali [sic] Busnach."[26] By August he had received news from Joseph, as he told Dié Brothers, that the Bacri and Busnach families had all been able to escape in two boats that had been loaded for Livorno, and that only Joseph and Joseph's son David were to stay in Algiers. Jacob remained, he confided, "in the cruelest confusion, waiting for subsequent news from which I will learn what has followed after this

23. ADBR 39 E 21, p. 144, 17 prairial an 12 (June 6, 1804), Jacob Bacri to Jacob Gozlan.

24. ADBR 39 E 21, p. 143, 28 floréal an 12 (18 May 1804), Jacob Bacri to Gozlan.

25. ADBR 39 E 21, p. 176, July 19, 1805, Jacob Bacri to Dié Brothers.

26. ADBR 39 E 21, pp. 176–77, 30 messidor an 13 (July 19, 1805), Jacob Bacri to Manuel de las Heras.

distressing event." Letters dated sixteen days after the events, which he received from Algiers via Barcelona, informed him that calm had been reestablished, and that all was peaceful.[27]

Jacob's financial situation continued to concern him no less greatly. In late July, he wrote to Courton, Ravel and Company in Paris. Going through his papers, he found an old account, from July 1797, eight years earlier. Had it been paid, he wondered, and if not, should he send the account to Paris or to their office in The Hague for his reimbursement?[28] Clearly, Jacob's need was becoming acute. He was now planning to return to Livorno, to attempt to get blood from the stone that was his older brother, Salomon. But first he had to await more news from Algiers. Joseph and David were now being held in prison, and Jacob was anxious to know the outcome. On November 14, he wrote to Dié Brothers in Alicante, to apologize for not having responded earlier to their letters from two months prior. He had, he explained, been "very worried" about his brother Joseph and his nephew David. "In such circumstances one is very happy to arrange things with a pecuniary sacrifice."[29]

On the other hand, Jacob had been forced to sacrifice a little too much. In mid-December 1805, he arrived back in Livorno, to once again seek funds from the older brother he called Shlomo. This was, he realized, the only way to "satisfy his debtors."[30] At first, Jacob wrote to Joseph Raphael Coen, to whom he had confided the management of his business in Marseilles, that while he had had "not yet concluded anything" with Salomon for the debts he had left behind in Marseilles, he believed that all would turn out well, and his creditors would be satisfied.[31] After five days of arbitration, however, his tone changed somewhat. He was "annoyed," he now wrote, not to have managed to persuade Salomon to agree to make payments. It was, Jacob told Joseph, "hard to get money out of him," but he lived in hope that his brother would "think again

27. ADBR 39 E 21, pp. 178–79, 21 thermidor an 13 (August 9, 1805), Jacob Bacri to Dié Brothers.

28. ADBR 39 E 21, p. 177, 11 thermidor an 13 (July 30, 1805), Jacob Bacri to Courton, Ravel et Compagnie, Paris.

29. ADBR 39 E 21, pp. 183–84, 1 frimaire an 14 (November 22, 1805), Jacob Bacri to Dié Brothers.

30. ADBR 39 E 21, pp. 196–97, January 24, 1806, Jacob Bacri to Joseph Raphael Coen.

31. ADBR 39 E 21, pp. 185–86, 30 frimaire an 14 (December 21, 1805), Jacob Bacri to Coen.

and see his mistake."[32] Michel Busnach was being reasonable, and the mediation organized by Salomon with David Busnach, Michel's brother, was to begin the following day. (Salomon and David had also agreed between themselves that they would pay their respective brothers nothing.) Jacob was not entirely confident to leave matters in the hands of others. After the mediation had been going for just a few days, he wrote to Jacob Toledano in Marseilles to clarify a misunderstanding regarding a transaction between himself and Michel Busnach, in which Toledano had been involved. "You will write me a letter in which you will confess the truth," Jacob wrote, "and I swear to you on my God that no one other than my brother, and his brother will see your letter, and if you do not want to give the truth that I demand of you, I will arrange things with Busnach, and you will live with the regret of having refused me a thing you cannot deny me."[33] On the same day he also wrote to Charles Rault with various instructions on the running of his affairs, both in the courts and before the government. He told Rault, also, that the news from Algiers was "very favorable." The dey had asked Thainville to write to his minister about the debt, and Jacob felt confident enough to ask Rault to approach the bankers, Doyen and Co., to act on the Bacris' behalf. He may well have been persuading himself as much as his correspondent. The recovery of the debt had, after all, been Jacob's job. And now he was in Livorno, forced to submit to the authority and the rulings of his brothers regarding his financial future.[34]

As it turned out, the brothers in Livorno did, in fact, propose a compromise, to which all parties agreed, initially. But by mid-January 1806, Michel had clearly begun to realize just how much he had stolen from Jacob and would be obliged to repay. On January 17, Jacob again wrote to Joseph Raphael Coen. Michel, he said, had been using delay tactics, trying to muddy the waters. While Michel sought to delay proceedings, creditors arrived in Livorno, threatening Busnach with prison if he did not pay the debts he had left behind in Marseilles. Busnach, to whom Jacob referred as the "dear man,"[35] decided to leave Livorno immediately, and return

32. ADBR 39 E 21, p. 186, December 26, 1805, Jacob Bacri to Coen.

33. ADBR 39 E 21, p. 188, January 3, 1806, Jacob Bacri to Jacob Toledano.

34. ADBR 39 E 21, p. 189, January 3, 1806, Jacob Bacri to Rault.

35. ADBR 39 E 21, p. 206, March 25, 1806, Jacob Bacri to Coen.

to Marseilles to file for bankruptcy, so as to avoid any liability for debts owed. This he did on March 18, thereby piling, as Jacob put it, "one difficulty on top of another" in their negotiations. Jacob had, he felt, no choice but to follow Busnach,[36] and by the spring of 1806, uncle and nephew were again back in Marseilles. Now Jacob tried a new tactic. Aware, perhaps, that personal appeals were failing, or perhaps because he simply had no one left to appeal to, Jacob sought recourse in the French court system.[37] Unfortunately for him, however, his efforts to funnel the dispute through official channels were to backfire. In September, in a coup for Michel, the court of appeal in Marseilles found that Jacob was indebted to Michel for 363,750 francs, plus interest. At this time, Jacob sold his Marseilles house in the rue Montgrand (Jacob's nephew Nathan would later buy it back in 1816), perhaps to raise funds. At the same time, Jacob sought to have the judgement annulled. In support of his claim, he gathered other judgements, his own written statement, and a description of Busnach's failure to swear the *more judaico*, or Jewish oath. The court of appeal in Marseilles had required Busnach to swear the oath, to support his claim that his demands on Bacri were legitimate, but there was a question over whether the oath had been administered correctly.

The *more judaico* was a special form of swearing oaths for Jewish litigants, witnesses, and jurors in civil and criminal judicial proceedings. This oath was accepted as conclusive proof, and the entire outcome of a case could rest on it. Its use was based on the assumption that Jews would not swear the oath falsely. Even after emancipation, the understanding persisted that "only a special Jewish oath would be considered binding by Jews." [38] Swearing of a special Jewish oath took various forms. Phyllis Albert Cohen has found that "fully synagogue ceremonies, which rabbis administered *more judaïco* on Torah scrolls, seem to have been encouraged by Napoleon's government as

36. ADBR 39 E 21, p. 196, January 17, 1806, Jacob Bacri to Coen.

37. Francesca Trivellato has described how merchants were among the greatest users of courts in early modern Europe, a trend continued by the Bacris. Trivellato, *The Familiarity of Strangers*, 272–73.

38. Albert, "The Jewish Oath in Nineteenth-Century France," 4. Clearly, in 1806, when this particular swearing took place, the practice was already established.

early as 1806."[39] The rabbi would take out the Torah scrolls from the ark where they were normally kept. The person swearing would place their hand on them, repeating the oath:

> I swear before God, who created heaven and earth, mountains, rocks, greenery, and all that exists through His power, and if I swear the opposite of the truth, may God make sulfur and tar rain down on me, as it rained on Sodom and Gomorrah, and if I swear the opposite, I wish the earth to open up and swallow me [. . .], and if I swear the opposite may I be turned into a pillar of salt, like Lot's wife when she turned to look at the city behind her, and if I swear the opposite may I become a leper, like Maris, Moses's sister, and if I swear the opposite, may I be crippled in all my limbs, may my blood leave my body, and may my bloodless body be forever deprived of a burial, and if I swear the opposite, may I be damned, and never be gathered in to Abraham's breast.

Following this, the Jew would answer, point by point, the questions put to him, while the clerk wrote his answers down. In the synagogue, a coffin would be laid out, covered by a black sheet, and a lamp lit.[40]

As part of this process, the person swearing also had to hear the *Kol Bo herem*.[41] The *Kol Bo herem* was a severe formula of *herem*, or excommunication, presented in the *Kol Bo*, an anonymous collection of Jewish ritual and civil law from the late thirteenth or early fourteenth century. Its title translates to "everything within." Yosef Kaplan has detailed its use in seventeenth-century Hamburg, including "a large number of curses taken from the Torah, and characterized by a rigorous and threatening style."[42] Anyone who transgressed would be subject to a series of unpleasant experiences, among which would be their excommunication from their Jewish community. "By decree of the angels," the rabbi would read, "and by leave of the holy ones, we excommunicate and forswear; anathemize and ban, curse and imprecate [. . .] Accursed be he by the mouth of God, the Great, the Mighty, and the Awesome [. . .] Lord,

39. Albert, "The Jewish Oath in Nineteenth-Century France," 5.

40. Laget, "Le Serment 'sur le coude' more judaïco," 118–19.

41. *Herem* is a historic Jewish practice of excommunication. In the history of Jews in Europe, the best-known and most high-profile case of *herem* was against Baruch Spinoza.

42. Kaplan, *An Alternative Path to Modernity*, 178.

God of all spirits of flesh, destroy him and annihilate him."[43] This ceremony also took place in the synagogue in Marseilles. But in Michel's case, "the truth," as the Marseilles merchant Jean-Baptiste Dupuy Samadet recounted to Pierre-Antoine Berryer, the Paris lawyer, was that the rabbi, who should have done several things, had done nothing at all. Perhaps most consequentially, he had not read the *Kol Bo herem.* He had not hung the synagogue with black fabric, and he had not given the litany of curses against traitors. And Busnach, instead of reading the oath in a loud and clear voice, mumbled, so that Samadet did not hear a single word. It was, Samadet reported, "a farce, and nothing more. The result is that Bacri has been condemned to pay a sum of 363,750 francs that he has no more received than you and I."[44]

It is unclear when Michel Busnach first arrived in France. At the time of the difficulties with Jacob, he must have returned to Algiers, since he was there when Naphtali was assassinated. Ordered by the dey to remain in the regency with Joseph and David after their brother's assassination, Michel had in fact escaped the regency in October 1805, on a French ship. He did not make himself popular with the dey at that time, and most probably not with his extended family either, since they bore the brunt of the dey's fury. An undated secret police report on the various members of the family living in places under French control described Michel as living in Livorno, possibly at the time of the 1808 sequestration. "He was a merchant," went the report, and, not wasting words, continued, "and squandered between 400,000 and 500,000 francs." "He is believed to have no great worth."[45] Thainville, for his part, did not have anything good to say about Naphtali's brother: "I have pointed out the intrigues of Mr. Busnach in my correspondence too often, for there to be any need of repeating it here; he has not been a stranger to all of the difficulties that the government has endured over the nine years I have been in charge in Algiers."[46]

43. Cited in Woolf, *The Fabric of Religious Life in Medieval Ashkenaz,* 72.

44. ADBR 39 E 21, p. 211, September 9, 1806, Samadet et Compagnie to Maitre Berrier, Paris.

45. AN F/7/6537, [no date], "Notes sur la famille Bacri d'Alger, Livourne, Marseille, et autres."

46. AMAE 8CCC/39, pp. 359–60, September 9, 1809, Thainville to Champagny.

Jacob, as events have shown, was not one to leave things to chance. He pursued all avenues, old and new. He addressed a petition on the matter to Napoleon. He made counterclaims against his nephew and pursued him through the courts. Matters now stretched through 1806 and into the following year, and Jacob continued to do all in his power to ensure an outcome favorable to himself. In January 1807, Jacob obtained a ruling from the commercial court in Marseilles that his brothers in Algiers and Livorno were to be declared as being in solidarity with him in business, and, therefore, required to pay off one of his creditors.[47] (Unsurprisingly, this judgement did not have the desired effect.) Three months later, Jacob inserted a note in the *Journal du commerce*, setting out the details of the judgement against him, and seeking to warn "bankers, merchants, and businessmen," that Michel Busnach had no "real, legal and legitimate claim" to the money owed by France to the House.[48] Busnach responded, equally publicly, stating that he had acted honestly, and that Jacob owed him 3,200,000 francs, which he had, he claimed, been trying to recover for three years. He threatened to pursue Joseph and Salomon for these funds.[49] The family appeared to have no qualms about using every means at its disposal, drawing the French legal system and the country's press into its orbit. Jacob's recourse to the court system meant that the family dispute now played out in the French public sphere.

Jacob was so comfortable with the family dispute playing out in public, in fact, that he treated court proceedings as though he were at home in Algiers, seeking to override process with a personal appeal. In July 1807, he took the extraordinary step of writing to Jean-Baptiste Cresp, a lawyer in Marseilles, asking him to withdraw from proceedings, due to take place in the civil court in Marseilles. "You do not know me," Jacob wrote, and yet, Cresp's friendship with Busnach's lawyers, who pursued their mission against Jacob "by an animosity and hatred against me that I did not provoke," could not but influence Cresp's opinion against him. "I know," Jacob conciliated to Cresp, that "you are a man of integrity." But partiality was

---

47. ADBR 13 B 264, judgement of January 14, 1807.

48. "Avis divers," *Journal du commerce, de politique et de littérature*, April 1, 1807, 360.

49. "Avis divers," *Journal du commerce*, April 5, 1807, 376: *Réponse de M. Michel Busnah à la note de M. Jacob Coën Bacri, insérée dans le* Journal du commerce *du premier avril.*

so difficult not to feel, and Jacob felt he had no choice but to beg the lawyer "to abstain from the case." "Your sensitivity will doubtless find repugnant the idea of occupying yourself with an affair in which, I believe, it would, with the best will in the world, be impossible for you to be completely impartial."[50] Writing to Arnaud, one of Busnach's lawyers, Jacob concluded on a similar climax: "I know that in addressing oneself to you as a private individual, one always obtains what the sensitivity and loyalty of a gallant man can permit you to grant."[51] Jacob's character is revealed, in parts, through this correspondence. He was unabashed and determined, at times desperate and angry. But he was also, ultimately, powerless, a reminder that it was their situation in the regency, as well as the circumstances of the war, that allowed the family to accumulate wealth. Perhaps, too, these events simply tell us something about Jacob. After all, in Livorno, his brother Salomon enjoyed both status and success.

As Jacob's fight dragged on at the Mediterranean's northern shore, in Algiers, things were also becoming very difficult for Thainville, as the relationship between him and the regency's elite deteriorated, and the consul ran out of options. In December 1807, Jean-Baptiste de Nompère de Champagny, minister for foreign affairs since August 9 (and later to become the Duc de Cadore), wrote to Antoine Claire Thibaudeau, the prefect of the Bouches-du-Rhône, Marseilles, as well as to Etienne Famin, in charge of foreign affairs in Marseilles. Champagny was concerned. He had not had a letter from Thainville since October. Knowing how punctiliously and correctly the consul fulfilled the requirements of his role, his long silence was cause for worry. Moreover, a ship's captain arriving in Barcelona had reported that France's consul in Algiers had been arrested, and the order given to Algerian corsairs to pursue French ships, several of which had already been caught. In order "to protect [Thainville] from the dangers to which he might possibly be personally exposed," Champagny was ordering that all Algerians in France be prevented from leaving. Algerian subjects were to be denied passports, and placed under

50. ADBR 39 E 21, p. 227, July 9, 1807, Jacob Bacri to Cresp.
51. ADBR 39 E 21, pp. 228–29, August 31, 1807, Jacob Bacri to Arnaud.

surveillance, so that they could not find a way to escape. This was a precautionary, but "appropriate" response.[52] Just over a month later, the minister's worst fears were confirmed. Thainville had managed to send word to Thibaudeau in Marseilles. The Dey Ahmed still refused to liberate the Genoese slaves claimed by France, and Thainville, having been made prisoner, along with all the French in the regency, had been unable to follow Napoleon's order to leave Algiers. He begged Thibaudeau to impose reprisals on all Algerian subjects in Marseilles.[53] Champagny received the prefect's report at the end of January. A few days later, he wrote to prefects in Livorno and Genoa, as well as to Thibaudeau in Marseilles, ordering them to prevent any Algerian subjects from leaving, and to place their property under surveillance, so that it might also be held. To Mathieu de Lesseps, *Commissaire général* in Livorno, Champagny wrote that "the Jews Busnach and Bacri, still influential in Algiers, have relatives in Livorno who are the guardians of all their riches."[54] (He had received this particular piece of wisdom from Thainville.) Even as the family was imploding, the idea of their centrality to the relationship between France and the regency persisted. Champagny's letter was timely. The Treaty of Fontainebleau, signed in secret between Napoleon and Charles IV of Spain in late 1807, had ceded the kingdom of Etruria to France. France annexed the kingdom (in modern-day Tuscany) on May 24, and just six days later, French bureaucracy created the department of Méditerranée, with its capital in Livorno. Bacris and Busnachs in that port were now also subject to sequestration measures, and Lesseps wasted no time, sequestering the offices and warehouses of Salomon Bacri and Moses Busnach, and placing both men under arrest.

Salomon had settled in Livorno in 1787, establishing a branch of the family business in the port city, "one of the most animated and dynamic mercantile centers in western Europe."[55] In Livorno, Jews, Greeks, Armenians, and Protestants lived together, alongside

---

52. AMAE 8CCC/38, pp. 294, 295, December 17, 1807, Champagny to Thibaudeau and Famin.

53. AMAE 8CCC/39, p. 16, January 13, 1808, Thainville to Thibaudeau.

54. AMAE 8CCC/39, 23, February 4, 1808, Champagny to Lesseps. Lesseps, the father of the better-known Ferdinand, had previously been French consul in Morocco.

55. Bregoli, *Mediterranean Enlightenment*, 16.

a devout Catholic population. Salomon lived in this densely populated and highly privileged community, where, notwithstanding occasional uprisings against the Jews by the Catholic population, Jews could rely on Tuscan authorities for protection, of their person as well as their property. They had complete communal autonomy, and "hardly any restrictions" on their economic life.[56] Salomon personified much that was typical of the Livorno Jewish community, and this may explain why he planted roots there, in a way that family members in France did not. He was very active in the Jewish community, marked by its diversity, as well as its high level of mobility. Livornese Jews were observant, while also, notably, acculturated and prosperous, a combination explained by their freedom, their sense of protection, and their "exceptional status." Livorno was "home to the very rich and the very poor; to rabbis and doctors, to criminals and prostitutes; to merchants who gathered in one of the coffeehouses of the port before heading to the theatre; to porters who worked in the docks; and to saintly kabbalists who spent their ascetic days in prayer and study."[57] In 1799, Salomon had been elected deputy head of the Jewish community,[58] later becoming head of the community for a short time. He lent money to the community, and its more needy members. Salomon, like his brothers, was an observant Jew. He was, consistently, among those capable of taking on the honor of *Chatan Torah*, literally bridegroom of the Torah, the one tasked with reading the final section of the Torah on the Jewish festival of Simchat Torah, when the five books of Moses are finished, and begun again. He served, too, as head administrative officer, or *parnas*, of the congregation. He was an administrator of the Jewish school. All of this, and perhaps his much-written-about great wealth, too, placed him among the community's elite. In 1806, his status was recognized when he was among a group of notables invited to attend a royal party, in honor of the young Charles Louis, then King of Etruria.[59]

56. Lehmann, "A Livornese 'Port Jew' and the Sephardim of the Ottoman Empire," 53.

57. Bregoli, *Mediterranean Enlightenment*, 17.

58. Archivio della Comunità Ebraica di Livorno (ACEL), Deliberazioni del Governo della Comunità, Registro cc. 112. N.a. L. 11, f. 33, cc. 21–23.

59. ACEL, Rescritti dal 7 febbraio 1806 al 10 ottobre 1808 (February 7, 1806 and October 10, 1808), n. IX.

Like his brother, Mordecai, and his nephews, Naphtali and David, for Salomon, prominence in the community went hand in hand with commercial success. Not much is known about the nature of Salomon's business. He clearly undertook trade, like forty-two percent of the Jews in the port: searches of his properties in 1808 found goods evidently for shipping or sale.[60] Livorno was a stopping point, where goods were moved on, in various directions. Trading Jews in Livorno maintained networks that matched the dispersal of Sephardi Jews across the world, to both the East and West. Markets would be identified for raw goods sent from Algiers. Luxury items requested from Algiers, including silks, muslins, jewels, fine pearls, watches and worked coral, would be assembled and shipped on. Salomon, working with his brothers in Algiers, would most probably have been a middle man. He could make extra on these movements of goods, working not only in trade, but also in the insurance of the ships that carried his family's cargoes.[61] Salomon was active in business in Tuscany. In 1807, he supplied forty thousand Spanish silver dollars as capital for the establishment of a business with another Algerian Jew and a friend of the family, Isaiah Arbib.[62] Over two decades he purchased several properties. An 1808 ranking of property ownership among all the citizens of Livorno listed Salomon in ninth place.[63]

Salomon was not the only member of the two families to settle in Livorno. In 1809, at the age of 50, Salomon listed his family as including his wife Ricca and four children: David, ten; Rachelline, seven; Fortunata, four; and Rosa, two. Another daughter, Aziza, was mentioned in his will. All were born in Livorno. In 1802, Salomon's nephew, Moses Bacri, the son of Mordecai, was admitted to Livorno with his mother, Stella, and his sister, Aziza.[64] Following the massacre in 1805, more family members arrived: Salomon's nephews,

60. Filippini, "Una famiglia ebrea di Livorno tra le ambizioni mercantili e le vicissitudini del mondo mediterraneo: i Coen Bacri," 293.

61. Filippini, "Una famiglia ebrea," 300. Francesca Trivellato has detailed, similarly, how Ergas and Silvera "were primarily involved in the exchange of local and imported commodities." Trivellato, *The Familiarity of Strangers*, 38.

62. Archivio di stato di Firenze, Camera di commercio, 1263bis, fols. 99r-v, 13 aprile 1807 (April 13, 1807). I am grateful to Francesca Trivellato for sharing her find with me.

63. Cited in Filippini, "Una famiglia ebrea," 295.

64. Filippini, "Una famiglia ebrea," 290–91, n. 10.

Nathan, with his wife, Rachele, and his young son, Angiolino; and Joseph, with his wife and children, Moses and Elia. Jacob's teenage son, also Joseph, arrived at this time too. There were Busnachs in Livorno also, and Salomon worked closely with Moses, who was probably a brother of Naphtali. They were part of a thriving Jewish community, which, in 1809, counted 5,300 members—approximately ten percent of the total population.[65]

Immediately following their imprisonment, both Salomon and Moses Busnach began petitioning to be released. They provided documents to prove that they had been naturalized Tuscan, and should thus, by virtue of French rule in Tuscany, be considered French. These documents were forwarded by Lesseps to Champagny. But both men were deemed to be outside the rules. Even if they had become Tuscan, they were found nonetheless, "by reason of their connections, and their business relations with the Bacris and Busnachs in Algiers," to come fully under the aegis of the decree.[66] "Their sin," as Richard O'Brien had observed of the 1799 sequester, was "that they have money."[67] Their request for release was denied. After all, in Algiers, the sequestration decree had, as Thainville reported, "caused a great surprise, and produced an admirable effect."[68] Thainville was an enthusiastic supporter of sequestration. With characteristic drama, he reported that the threat of this measure was "dreaded in all Algiers, and even in the palace, which appears to fear nothing, [and] would ruin the country in six months and bring it infallibly to a revolution."[69] In 1809, with Thainville's departure from the regency still blocked by the new dey, Hadj Ali, the French consul wrote to Champagny that while it was not his place to "indicate to the government what measures to take," the Minister would "doubtless judge it appropriate to undertake reprisals against Algerian subjects in France and Italy, and renew the measures taken last year."[70] Champagny did, in fact,

65. Lehmann, "A Livornese 'Port Jew' and the Sephardim of the Ottoman Empire," 53.

66. AMAE 8CCC/39, p. 108, March 18, 1808, Champagny to Lesseps.

67. NARA Atlanta M23, roll 5, vol. 4, p. 102, April 24, 1799, O'Brien to Pickering.

68. AMAE 8CCC/39, p. 110, March 27, 1808, Thainville to Champagny.

69. AMAE 8CCC/38, p. 194, January 7, 1807, Thainville to Talleyrand.

70. AMAE 8CCC/39, p. 259, April 23, 1809, Thainville to Champagny.

judge it appropriate.[71] On this occasion, and over the next three years, seals were placed on Salomon's house no less than four times: from February to April in 1808; for a month in 1809; for three days in late June of 1810; and again from late October to early May 1811; and lastly, in January 1812.[72]

Like his brother Salomon, Jacob was also caught by the 1808 sequestration. Following the announcement of the decree in Marseilles, Jacob had gone to the police to present himself, along with Michel Busnach, Jacob Gozlan, and Simon Coen Solal. The three others were freed, but Jacob was detained. It must have been galling for him to watch Busnach and Gozlan, with whom he remained in a bitter financial dispute, walk free. But the prefect deemed Jacob too important to release: his family was "in great favor" with the dey, and his detention, therefore was "necessary."[73] Jacob's actions probably only served to reinforce this belief. Like Thainville in Algiers, Jacob, too, was running out of options. Following his imprisonment, Jacob, of course, wrote to the authorities. He recited a history of all the good his family had done for France since the famines of 1794. He had, he stated, brought more than eighty thousand loads of wheat to France, supplied the armies in Italy, Egypt, and the Rhine, made loans to generals, so that they might speed up military recruitment, and undertaken the provisioning of Malta, which, he argued, had allowed France to keep the island for longer. And making a personal appeal, bitterly summing up the past five years, he wrote that he hoped his release might allow him a chance to reconcile with his family; the estrangement from them since 1803, had left him, he said, "in complete abandonment and destitution."[74] According to his nieces and nephews, in May 1808, Jacob declared his intention to settle in France permanently, with a view to gaining French citizenship. Before the mayor of Marseilles, he gave his address as 41 rue Grignan, near the port. It may be that this declaration of intent to settle was calculated to guard against

71. AN F/7/8524, 19 June, 1809, Champagny to Denis Decrès, Ministre de la Marine et des colonies.

72. Filippini, "Una famiglia ebrea," p. 291, n. 14.

73. AN F/7/8524, March 31, 1808, "Département des Bouches du Rhône: Rapport: Fin mars 1808 séquestre levée."

74. AN F/7/8524, March 26, 1808, Jacob Bacri to Police Minister Joseph Fouché.

further sequestrations. For if Jacob were seeking French citizenship, surely the regime would not imprison him. But Jacob did not stay to pursue citizenship, leaving France in 1808, seemingly to return to Algiers. Perhaps he sought to avoid further sequestrations. Perhaps he was simply abandoning a mess.

Either way, Jacob might have run too soon. He was not present in Marseilles to witness the final ruling of the civil court in his dispute against Busnach. On October 8, the court pronounced in favor of Jacob, against Busnach, for the sum of 823,000 francs. Jacob had left Marseilles before the judgement was pronounced, and so it was his proxy, François Eyrand, who wrote to Salomon in October 1808, to let him know this outcome. Eyrand reported that the judgement had left "Busnach desperate, and his creditors furiously indisposed against him."[75] Busnach's legal team deserted him.[76] The archives that might have shed light on whether the ruling against Busnach was upheld and carried out have not been preserved. What we do know is that Michel Busnach had been able to pay off his debtors in early 1809, with help from his brother David. Almost thirty years later, however, Salomon's children were still pursuing Busnach for restitution. They brought a case to the magistrate's court in Marseilles, claiming that jewels and precious goods, promised by Jacob to Salomon as security, had never been released by Busnach.[77] Trouble was to haunt the family for years to come.

To Thainville in Algiers, it must have seemed that trouble had come to stay as well. Relations between France and the regency were breaking down, and the French consul found himself caught between Napoleon's repeated refusals to make any concessions and the Dey Hadj Ali's growing frustration. Napoleon's refusal to give gifts according to the practice and expectation in the regency was understood to be one cause of the breakdown in relations. In the report he authored before his departure from Paris, Thainville's successor Pierre Deval wrote (somewhat reassuringly) that the former

75. ADBR 39 E 21, pp. 236–37, October 15, 1808, Eyrand to Salomon Bacri.

76. ADBR 39 E 21, p. 238, October 12, 1808, [Eyrand] to Jean-Baptiste Samadet, Prefect of the principalities of Lucca and Piombino.

77. Bibliothèque nationale de France (BNF), May 25, 1832, "Jugement dont est appel, rendu par le tribunal de première instance de Marseille, le 25 mai 1832, entre les héritiers de feu M. Salomon-Coën Bacri, le Sieur Jacob-Coën Bacri, et le Sieur Michel Busnach."

ruler's "incompetent tact" in stopping the ritual, a custom "since time immemorial with Oriental peoples, and which no nation having relations with them has yet refused," had lost France its dignity, as well as its commercial advantage in the regency.[78] Indeed, much of Thainville's period of service had been taken up with prevarication. Payments of dues for the rights enjoyed under the concessions, the distribution of gifts, and the settlement of the Bacri debts would regularly be demanded of him.[79] Until the dey received gifts and a letter from Napoleon, Thainville reported in 1806, the release of 106 slaves being claimed by France would not take place.[80] One dey after another maintained this demand. Thainville was regularly threatened with slavery and hard labor.

The dey turned to sequestrations to express his impatience with France, and each time, France retaliated. Thainville came increasingly to rely on sequestrations of Bacri livelihoods to manage relations, and in particular, Jacob Bacri, after he had returned to Algiers. The relationship between Thainville and the Bacris was now equally difficult—from Thainville's perspective, at least. His strategy, and his deteriorating standing in the regency, mark the beginning of the end of Thainville's adventure as consul. Thainville's world was becoming ever smaller, and the Bacris now sat firmly at its center. In the middle of 1810, in the midst of ongoing arguments with Thainville regarding France's refusal to pay a ransom for the release of Genoese slaves, Hadj Ali sequestered eleven captures that had been brought into the port of Oran by French armed vessels, and then proceeded to sequester a considerable sum being kept in the chancellery of the French consulate. Thainville found himself in a "difficult position."[81] On one November morning, a divan took place at the marina. Its results were communicated to Thainville, sick in bed: the Dey Hadj Ali wished the consul to pay a twenty-five percent deposit on the money owing to the Bacris, with two months to receive the balance from his government. On Thainville's refusal to settle the debt, he was informed that he was now a prisoner of the regency. The dey now "demanded that all sums claimed be paid." Thainville refused and

78. AMAE 8CCC/42, p. 158, October 25, 1815, Deval, "Affaires d'Alger."
79. AMAE 8CCC/38, p. 143, September 25, 1806, Thainville to Talleyrand.
80. AMAE 8CCC/38, p. 143, September 25, 1806, Thainville to Talleyrand.
81. AMAE 8CCC/40, p. 277, November 21, 1811, Thainville to Champagny.

was informed that the dey "would send me, tomorrow, laden down with sixty pounds of chains, to carry stones in the mountains. I am writing to Your Excellency in the night; tomorrow I will probably be at hard labor. Long live the emperor!"[82]

In response, Champagny promulgated an imperial decree that sequestered all Algerian property found in France. Once again, this was to act as a surety for any French property seized in the regency. To this end, Thainville counselled, the best course of action was to focus on the Bacris and Busnachs in Livorno. Salomon and David were the "richest" of a population of "Algerian merchants, very wealthy, who have properties, capitalists, subjects of the dey," to be found in that port. But Salomon and David were also "related and linked in business with high and powerful subjects of the dey in Algiers." This was a tried and tested exercise, Thainville stressed: sequestration would place Salomon and David in a difficult position, and they would, in turn, put pressure on their brothers in Algiers to help France—and by extension, Thainville— "in every way possible." This was how sequestration had played out on previous occasions, and Thainville trusted that it would work this way again for him.[83] Thainville, unable to understand or to see the process of family breakdown, simply assumed that relations between family members were good. It was perhaps on his recommendation that French police undertook secret investigations into the members and associates of the Bacri and Busnach families in France and French-occupied Tuscany.[84] Their report noted that Salomon was "infirm and very unwell," living in seclusion and simplicity, although he had "a reputation and external appearance of a great fortune." Salomon's wealth was calculated at 800,000 francs, including four houses, which he owned with David Busnach, whom the police described as being "very highly esteemed in Livorno."[85]

In February 1812, Thainville was again able to report that this new sequestration had met with success. Ever given to drama, he

82. AMAE 8CCC/40, pp. 279–80, November 21, 1811, Thainville to Champagny.

83. AMAE 8CCC/40, pp. 141–42, November 26, 1810, Thainville to Champagny.

84. AN F/7/6537, "Notes sur la famille Bacri d'Alger."

85. AN F/7/6537, "Notes sur la famille Bacri d'Alger." This police report describes David Busnach as Salomon's brother-in-law. The consensus in other sources is that this David was in fact a brother of Naphtali, making him Salomon's nephew.

reported to Bassano that he had been "under attack." Jacob, who had returned to Algiers in 1808, and worked alongside his brother Joseph and his nephew David, was making Thainville's life a misery. In a coded message to Bassano, Thainville described Jacob as despicable, "the friend of all intrigues and plots against France, whose complaints grow each day, to whom must be attributed the infamies without precedent, which, in several circumstances, placed me in imminent danger of losing my head." But the Jews had just learned of the sequestrations in France and in Livorno. They were "beginning to tremble," and the regency itself was fearful of receiving an angry message from the Sultan.[86] By May, Thainville wrote, again in code, that for the first time in a while, he was able "to breathe"; thanks to the sequestrations, the Bacris had ceased all their intrigues against him, and he now enjoyed the upper hand. Joseph had gone so far as to throw himself at Thainville's feet, begging him to write to the government in the family's favor. If the despicable Jacob had not yet presented himself at the consulate, he nonetheless trembled for his head. Thainville begged Bassano not to "relax the rigor" of their sequestrations.[87]

The authorities were indeed maintaining a rigorous sequestration, as Bassano reported to Thainville. Nonetheless, a nagging concern remained: had the Bacris been able to outsmart the nation? In Livorno, the right people had been arrested, and seals placed "with all appropriate care and strictness," but the state of Salomon and David's fortune in Livorno had "not been found to be nearly as considerable as was to be supposed," all the more so since it was known, as Bassano stated, "that they were the keepers of a part of the fortune of the Bacris in Algiers."[88] It could only be that they had found a way to hide their true fortune from the police. The French authorities believed fully in the power and danger of the Bacris. If Hadj Ali was refusing to communicate directly with Thainville, this was, as Bassano wrote, the fault of the Bacri Jews: they were the ones who pushed the dey

86. AMAE 8CCC/40, p. 295, February 25, 1812, Thainville to Bassano.
87. AMAE 8CCC/40, p. 311, May 11, 1812, Thainville to Bassano.
88. AMAE 8CCC/40, p. 300, April 30, 1812, Bassano to Thainville. On Salomon's death, his son-in-law and nephew, Moses Bacri, reported the value of his estate to be 457,924.20 francs, of which real estate to the value of 410,140.20 francs. Filippini, "Una Famiglia Ebrea," p. 292, n. 16. Filippini considers that this was clearly an undervaluation.

"to all of the excesses for which we reproach him," and together with Britain, corrupted the dey's ministers.[89] Bassano saw the sequestrations as "a just punishment." "Nevertheless," he wrote to Thainville,

> This punishment should be inflicted in such a way as protect us from perfidious insinuations that our enemies might profit from events to spread. To this end, we will ask that the Bacris only be imprisoned until the falseness of their allegations has been demonstrated. After that, the measures we undertake as regards them will be those which are adjudged to be appropriate.[90]

(In fact, in his suspicions of Britain, Bassano was closer to the truth than he knew. Perhaps seeing an opportunity, the Prince Regent had sent a letter to the dey in early 1812, amounting to what a later US consul, William Shaler, called "an obligation of defensive alliance."[91] Britain had once more made a bid for favorable treatment from the regency. The Prince Regent promised to protect Algiers, as long as the dey respected the treaties between the two powers.) Above all, Thainville repeatedly asserted, the sequestrations had to be maintained. Livorno was particularly important. According to information published in Algiers, Thainville wrote, Salomon Bacri's fortune was valued at twenty-five million francs. Resorting yet again to an idea of Jews as duplicitous, Thainville reported that he had been positively assured that hidden in the walls of Salomon's home were "a great quantity of diamonds."[92] (Bassano forwarded this particular piece of information to the police minister.)[93] Thainville raised the matter again in June. The Jews were trembling still: Jacob for his head, and Joseph, "for his piasters in Livorno." This was all the more reason for France to keep hold of the same piasters. This was a happier letter than those from earlier in the year. Now, the British were losing influence in Algiers daily, "by reason," Thainville wrote, "of that which I regain."[94] From his position, camped in Vilna with

---

89. AMAE 8CCC/40, p. 300, April 30, 1812, Bassano to Thainville.

90. AMAE 8CCC/40, p. 307, April 30, 1812, Bassano to Thainville.

91. Shaler, *Sketches of Algiers*, 118.

92. AMAE 8CCC/40, p. 319, May 17, 1812, Thainville to Bassano.

93. AMAE 8CCC/40, p. 356, August 8, 1812, Bassano to the Duc de Rovigo, Minister of Police.

94. AMAE 8CCC/40, p. 342, June 5, 1812, Thainville to Bassano.

Napoleon's *Grande armée*, pursuing the Russian campaign, Bassano took the time and the trouble to write, just as positively. The detention and sequestration that had been ordered against the Bacri Jews in Livorno would be maintained, as long as France's needs in Algiers demanded it. But Bassano wanted to be sure, too, that Thainville would "not neglect the overtures of rapprochement being made to you by this family."[95] The Bacris and Busnachs in Livorno were important enough to sequester, because their relatives in Algiers could make Thainville's life a misery. But they could make it a good deal easier too. Bassano must have received Thainville's letter by August, since he reported from Eastern Europe, in the midst of the invasion of Russia, to the police minister, the Duc de Rovigo, that "measures taken in Livorno against the Bacri Jews have produced an impression on the members of this family in Algiers whose effect has not been devoid of use in the re-establishment of our affairs in this land."[96] Among those in government in France, it continued to be understood that that the Bacris were central to the relationship between France and the regency.

But the Bacris had other concerns. The dispute between Michel and Jacob had placed great strain on the bonds that held the family network together. The death of Salomon was to break them altogether. Under this round of sequestration, Salomon, elderly and frail, died in his home at the age of seventy, while under arrest. His death was reported by a close friend on March 3.[97] When the news hit the family, Joseph came to see Thainville again. This time, Thainville reported, Joseph was "screaming horribly against the government (the expression is exact), and accused me of having caused his brother's death." Thainville had been waiting some time to write a letter such as this. Once again, he demonstrated his prodigious memory (and perhaps also his creative mind), recounting, word for word, the speech he had made to Joseph. It was triumphal, and the handwriting, unlike his usual, careful script, was a hurried scrawl. Thainville was having his day, and he rushed to commit the intensity of his feelings to paper. The consul did not seek to spare the

95. AMAE 8CCC/40, p. 346, July 5, 1812, Bassano to Thainville.

96. AN F/7/6537, dossier 1633/2, August 8, 1812, Bassano to Rovigo.

97. ACEL, "Anagrafe della Nazione ebrea di Livorno per gli anni 1808–1814, estratti dai registri del comune di Livorno compilati secondo la legge napoleonica dell'anno 1807."

grieving man's feelings. "In the harshest terms," he reminded Joseph of all the insults he had borne over the last months. Joseph sought to shift the blame on to Jacob, but Thainville would have none of this, accusing Joseph of being his younger brother's accomplice, and proceeding to list all of the wrongs that the two had recently committed. Joseph was not crying for his dead brother, but for his piasters, sequestered in Livorno to guarantee Thainville's safety in Algiers. When Joseph claimed that the family had been ruined by France, Thainville, drawing on all the tropes of greed and duplicity, accused him of hypocrisy:

> where did the colossal fortune of your houses in Algiers and Livorno come from, if not your plundering in France and Italy, during the revolution, and without any type of motive, you dare to demand twelve million for supplies that have been largely paid for. And who, more than you, since my departure from Algiers especially, showed themselves to be France's greatest enemy, who fueled the agents of the Spanish insurgents? You, to whom they owe more than 100,000 piasters, who sends the kingdom's wheat to the Spanish and English armies daily? The house of Bacri. Who provoked the French vice-consul's expulsion? You, and you alone. And you come here today, to demand favors from the French government for your relatives? On what basis? What rights do they have? Have they not always been accomplices to your intrigues in Algiers?

Joseph's response, "convulsing with hypocritical tears," was to apologize humbly, and to promise, "in the most solemn fashion, to stop all of Jacob's intrigues."[98] Clearly, the brotherly relationship was still fraught. Three months earlier, Joseph had complained to Thainville about Jacob who, with his friend and associate Moses Amar, "pursued all intrigues with perseverance."[99] The problems between the brothers were just one part of broader family issues. The relationship between Bacris and Busnachs had begun to break down with Naphtali's death, and the financial disputes between Jacob and Michel were the final straw. Now, with Salomon gone, the two families had lost all points of collaborative contact. In 1813, Thainville wrote that

---

98. AMAE 8CCC/40, p. 318, May 17, 1812, Thainville to Bassano.
99. AMAE 8CCC/40, p. 296, February 25, 1812, Thainville to Bassano.

the "greatest enmity" now existed between the two families.[100] He even claimed that the Bacris had "seized the entire fortune" of the Busnachs, reducing them to beggary.[101] Thainville, of course, was given to the occasional bout of hyperbole. But it can be said that the extended family network that took in brothers, and then nephews, and Busnachs, was no more. By 1813, only Joseph and Jacob remained, and relations between the brothers were strained.

While in the regency, the assassinations of Naphtali and David had led to the breakdown of the family business network, events in Europe were to bring about Thainville's final ignominy. The war had turned: in June 1812, Wellington's forces had defeated the French in Spain, bringing their kingdom there to an end, and opening up southern France to attack. The Austrians now joined the allies, and Napoleon found himself ranged against all the major European powers, including the British navy. By late 1813, the allied powers had pushed French forces back out of Germany and were in a position to propose peace, if Napoleon agreed to remain within France's natural boundaries of the Alps and the Rhine. He refused, and by early 1814, German forces had crossed into France from the north and the east, and were moving toward Paris. The capital surrendered in March, and Napoleon was forced to abdicate shortly afterwards. By early May 1814, he was in Elba, the island between Corsica and the Italian mainland. Louis XVIII, the younger brother of the beheaded Louis XVI, was now in Paris.

In March 1814, a British corvette brought the first news to Algiers of the defeats being suffered by the French army. Thainville responded indignantly, rushing to expose these lies. It was frankly "impossible" that they could be true.[102] But two months later, a French frigate moored in the harbor. It was flying the white flag of the Bourbons, and Thainville was obliged to change his tune. When the captain, Maynard, came ashore, he handed a letter to Thainville announcing the memorable event that, as a diplomatic Thainville now stated, in returning "the August family of the Bourbons to France and to the French, had ensured the nation's happiness, and

100. AMAE 8CCC/41, p. 90, July 20, 1813, Thainville to Bassano.

101. AMAE 8CCC/41, p. 293, November 2, 1814, Thainville to Talleyrand.

102. AMAE 8CCC/41, p. 166, March 5, 1814, Thainville to the Marquis de Caulaincourt, Ministre des relations extérieures.

the blessings of peace to all the nations of Europe." As his words suggest, Thainville hastened to embrace the new regime, and to fulfill his instructions. He reported carefully to the Count de la Forest, the new minister for external relations, that he had taken care of the replacement of the tricolor with the white flag, he had gone with the ship's captain and his officers to the dey to announce the change of regime, and he was happy to be able to report that the dey responded with pleasure. "No news could have pleased him more." He expressed his hope that the return of the Bourbons would also be a return to peace and to strong relations with France, both removing all hindrances to trade.[103] Louis XVIII's government was to be in complete agreement.

Thainville, meanwhile, had written to all of the other foreign consuls in the regency. He received gratifying responses, all of which he copied for the minister's edification. Several consuls, he reported, had hosted dinners and celebrations in their country houses, "in an atmosphere of the liveliest gaiety and the most open cordiality." Toasts were made, "with the greatest enthusiasm," to the general peace.[104] None of these festivities, however, would rival Thainville's own. On August 25, he held a great celebration for the king. All of the French in Algiers gathered, together with the foreign consuls and their nationals, as well as other Europeans of distinction. Some of the city's main Jewish families were admitted, although not as many as had requested that honor. It was Ramadan, so the "outstanding" Muslims of the regency were unable to attend, although they did make known their regrets. The beautiful consular house was elegantly decorated with foliage and flowers, decked out with the flags of His Majesty and of the foreign consuls. There was a dinner, and toasts were proposed: to the king, to the royal family, to the general peace, to the good men, to the ladies, to the rulers whose agents were present—all with the liveliest enthusiasm. A ball followed, and the dancing carried on until dawn, interrupted only by a most elegant supper, served at one in the morning.[105] The event came to a close with "a very festive breakfast" the following morning,

103. AMAE 8CCC/41, p. 180, May 7, 1814, Thainville to the Comte de Laforêt, Ministre des affaires étrangères.
104. AMAE 8CCC/41, p. 182, May 7, 1814, Thainville to Laforêt.
105. AMAE 8CCC/41, pp. 259–60, August 27, 1814, Thainville to Talleyrand.

shared by Thainville and the English and Spanish consuls.[106] Never before had Algiers witnessed so touching a union.

Thainville's position in Algiers, "so difficult for so long," had completely changed.[107] He had reconciled with the British agent, MacDonell, and now the two men saw one another constantly. Where he had endured derision, now he was treated with esteem.[108] Keen to show himself worthy, Thainville carried out his new instructions with his usual assiduity. His first task was to obtain a full renewal of the treaties. This he did, ensuring that the British might never again steal the concessions. His second was to provide information on the Bacri debts, so that a decision might be reached regarding the merit of their claims. On this "very complicated and very delicate affair,"[109] Thainville had very firm opinions. If trade were to be opened for France in the regency, the Bacris could not be trusted or believed, and their power, now two decades old, had to be destroyed.[110]

But with a new regime in Paris had come a change of policy concerning relations with the regency. Just one month after he had returned to Paris, as the widely quoted phrase would have it, "in the baggage of the Allies," Louis XVIII was writing to all of the Barbary States, assuring them of his desire for lasting peace, and seeking the renewal of the treaties. Peaceful relations would mean that trade and sea traffic would be sheltered from risk and danger, which in turn would ensure stability in France.[111] While Thainville was reviewing the Bacris' claims in Algiers, his newly appointed replacement, Pierre Deval, was writing a report on the history of the debt in Paris.[112] Thainville remained convinced that almost all of the monies claimed by the Bacris to be owing were "illusory."[113] This was to place him out of step with views in Paris. In the months

106. AMAE 8CCC/41, p. 287, November 2, 1814, Thainville to Talleyrand.

107. AMAE 8CCC/41, p. 187, May 14, 1814, Thainville to Talleyrand.

108. AMAE 8CCC/41, pp. 285–86, November 2, 1814, Thainville to Talleyrand.

109. AMAE 8CCC/41, p. 226, July 12, 1814, Thainville to Talleyrand.

110. AMAE 8CCC/41, p. 204, June 23, 1814, Thainville to Talleyrand.

111. AMAE 8CCC/41, p. 194, May 25, 1814, Thainville to Talleyrand.

112. Pierre Deval (1758–1829) was to be the last French consul in the regency. Deval had been assigned the consulship in Algiers in late 1791, but he only lasted six months, being sent away at the Dey Hussein's request. He spent the revolutionary years in exile in Constantinople, returning to France in 1803.

113. AMAE 8CCC/41, p. 293, November 2, 1814, Thainville to Talleyrand.

following the change of flags, Thainville returned to his central concern, warning of the Bacris' power, and the risk that they would
turn the dey against France, and, more particularly, against himself.
In his eyes, he was to be proved right, and in spectacular fashion.
Thainville was prone to overstatement, but it is nonetheless true,
perhaps, that members of the Bacri family were much more in their
element, and thus much more capable, in Algiers. The contrast
between the Jacob who wreaked havoc for Thainville at home, and
the Jacob whose Paris and Marseilles ventures collapsed so spectacularly, is striking, and also telling.

A war of twenty-two years does not simply stop, and its echoes could
still be heard in Algiers six months after its official end. Nor could
years of enmity between two consuls be mended in the course of one
all-night party. Relationships would continue to be fraught. And nor
did the regency observe the end of hostilities, necessarily, when war
had been so beneficial to its coffers. Tobias Lear observed to Robert
Smith, his secretary of state, that the regency did not appear to be
influenced by the events of the war, but rather, that they understood
"the game they have to play between Britain and France too well to
give themselves entirely up to one or the other."[114] In late October,
the British consul, MacDonell, reported that Thainville was refusing to pay the value of a load of wheat, shipped from Algiers on a
neutral Algerian vessel, for the use of British armies in Portugal, and
which had been captured by a French corsair. Although the dey had
assured MacDonell that Britain should indeed be paid the value of
the wheat, sold off in Malaga, Thainville had been prevaricating for
no less than two years. Most recently, Thainville claimed that he did
not have sufficient authority from his government, and therefore
could not comply with the demand made upon him. The dey would
not have this. "Without otherwise dissolving the friendly relations
subsisting between the two countries," as MacDonell observed, the
dey ordered Thainville to depart, which he did on October 19.[115] The
dey sent a request to France for a new consul.

114. NARA Atlanta M23, roll 10, vol. 8, n.p., November 1810, Lear to Smith.
115. TNA FO3/16, p. 64, October 30, 1814, MacDonell to Sir Henry Bunbury, Under-
Secretary of State for War and the Colonies.

Thainville's report on the same events was somewhat different. Writing from the Bay of Mallorca, he attributed his expulsion—predictably—to the Bacris. The captured wheat was theirs, sent in one of their ships, and they had conspired with MacDonell to retrieve its value. With hindsight, he noted that he had perceived "a secret jealousy" in the British agent, even though their relations appeared open and cordial.[116] In October, he was ordered to pay for the cargo.

> I repeated what I had already stated: that I could not settle anything without orders from the king, that the dey had given me three months, and that I was going to send urgent letters to France.
>
> The next day, I was told to pay before midday, and that if I did not have money, I should borrow from the Jews, and give them bills of exchange. My dragoman was threatened with strangulation. I stayed in my home with the doors locked.[117]

On October 17, he was given three days to leave Algiers. On the eighteenth, word was sent to him from the dey that he was to depart immediately. Thainville had his bags packed and sent to the ship that he had chartered (this was a ship owned by the Bacris). By the dey's orders, Thainville's bags were taken off the ship and brought to the palace, where they were opened, and their contents examined, piece by piece. The next day, at 9:00 a.m., Thainville left his house:

> accompanied by my friends, and by a large number of Europeans. If my return to Algiers had been a day of celebration, my departure, I assert, was truly a day of mourning. I crossed the town, followed by a large crowd, in the most mournful silence, and the marina in the midst of all the unfortunate slaves who threw themselves at my feet with cries of long live France. I embarked on the *Lis* and sailed. I was not saluted by any cannon fire.[118]

Even though Thainville no longer wished to remain as consul, he did want to replay his final moments. His departure in mid-October had not been the grand exit he so often described in his

116. AMAE 8CCC/41, pp. 286–87, November 2, 1814, Thainville to Talleyrand.
117. AMAE 8CCC/41, p. 289, November 2, 1814, Thainville to Talleyrand.
118. AMAE 8CCC/41, p. 290, November 2, 1814, Thainville to Talleyrand.

letters, where he was accompanied down the hill to the port by an adoring crowd of locals and seen off with a salute from the cannons in the fort. Indeed, in the end, his final departure was a grand anticlimax to the fourteen years he had spent serving France in Algiers. Thainville's vision for the taming of Algiers involved a show of military force: he was to be sent back to the regency in state, accompanied by a division (a ship of the line and two frigates would be "all the more imposing"). He would carry a stern letter from the king to the dey, "expressing His Majesty's surprise at what has just happened, and revealing, in a concise manner, the intrigues I have just described." Thainville would deliver this letter to the dey in person. And if differences could be settled, then he was to be granted the power to take up his post in Algiers once again, only briefly: just long enough, in fact, to demand the salute that was refused him when he departed so unceremoniously.

Thainville was not to have the send-off he craved. In July 1815, after Napoleon had returned from Elba and then been seen off, yet again, the dey wrote to France. With the return to power of his old master for one hundred days, Thainville had sought to return to his post. Omar had found a pretext to prevent Thainville from landing. He did not want Thainville. "A consul who resides among us must be a prudent person, capable of managing affairs, observing correct procedures, [. . .] your consul possesses none of these qualities; and for this reason we have sent him back to France."[119] In August 1815, Ferrier, the secretary and most senior functionary in the consulate in Algiers, wrote to Talleyrand that the dey impatiently awaited the newly appointed consul Pierre Deval, and hoped that the new consul would "see an end to all these unfortunate monetary arguments, which should have been settled long ago."[120] Charles-François Dubois Thainville was fast becoming a distant memory, left behind by change. He returned to Paris and died shortly afterwards, in 1818. After his death, his widow and children spent years petitioning the ministry for a pension; a request that was never granted.

Well before the invasion of 1830, France and the regency were entangled in a complex relationship. It was maintained by France's

119. AMAE 8CCC/42, p. 94, July 1815, "Rapport au gouvernement."
120. AMAE 8CCC/42, p. 111, August 26, 1815, Ferrier to Talleyrand.

continuing need for raw produce, the outstanding and ever-mounting debt owed to the Bacris and the dey, and the repeated tit for tat of sequestrations. France saw the Bacris at the center of this relationship. But the Bacris had their own difficulties, and when events challenged Thainville, or members of the extended Bacri family, they did not rise to the challenge. They were unable to move with changing events, and to understand their context. Thainville, over and over again, was profoundly shocked by the ability of Bacri brothers to come back from misfortune. He did not comprehend the nature of relations in the regency, and the ways in which the Bacris, as Jews, and specifically as *muqaddem*, were able to profit from these relations. Head down and blinkered, he persisted, in increasingly dogged terms, in insisting on French supremacy, British perfidy, and the awful malign power wielded by the Bacris. Ultimately, he was to fall victim to rapid regime change in France.

The Bacris, likewise, did not understand different contexts. Jacob did expand his repertoire to make use of the French judicial system in his attempts to pin Michel Busnach down. But he saw this, also, as an opportunity to establish and make use of personal relationships, writing to lawyers he felt would not support his cause, and asking them to stand down. His strength in Algiers—his ability to establish and draw on personal and business relationships with those in power—was a weakness in France, where he did not have the standing to profit from such clientelism as was practiced. Jacob's misfortunes, and his increasingly difficult relations with family, reveal in vivid detail the multiple, overlapping norms and jurisdictions that continued to exist in the postrevolutionary world, from family relations, to religious practice, to law, and to the public sphere. In the dispute between Jacob and Michel, what had been festering mistrust between members of the extended family became open accusations, as family members were first drawn in, and then sought to break away, from Jacob's maelstrom. The family broke apart, and ultimately only Jacob and Joseph were left, the last Bacris in Algiers. The final break, and perhaps Jacob's final revenge, were to come.

CHAPTER FIVE

Diplomacy, New and Old

PIERRE DEVAL, the new French consul, reached Algiers in early 1816. Between Deval's appointment in September 1814, and his arrival at his posting, Europe had lived through two extraordinary, transformative years. In early 1814, after twenty-three long years of total war with just one short break, the allied armies of the sixth coalition defeated Napoleon's forces. The emperor abdicated, albeit reluctantly, and was given the nominal title of ruler of the island of Elba, off the Tuscan coast. For the first time in twenty-five years, all of Europe's major powers—including the French—gathered together in peace, in Vienna. From late September 1814, delegates from Prussia, Russia, Austria, France, and Great Britain assembled in the Austro-Hungarian capital. The European powers needed to remake Europe, and they agreed to act in concert, to ensure that France could never again pose a threat to stability. This was no less a task than coming together to decide the destinies of some thirty-two million people, and the status of almost every border, in territories that had been conquered by Napoleon, but that now lay outside the borders of France. The meeting was imagined as a formal, brief gathering, its purpose to confirm the Paris Peace Treaty, and to take care of smaller issues. What came to be known as the Congress of Vienna lasted nine months: a series of parties, concerts, spectacles, and endless intrigues, which Mark Jarrett has termed "a joyous ritual cleansing" at the end of more than two decades of war.[1] It

1. Jarrett, *The Congress of Vienna*, 69.

was an extraordinary time, of exhaustion and elation, of large-scale mopping up and reckoning, and of looking forward, imagining an idealized new reality. This is the setting for this chapter.

Both the regency and the Bacris had benefited from the war. Over the long period of war, they had become accustomed to taking advantage of hostilities among European powers to play one off against the other. The war caused chaos in the Mediterranean, and the regency took advantage of this, declaring war on one or another of the minor powers, in order to profit from the capture of its ships. Corsairing, as well as slavery, had blossomed anew. But with the end of the war, everything was to change, as the fog of war lifted, and the countries of Europe entered an era of determined cooperation. Even before the congress began, the allied statesmen who were to be its main characters had already begun to describe themselves as acting "in the name of Europe."[2] They would make the world anew: a united Europe would stamp out the corsairing that damaged trade, and the enslavement of Europeans, that was nothing less than an affront to national dignity.[3] No longer would the regency have the power to hold them hostage, setting prices for the return of ships and citizens. Or so "Europe" wished to believe. In this program, diplomacies new and old were brought together. On the one hand, a united Europe sought to rewrite the rules of state-to-state relations. On the other, Jacob and the regency kept to age-old ways—regency ways—in the personalization of diplomacy. All the Bacris had profited from the war, in many ways. So how does their story change with the coming of peace? What happened when this new Europe at peace, determined to create order, met those who wished to maintain disorder? In this chapter, two contrasting ideas of diplomacy meet, head-to-head, free of the urgency and desperation of war. Where nations formerly in conflict now came together as Europe, and sought to install order and orderliness, Jacob, together with the dey, wished for circumstances to remain as they had always been. The story of who emerged triumphant and why is at the heart of this chapter.

2. Jarrett, *The Congress of Vienna*, 69.
3. See Weiss, *Captives and Corsairs*, 132.

With the Congress of Vienna, Europe's self-image began a process of transition. At Vienna, the delegates inaugurated a "new diplomacy":[4] the idea that coming together regularly to act in concert could "promote repose, prosperity, and peace."[5] The British and their allies, together with France, made a concerted effort, acting as Europe in the face of Muslim Africa, and reorganizing the framework of economic interaction. They assembled at the Congress in unprecedented fashion: not to settle a dispute, but rather, to organize and affirm an already existing peace. This also allowed them to imagine themselves as the harbingers of a new era of civilization. It suited the European powers, newly emerged from these wars and inaugurating an age of cooperation, to see Muslim corsairing "as a barbarous relic of a previous age."[6] It is true that corsairing had constituted part of an informal but sanctioned international economy for centuries. At the same time, the practice interrupted trade, and posed a threat to the safe passage of merchant ships. Corsairing had declined over the eighteenth century, but it flourished again in the chaos brought on by the wars. The French and British profited from it in the war, using corsairs as a proxy measure against competitors: if Algerian corsairs were pursuing the ships of minor powers, it saved them this trouble, and as long as Algerian corsairs were attacking the same ships, then British and French shipping was safe. Throughout the wars and beyond, American consuls grumbled over British behavior in particular, claiming that they deliberately directed Algerian corsairing against American merchantmen. But with the peace came an era of economic protectionism, and the belief that it was now reasonable to expect a controlled, reliable supply of goods.

When Deval arrived in Algiers, the regency, too, had been through turbulent times. Food shortages caused economic and social instability, as elites sought to maintain the high and profitable volumes of grain exports.[7] This instability made for an unlucky few years for deys, as several were murdered in quick succession, often by their successor. Hadj Ali had come to power in

4. Aprile, *La Révolution inachevée*, 229.
5. Schroeder, *The Transformation of European Politics*, 557.
6. McDougall, *A History of Algeria*, 48.
7. McDougall, *A History of Algeria*, 46.

1809. He was known for his cruelty, and he murdered many of the elite, and humiliated his ministers. They plotted their revenge. On March 21, 1815, when Ali took his bath, servants, who numbered among the conspirators, shut the doors tightly, and fed the fire, causing Ali to suffocate.[8] His successor, the elderly Muhammad Khaznaji, "decrepit and infirm," managed to rule for only seventeen days, before he, too, suffered a violent death, strangled in early April.[9] Omar followed, ruling for a relatively long period of two and a half years. It was Omar who was in power when Deval came to Algiers.

There had been upheaval in the Bacri family, also. Relations between the last two surviving brothers had broken down. In January 1816, Omar exiled Joseph. Jacob, the last brother left in Algiers, gained possession of all Joseph's assets, and became *muqaddam* in his brother's place.[10] Before leaving Algiers, Joseph wrote an official protest and had it registered and deposited at the Spanish consulate, where he had been financial agent. By order of his government, the protest read, he had been deprived of his house, his worldly goods, and his very freedom. He had been dispossessed of his title as head of the Jewish nation in the regency. He was obliged to depart with "nothing other than the clothes on his body, without being given the time or the ability to dispose of some of his goods, accounts, and debts." With the same bitter anger he had shown after David's death, Joseph asked the Spanish consul to receive the formal, solemn, and public protest that he made against ten members of the Algiers Jewish community. These were his enemies: "The instigators and authors of all the harm that my absence and my abandon cause, and will cause to suffer to all my own belongings, real, negotiable, or on account, as well as those goods coming from the inheritance of my deceased son David Coen Bacri and those of my correspondents and friends which could be linked to mine." Joseph accused them of having refused him his right, before divine and human law, to seek justice, and he held them responsible for any harm that might befall

8. Khoja, *Aperçu historique et statistique sur la régence d'Alger*, 132.

9. Camille Rousset, *La Conquête d'Alger*, 6.

10. Archivo Histórico Nacional (AHN), Madrid, Archivo del Ministerio de Asuntos Exteriores (AMAE), Política Exterior, leg. 2309, January 23, 1816, "Sobre el destierro del Ebreo, José Cohen Bacri, y su demanda de ser reconocido como súbdito Español."

him as he made his way to Livorno. He promised to detail their machinations in full once he reached there.[11] On arrival at the port of Mahon on the island of Menorca, Joseph drew a bill of exchange of 1,950 piasters on Jacob, but his brother did not pay it. Perhaps Jacob, too, was vengeful, taking full advantage of an opportunity to leave his older brother destitute, just as Joseph had deserted him in the midst of his battles with Michel Busnach. Joseph's humiliation was complete: he was never able to return to Algiers, or to recover any of his fortune. He lived a few more years in Livorno. In Algiers, Jacob was now the last brother left, in full power. He continued to import and export goods and enjoyed the monopoly over the export of wool and wax, a "very significant sector" of the regency's business, which he managed on its behalf.[12] His had been the final name on Joseph's list of his ten enemies.

After unfortunate adventures in Europe, Jacob was back in his element, conducting and using diplomacy in the only way he knew how—through personal relationships. France and Britain may have wished to believe that they were imposing a new order in the post-Napoleonic world, but, together with their fellow longtime presence in the regency, Spain, they owed money to the House of Bacri and its last surviving member: Jacob. All three powers were to be embroiled in diplomatic spats over payment. They still needed the regency: a disastrous summer that brought food insecurity, exacerbated by returning troops, meant that finding reliable sources of raw food-stuffs remained a priority. Jacob found ways to bring all three governments back into old patterns and interactions. He used tried and tested methods to force repayment, involving the dey and the elite of the regency, and thus elevating a financial issue to the great heights of state-to-state relations, or diplomacy. This had always been the genius of the Bacris, to make the dey the public face of their business, so that their business matters would become a diplomatic matter. And where states now sought to change the nature of relations, Jacob was not ready to do so. It is possible, of course, that Joseph was right about his brother. Jacob now had total control of all monies owed

11. Bloch, *Inscriptions tumulaires*, 118–19.

12. AMAE 8CCC/46, p. 5, February 4, 1822, Deval to the Vicomte de Montmorency, Ministre des affaires étrangères.

to the family. Omar and his successor, Hussein, pursued the Bacris' debtors assiduously, on Jacob's behalf. The dedication of both deys to payment of these debts suggest that they might have had a stake in them. Did Jacob promise them a cut, if they helped him to recover the funds he was owed? He was clearly doing business with the regency's elite. Or could it be, as some sources claim, that Jacob, deep in debt, had been forced, for the sake of his head, to sign these debts over? These were considerable amounts, which the regency took striking pains and risks to recover.

When it came to debt, France, Britain, and the United States— as well as Spain—vacillated between a perceived need to woo the regency with payments so as to ensure stability and supply, and the desire to force the regency to adapt to the newly reordered world: to stop corsairing, slavery, and constant demands for gifts. All found this balance difficult to strike, but it was perhaps France that faced the greatest challenges in seeking to renew its relationship with the regency. As the war came to an end, France still owed money for the wheat that the Bacris had sent, a debt now more than two decades old. The new regime in France under Louis XVIII was prepared to pay, and consul Pierre Deval was instructed to organize settlement of the Bacri debts, so as to reestablish the good relations that would allow France to enjoy full control over the concessions. The debt was causing bad feeling between France and the regency, and Omar would not return full control of the concessions to France until it was repaid. On March 1, in his first letter to his minister, the Duc de Richelieu, Deval gave an account of his inaugural interview with Omar, and the elite of the regency. In late February, Deval and Jacob had been called to the divan. Here, Jacob bore witness to the outstanding debt owed to his trading house. Jacob ensured the debt would be understood as part of state relations. This was, he complained, the hundredth time that he had been asked to produce his accounts. Now, he "invoked the justice and protection of the regency, and the treaties with France, for the immediate liquidation of his accounts, by the French consul in Algiers."[13] Jacob's approach was successful: the regency's elite agreed that the debt was a question of

13. AMAE 8CCC/42, p. 214, March 1, 1816, Deval to the Duc de Richelieu, Président du conseil et affaires étrangères.

diplomacy. Of all the "litigious affairs existing between the regency" and France, Deval reported being told, the Bacri debt was the "main affair." Now, with its age and the failure of the previous regime to pay, the debt had also become the "most urgent, and the most important."[14] The *vekilardgi*, or prime minister, pronounced that the regency found Jacob's claims to be correct and justified, and it was up to Deval to beg his minister to communicate this to His Majesty Louis XVIII.[15] If the French government truly wished to render full and complete justice to Algerians, they would not, surely, forbid the French consul from hearing the regency's claims and communicating them to his government. It was reasonable for Jacob to name a proxy in Paris in preparation for the full liquidation of the debt, and to report to the regency if he did not obtain full satisfaction. Deval was caught. All of the members of the divan, he reported to Richelieu, were in agreement.

From France's perspective, the advent of a new regime allowed them to establish a different narrative of relations with the regency: one that laid full diplomatic skill at the feet of the Bourbon Monarchy. France effectively folded the debt into its new understanding of itself. Under its kings, so the narrative went, France's political relations with Algiers had been "in line with the dignity of the crown and the nation's commercial interests." During the revolution and the years of Napoleonic rule, wisdom had been abandoned. For the sake of diplomacy, it was of little consequence, now, whether the Bacris' claims were "exaggerated or unjust." What did matter was that the Bacris' personal interests had become "a public grievance for the regency," and this, in turn, had served as a motive for "highly deplorable reprisals." The regency's grievances had been increased by further incompetence and tactlessness on the part of France when Napoleon brought an end to the custom of gift-giving. As a direct result of "these imprudent undertakings," and "dangerous innovations," along with "the unfavorable influence of agents of those powers with which France was at war," France was no longer able to contain the regency, and political relations were "ruined." In 1806, France's concessions were taken away. According to the

14. AMAE 8CCC/42, p. 214, March 1, 1816, Deval to Richelieu.
15. AMAE 8CCC/42, p. 218, March 1, 1816, Deval to Richelieu.

report, this was "on the instigation of the Bacri Jews who thought that by this means they had found a way to recover some of their debts with the French government." The concessions were given to the British.[16]

France needed the regency. But it was by no means a given that France would be willing, much less able, to pay Jacob what it owed. By 1814, French society had been completely restructured and destabilized, the fabric of old regime life torn apart by the abolition of the monarchy, the delegitimization of the church, the Terror, and protracted civil war that had left "livid scars" in France. 1.3 million people had died over the course of the Revolutionary and Napoleonic Wars; among these, forty percent of men born between 1790 and 1795. The nature of war itself had been transformed. For the first time, politics and war fused, as combatants fought for or against the revolutionary cause. Fighting was driven by a political agenda, which meant that the stakes became higher, and battles could only end in total victory, or total defeat.[17] Even for France's great adversary in these wars, the prospect of losing was unthinkable. The war was highly strategic for Britain. It was also ideological, a war to the death,[18] "a desperate struggle to defend rank, and above all, property."[19] But the war was not quite over, and more uncertainty was to come.

Napoleon's exile to Elba in 1814 was, as it turned out, a defeat that was lacking in totality. After his departure, Louis XVI's younger brother had reclaimed the throne as Louis XVIII. But France, at war for so long, was in foment. Napoleon, hearing of the unrest, escaped his island prison on a ship, appropriately named the *Inconstant*, and landed in the south of France. As he marched north, he gathered support—and an army. The King's soldiers defied orders to fire on Napoleon, and instead took up arms for his cause. He reached Paris on March 20 and resumed rule in triumph. Louis fled to the Kingdom of the Netherlands. But the allies, now in an established pattern of working in concert, were not prepared to trust Napoleon's professions of peace. They mobilized against him once again, and British and Prussian forces met a tired and poorly

16. AMAE 8CCC/42, pp. 158–59, October 24, 1815, Deval, "Affaires d'Alger."
17. Bell, *The First Total War*, 7–8.
18. Hilton, *A Mad, Bad, and Dangerous People?*, 87.
19. Colley, *Britons*, 152.

equipped French army for battle in the Dutch Kingdom (today's Belgium), in mid-June. Two preliminary battles were inconclusive, but on June 18, the French were decisively routed at Waterloo. Napoleon abdicated once again four days later. This time, he was definitively exiled, to one of the world's most remote islands: St. Helena, in the Atlantic Ocean, where he would remain until his death in 1821.

In France, Louis XVIII's regime sought some sort of stability. Commerce and industry were in shambles. Investment was slowed by the occupation of France by more than a million allied soldiers, as part of the Allies' "occupation of guarantee" to guard against any further political instability.[20] Political and economic difficulties were only to be exacerbated by a climactic crisis. In the early nineteenth century, economies across Europe remained largely agricultural. This meant that Western economies were vulnerable, both to agricultural productivity, and to food prices.[21] In 1816–17, the northern hemisphere experienced an extended period of unusually cold temperatures—"among the lowest in the recorded meteorological history of the western world."[22] The cold damaged crops right throughout Europe, and much of the Western world, bringing on a subsistence crisis.[23] From the beginning of autumn 1816, to the end of spring 1817, France had severe shortages of basic subsistence provisions. The price of cereal, the staple that could claim half of a laboring family's income in times of plenty, doubled, or even tripled. It was not only in France that populations suffered. The high cost of food led to dearth and scarcity, and, in some places, to deaths from starvation, just as European economies were having to adjust after the dislocation of two decades of war. The return home of millions of men, released from the armed forces, intensified the crisis for families struggling to buy food, and put pressure on a labor market that struggled to absorb them. Governments were forced to look abroad for grain, and a worldwide search for provisions began. The subsistence crisis marked the shift in the grain trade, from the Baltic to the new port of Odessa on the Black Sea, ice-free. Supplies of

20. Haynes, *Our Friends the Enemies*, 2, 211.
21. Post, *The Last Great Subsistence Crisis*, 141.
22. Post, *The Last Great Subsistence Crisis*, 1.
23. Caron, *An Economic History of Modern France*, 119.

grain through this channel were abundant, but remained inaccessible until transports began in 1812. In the autumn of 1816, some six hundred ships left Mediterranean ports to collect grain from Odessa.[24] The need for stability in the Mediterranean was indeed great, but even this endless supply of precious foodstuffs was not guaranteed. Ships carrying cargoes from the Black Sea were regularly seized by Ottoman corsairs.

France was also trying to fulfill the financial obligations imposed by the victors, to relaunch industry, and oversee the recovery of the French economy. This required "a rethinking of political economy,"[25] and with it, the place of debt. Baron Louis, the finance minister, saw his primary duty as being the scrupulous repayment of all "engagements contracted in the name of the state."[26] Strong, safe port stations in North Africa could resolve many of France's issues: if the government could restart the trade concessions, it could control supply of raw goods from Algiers, and thus pricing, while also avoiding the problem of shortages. The regime had good cause to feel both nostalgic and optimistic about the Royal Africa Company. Running between 1741 and 1793, its success during this period—one, it must be said, of political stability and plenty in Algiers—was unequalled, and unique in the history of French monopoly companies.[27] Even if the concessions were now losing money for France, they could still act as a trade incentive for France's southern departments and make French influence on the African coast preponderant. In Algiers, Deval was enthusiastic. These advantages, he felt, would surely be ample compensation for any loss.[28]

The French were not the only European power concerned to ensure good relations with the regency, and to secure shipping in the Mediterranean. The British had managed better in financing the war, but it had nonetheless cost them dearly, approximately six times their prewar national income.[29] Like France, Britain, too, had experienced a crisis, and a period of commercial stagnation.

24. Post, *The Last Great Subsistence Crisis*, 55.
25. Haynes, *Our Friends the Enemies*, 212.
26. Cited in Haynes, *Our Friends the Enemies*, 214.
27. Touati, "L'Algérie au 'siècle du blé.'"
28. AMAE 8CCC/46, 250, March 1824, "Rapport au ministre."
29. Colley, *Britons*, 152.

The sea blockades of the war had created new trade monopolies for Britain in continental Europe, but these had now been lost. The broader effect of this downturn was the increase in unemployment in "almost every branch of industry," as manufacturers were forced to suspend or reduce production.[30] An overproduction of grain caused further problems. In wartime, with prices high and no foreign competition, Britain had added five million acres to its wheat-producing capacity. But with the return of competing grain supplies, particularly from Baltic ports, as well as ample yields in Britain, by early 1816, the price for wheat was the lowest average since 1804. One-third of the British population worked in agriculture, but the rural depression spread: "The tradesmen, innkeepers, and shopkeepers of country towns also suffered from the agrarian depression, and blacksmiths, wheelwrights, collar-makers, harness-makers, and carpenters found no work."[31] Following mass demonstrations in London at Spa Fields in November and December, social protest became a matter for concern in government. The combined effects of the flooded market, and social unrest caused governments to retreat into protectionism. In 1815, Britain introduced tariffs and restrictions on imports of grain, known as the corn law; France followed suit in 1819. Keeping foreign competition in check would protect domestic producers. But the prevailing wisdom was that periodic supply shortages through failed harvests were unavoidable. This was a lesson learned by times of scarcity in 1795–96, 1800–1801, a mini–ice age in 1810, and famine in the summer of 1812. Throughout the first half of the nineteenth century, "food supply was the most anxious priority of governments."[32] Domestic production could not be relied upon, and it was vital to find and secure overseas sources of staples, should the harvests fail again. In most years, need could be covered by crops. Shortages leading to famine occurred every fifteen to twenty years only. Clearly, though, this was sufficiently regular to create a mentality of fear, especially after the upheavals of the French Revolution.

30. Post, *The Last Great Subsistence Crisis*, 28.
31. Post, *The Last Great Subsistence Crisis*, 28.
32. Hilton, *A Mad, Bad, and Dangerous People?*, 264.

Britain, like France, was very keen to secure supply. Shortly after the victory at Waterloo, control of British consuls in the Barbary States was given to the Governor of Malta, Sir Thomas Maitland. His first instructions to MacDonell, the British consul in Algiers, were all about trade. The consul was to send a full report on all trade carried out in the regency, to suggest any means that might occur to him, by which British commerce could be increased, and to inform Maitland what supplies of grain and cattle might be available to the British government.[33] Britain was seeking markets, not just for supply, but also for export. With the renewal of peace, the Levant Company, based in Egypt, enjoyed unprecedented prosperity.[34] Algiers turned out to be a profitable export market too. Algerian traders imported British textiles from London and Gibraltar, and colonial goods from Livorno and Malta. And Britain, according to Deval, established a coral fishing company, and acquired permission to fish off the coast of Tunis. Deval was obliged to report that British boats would regularly stray across the boundary that marked the French concessions. At the same time, the British sought to block any competition, repeatedly asking Dey Hussein to close off Algerian waters to fishing if they had not been ceded to France.[35] The Algerian coast was in demand.

While France and Britain undertook a dignified wooing of the regency, the United States was the first to use force against it. The United States had had a difficult relationship with the regency for some time. Congress had decided to manage its relationship with the Barbary States with the payment of tributes. But this had left them powerless and exposed. Algerian corsairs were regularly sent out to cruise against US ships. Disputes over these captured boats and crew on the US side, and regular accusations and threats relating to payments in arrears on the Algerian side, flared up sporadically. In 1812, war was only averted when Joseph agreed, on behalf of the United States, to pay money being demanded by Hadj Ali, for tributes he claimed were outstanding. In 1814, Jacob was the intermediary in another negotiation between the United States

33. TNA FO 3/20, p. 14, October 15, 1815, Maitland to MacDonell.
34. On the Levant Company, see Wood, *A History of the Levant Company*, 191–98.
35. AMAE 8CCC/47, p. 297, September 29, 1825, Deval to the Baron de Damas, Ministre des affaires étrangères.

and the regency. Raynal Keene, an American living in Spain, was deputized to travel to Algiers to negotiate the freedom of enslaved Americans. Aaron Cardoza, an elite Jewish trader in Gibraltar, gave Keene letters of recommendation to the Bacris. Keene met Jacob and found him "every way polite and accommodating."[36] The dey was demanding two million dollars from the US government for the right to pass the Strait of Gibraltar unimpeded. On the payment of these funds, the most recent treaty would then be renewed. Keene was inclined to trust his intermediary. Jacob, he felt, was vain enough to wish to demonstrate "the high consideration he held in relation to the cabinet, by being let into the secret of their views." Keene believed Jacob's display. He had "ample evidence" that the connection between the Bacris and the regency elite was "close, intimate, and confidential."[37]

But disputes continued to arise, and the payment of tributes proved very costly. In 1801, Thomas Jefferson had pursued an aggressive policy in the Mediterranean against Tripoli. Jefferson had three goals in his foreign policy: "Securing the nation's trade routes, protecting its rights as a neutral power to undertake commerce between European belligerents, and building a naval force sufficient to defend and advance these commercial interests."[38] He put these goals into practice in America's First Barbary War (1801–5), in order to protect American shipping. Eventually, Jefferson's policy was adopted again, this time in 1815, just one week after the three-year war with Great Britain came to an end. The US congress, urged on by President James Madison, passed an act declaring war on Algiers. Commodore Stephen Decatur sailed with a squadron on May 20, arriving at Gibraltar the following month. He bore a letter addressed to Omar from President James Madison, stating that Congress had declared war on the regency, but that Madison hoped Omar would accept the United States' conditions, and choose peace. Decatur was a celebrated and highly experienced veteran: he had fought in the war against Tripoli, as well as in the War of 1812–15, against Britain. He quickly captured the *Mashuda*,

36. Cited in Noah, *Travels in England, France, Spain, and the Barbary States*, 149.
37. Cited in Noah, *Travels in England, France, Spain, and the Barbary States*, 150.
38. Sofka, "'The Jeffersonian Idea of National Security' Revisited," 163.

belonging to Reis Hammida, the Algerian admiral, and he sailed into port at Algiers with the ship and several hundred prisoners. Hammida himself had been killed. Negotiations, undertaken by the Swedish consul Norderling, were brief. Omar had not long been dey, and his most recent predecessors had met unpleasant ends. Perhaps he reasoned that the best path was to avoid conflict at all costs. He signed a treaty providing for the total abolition of tribute payments, whether in cash or goods, and the release of Americans being held in the regency. Omar was to pay ten thousand dollars in compensation for US property seized by the regency. And he had to agree to emancipate any Christian slave in Algiers who escaped to a US ship, and for all future captives to be treated as prisoners of war, and to be exempted from labor. Decatur had brought an impressive fleet. It included the first US ship of the line to show the new republic's flag abroad, as well as a sloop and a frigate captured from the British and recommissioned for service in the US navy. The Second Barbary War convinced US authorities that it was worth the investment to maintain a permanent naval base in the Mediterranean.[39] This was the United States, out and about in the world. It should come as no surprise that Decatur was received as a national hero, and his campaign gave an extraordinary momentum to US nationalism.[40]

Britain, acting as and on behalf of Europe, followed the lead of the United States. In amongst the discussions on abolition that took place in Vienna, the question of the continued enslavement of white Christians by the Muslim states rumbled in the background. This was not the first time that the Christian powers of Europe considered the idea of joining together to fight the Muslim, Barbary States. Such notions had been circulating for two hundred years, and France had, indeed, attempted to teach the Barbary corsairs a lesson, on more than one occasion. On this particular occasion, while France was in favor, in principle, of forcing an end to Barbary corsairing, lingering mistrust of Britain made France reluctant to join a renewed effort. French officials suspected that the British sought greater dominance in the Mediterranean, both

39. Camps, "Minorca," 148–49.
40. Field, *America and the Mediterranean World*, 60.

on sea and land.[41] The allies at Vienna, perhaps not much inclined to take French concerns into account, felt no such doubt, and they delegated Britain to take action. Weiss argues that they were influenced in this course by Stephen Decatur's successful campaign for the United States.[42]

The British were certainly aware of Decatur's success. In April 1816, Admiral Edward Pellew, Lord Exmouth, was appointed to act as an intermediary between the Barbary States and concerned governments. His mission was to negotiate new treaties on behalf of Sardinia and the Kingdom of the Two Sicilies, as well as the release of all slaves. Mediterranean peoples were still vulnerable to enslavement: in October 1815, corsairs had attacked the small Sardinian island of Sant'Antioco, taking 160 men, women, and children prisoner. At the same time, fresh from war, Exmouth sent Captain Warde to reconnoiter the port of Algiers, in case it should come to a necessary bombardment. In Tunis and Tripoli, he secured the freedom of hundreds of Sicilians, Genoese, Neapolitans, and Sardinians, and a promise to stop taking slaves. In Algiers, Omar, perhaps regretting having given way so easily to the United States, prevaricated. He agreed to ransom some slaves at a rather inflated rate, but refused to make any promises. Exmouth had been ordered to lodge a protest with the dey over the US treaty—Decatur had secured an exemption from the payment of tributes, but Britain was still obliged to pay. Here, Omar was happy to be conciliatory. That treaty, he confided to Exmouth, had been imposed on him unfairly. Either the United States would have to revert to the 1796 treaty, which required tribute payments, or Omar would declare war. He could not afford to be so decisive about slavery. To cease altogether, he claimed, he would have to obtain permission from the Porte.[43]

Exmouth departed on this uncertain note. As he reached Britain, news came that two hundred Corsican and Sicilian coral fishermen had been massacred at Bona, when they were attending mass. Exmouth turned around and sailed back to the

41. Weiss, *Captives and Corsairs*, 150.

42. Weiss, *Captives and Corsairs*, 151. Why the British agreed to the mission, however, is less clear.

43. Gale, "Beyond Corsairs," 235.

Mediterranean, with the aim, this time, of teaching Omar a lesson. Armed with Warde's advice, he arrived back at Algiers on August 27, shortly after Deval came to take up his post. Exmouth had a fleet of ten British ships, together with a Dutch squadron of six vessels. A battle ensued. A Victorian "boys' own" account of the battle describes how the "Algerines" fired first, using the many guns that were fortifying the port city. The British fleet's flagship, the *Queen Charlotte*, answered fire, and the attack had begun. Bomb vessels launched shells that set fire to the city. A sloop loaded with 143 barrels of powder was run on shore, close to a battery. It was set alight and exploded. The bombardment continued into the night, creating a spectacle described by one British witness as "exceeding grand": "The burning ships illumined the atmosphere, while a heavy thunderstorm, with bright flashes of lightning, added to the grandeur of the scene."[44] Two days later, Omar signed a treaty with Captain Brisbane, commander of the *Queen Charlotte*. Christian slavery was to be abolished. Twelve hundred Christian slaves were to be released. 382,500 silver dollars, money paid to the regency by Sicily and Naples for the redemption of slaves since the beginning of 1816, was to be repaid. Thirty thousand dollars were to be paid to the British consul in compensation for his loss of property. A public apology was to be made to him for his imprisonment. Britain would deal with "barbarians" with brute force. This suited a narrative of British diplomatic and naval power, and Exmouth, like Decatur, was celebrated as a hero.

As the British were to discover, they could not have things entirely their way. This was the second attack on the regency, and just as the concessions achieved by the first were soon to be reversed, the effects of the bombing were similarly short. In November, MacDonell wrote to Henry, Earl Bathurst, who was secretary of state for the colonies, that the "impressive lesson" Exmouth had given Algiers had failed to teach its elite "wisdom or moderation."[45] The regency had been humbled, but while corsairing and the enslavement of white men did slow, neither practice stopped altogether. Algiers rebuilt the destroyed port fortifications

44. Brett, *Brett's Illustrated Naval History of Great Britain*, 315.
45. TNA FO 3/19, p. 5, November 10, 1816, MacDonell to Bathurst.

and reestablished its fleet. Very soon after the bombing, Barbary corsairs left the port to cruise the Mediterranean. William Shaler, the former secret agent and new US consul in Algiers, did not see the bombing of Algiers as a triumph. The 1816 attack was nothing more than "an unequivocal display of power over a most contempt-ible enemy." It might have humbled the regency "to the dust," but it also taught them that as long as the interests of France and Britain were respected, they were free "to prey upon the rest of the world"—including, of course, the United States—at their discretion.[46]

As far as Omar was concerned, he was also dealing with "barbar-ians." As he told the Sultan, he was not prepared to stop corsairing and enslavement just because "the infidel peoples" wished him to do so.[47] Exmouth had asked Omar to make peace with enemy coun-tries, without receiving any money from them. But payment—along with war, corsairing, and slavery—was simply "the example given, from the time of the Prophet to the last of the Sultans." The British had used trickery, flying a white flag and then attacking, destroying the port and the forts. Omar had been obliged to accept their con-ditions, and to renew the peace treaty.[48] Notwithstanding Omar's protestations, Exmouth's attack on the regency did have one lasting consequence: it spelled the end of Omar's reign. The treaty that the British had forced him to sign following the bombing led to his downfall, in September 1817. On the morning of September 8, the janissaries came. Omar was strangled and buried within an hour.[49] After he was murdered, Ali Pasha was named dey. His reign lasted for a thankfully short six months. Noted for his violence, he was also greedy, and sought to drain the treasury. One night, he moved all of the regency's valuables to the casbah: the "threatening, domi-nating citadel,"[50] and confined himself within. He died there, of the plague, on February 28, 1818. Hussein followed, and he was to be the last Dey of Algiers, ruling from 1818 until the French invasion.

46. Shaler, *Sketches of Algiers*, 104–5. Shaler had previously been a secret agent in Cuba and Mexico, and member of the delegation in Ghent, sent to negotiate peace in the 1812 war with Britain.

47. Letter from Omar to the Sultan, September 12, 1816, cited in Temimi, "Documents turcs inédits," 125.

48. Temimi, "Documents turcs inédits," 125–27.

49. Rousset, *La Conquête d'Alger*, 7.

50. Rousset, *La Conquête d'Alger*, 7.

Hussein was from Smyrna and had studied in Constantinople. He came to Algiers in 1815, and his literacy saw him appointed secretary of the cavalry (*khodja-cavallo*), head of the scribes, and third in rank after the dey.[51] Hussein was, by all reports, an "honest and moral" man, and a popular choice, chosen to rule by the divan following Ali's death.[52] He took care to reconcile with the janissaries. Under Hussein's rule, in the approving words of a French commentator, Algiers "enjoyed unprecedented order and security."[53]

Eight more attacks by outraged European states would take place after Decatur's 1815 campaign, and the Exmouth-led bombardment in 1816. But brute force, it was clear, was not going to work against the regency, and the united powers of Europe turned to high-handed threats. The decision to impose their will in this way was made at another congress. In late 1818, the four allied powers of Britain, Russia, Prussia, and Austria met again, this time in Aix-la-Chapelle, or Aachen. The French foreign minister, the Duc de Richelieu, represented France. The principal aim of the allies was to decide on a timetable for the evacuation of their forces from France. By the end of November, when the meeting broke up, the powers had agreed to two measures, both calculated to preserve the peace. These were, first, a secret protocol confirming and renewing the quadruple alliance (a preemptive measure, should France threaten the European peace again), and a public "declaration" of their intention to maintain their intimate union. The attendees also concerned themselves with a number of questions left unresolved in the hurried winding up of the Congress of Vienna. The most important of these involved the two—now linked—issues of the slave trade, and Barbary piracy.[54]

At Aix-la-Chapelle, the delegates agreed that two of the powers would take on the task, in the name of all, "of seriously making clear to the Regencies of Algiers, Tunis, and Tripoli, to make them bring a stop" to so-called piracy—in reality, corsairing.[55] France and Britain

51. Rousset, *La Conquête d'Alger*, 3.

52. Khoja, *Aperçu historique et statistique sur la régence d'Alger*, 134–35.

53. Rousset, *La Conquête d'Alger*, 12.

54. On the linking of abolition and white slavery, see Vick, "Power, Humanitarianism and the Global Liberal Order."

55. AMAE 8CCC/44, p. 300, July 8, 1819, "Instructions pour Monsieur le Contre-Amiral Jurien."

were nominated, "as the two courts whose influence over these regencies was the most powerful," but perhaps the choice of participants was also with an eye to the reestablishment of peaceful relations, a priority for the Congress. France had been reluctant. Where corsairing was concerned, they had nothing to fear from the *barbaresques*, as Richelieu stated, and so "had really no interest in pressuring other powers to unite against them."[56] He nonetheless agreed to France nominating Rear Admiral Pierre Roch Jurien de la Gravière (Jurien). Vice-Admiral Sir Thomas Francis Fremantle, commander in chief of the Mediterranean fleet, was to represent Britain.

After some months of discussion, the two powers agreed that Jurien and Fremantle would meet in Mahon on Minorca on July 28. From there, they would undertake a joint mission. They were given a declaration, from Europe to the regency, that threatened the regency's end, and promised friendship, if the dey would only agree to cease piracy. The declaration informed the Barbary regencies, "in the strongest terms," that all the powers of Europe, together in a "general league," were ranged against them and their piracy. It spoke down from a great height, threatening that the continuation of this impediment to trade would place the regency's very existence in danger. If, on the other hand, the regency were prepared to give up the practice, the powers of Europe would be prepared "not only to maintain relations of good intelligence and friendship with them," and perhaps with an eye to wooing Jacob, they went on, "but to encourage all types of trade relations which could be advantageous to their respective subjects as well."[57]

In Algiers, Hussein refused to play the role allotted him, and here was where Europe's "new" diplomacy of combined powers and general leagues met the "old" diplomacy of personal relationships. It was to be Deval's job to ensure that Hussein would comply. But Hussein would not. The delegates moored at Algiers on September 3, 1819, and had their first audience with Hussein soon after. Having been asked by the delegates if he was prepared to give them

56. Weiss, *Captives and Corsairs*, 153, cited in Julien, *Histoire d'Algérie contemporaine*, vol. 1, 30.

57. AMAE 8CCC/44, pp. 301–2, July 8, 1819, "Instructions pour Monsieur le Contre-Amiral Jurien."

a categorical answer in writing, he "had the dragomen tell the emissaries that he had never done any wrong to any European nation, and that, according to his principles, it was his intention always to act in the same way towards foreign powers, but that he didn't see any need to give this response in writing."[58] In diplomacy, Hussein saw himself as their majesties' equal. He refused to put anything in writing, or to sign any statement, because he had not received any official document signed by their majesties. Yet for Jurien, Hussein was merely the "head of an insolent militia," whom the delegates were obliged to address as "Prince."[59] Jurien reported to his minister, Count Portalis, that Hussein was not prepared to forego the right to "visit" all ships, so as to work out, as Hussein put it, who were friends and who were enemies, and to confiscate any ships whose papers were not in order. Flags alone, often falsely raised, could not determine this. (Jurien observed, in his memoirs, that Hussein "had doubtless drawn his ideas of maritime law from the works of some English jurisconsult.")[60]

Hussein renewed the demands of his predecessors that debts owed to his subjects be paid. As well as France, Spain, too, had borrowed funds from the Bacris. Spain had a longstanding presence in the regency. It had occupied Oran, on the northwest coast, on and off for centuries. In the eighteenth century, in a change of policy toward Muslim lands, Spain began to install consuls, in order to further trade. Many Jews who had escaped to the Ottoman Empire from the Iberian Peninsula refused to have any dealings with Spanish authorities or representatives. The Bacris, in contrast, were happy to do so, and this may suggest that they were, in fact, originally Arab Jews. Joseph had a particularly close relationship with Spain. In typically acerbic tones, Shaler described how under the government of Joseph-Napoleon in Spain, the expenses from Spain's relations with Algiers, "which have ever been enormous," were defrayed by loans from Joseph Bacri, who enjoyed a close relationship with that country's representatives in his own. Joseph's interest rates, according to a hostile Shaler, were "exorbitant," and thanks to

58. AMAE 8CCC/44, p. 359, September 9, 1819, "Rapport de la dernière audience de MM les commissaires."

59. Jurien, *Souvenirs d'un Amiral*, 227.

60. Jurien, *Souvenirs d'un Amiral*, 229.

"compound usury," Spain's debt was enormous.[61] Notwithstanding Shaler's penchant for editorializing, the debt was considerable, and it was to drag the Spanish regime into long-running disputes, both with the regency and with different family members, who claimed the funds for themselves.

Debt was the sticking point in the relationship between the regency and the "general league." It made diplomacy personal. And because Jacob and Hussein were business partners, it made Jacob, and Jacob's needs, pivotal. It was principally because of debt that Jacob and the dey kept pulling the would-be "combined powers" back into "old" diplomacy. In a general sense, it was not out of place for these states to be in debt. Debt had been a commonplace in late eighteenth-century trade; the former, in fact, facilitated the latter. In a period when banks were not widespread, credit was intrinsic to long-distance trade.[62] In France, any merchant's business depended largely on instruments of credit, such as "private promissory notes, *obligations* (formal IOUs), or bills of exchange."[63] This was especially true of the flourishing luxury or import-export trades, as well as in the realm of high finance. In the metropoles of London and Paris, credit sat at the foundation of all business. Merchants, and particularly those operating on a large scale, took credit for granted.[64] It would be fair to say that a culture of credit had long existed, and was prevalent in eighteenth-century France and Britain. A person's reputation could rest on their ability to obtain loans, implied, as Hoffman, Postel-Vinay, and Rosenthal have put it, "by the very word *crédit*."[65] In Britain, too, the term "credit" had a social meaning. It implied a household's reputation "for fair and honest dealing," and thus their trustworthiness.[66]

In eighteenth-century Paris, as in Britain, the unspoken rules of these relations were understood: they were so much part of the structure of life in the ancien régime, that they were barely visible.

61. Shaler, *Sketches of Algiers*, 162.

62. Price, "What Did Merchants Do?," 273.

63. Spang, *Stuff and Money in the Time of the French Revolution*, 12.

64. Hancock, *Citizens of the World*, 247.

65. Hoffman, Postel-Vinay, and Rosenthal, "Private Credit Markets in Paris, 1690–1840," 294.

66. Muldrew, *The Economy of Obligation*, 148.

Systems of credit were not only "in place and working,"[67] they had developed to become highly sophisticated, complex structures, supported by the state. They supported ever-growing networks with the bill of exchange. This was a measure of necessity. Boats spreading around the globe stretched the bonds of personal networks to breaking. Communication did not become more straightforward as trade expanded. As we saw in chapter 1, trade could not take place without the widespread use of the bill of exchange.[68] It benefited states, too, allowing them to expand dramatically, beyond their own borders.

In Algiers, a different idea of credit reigned, and this mismatch in understandings manifested as mutual miscomprehension in diplomacy. Debt could be woven into the gift relationship. This could include payments due for concessions or as a condition of treaties, but also, of course, the Bacri debt. Given that access to trade was granted in return for gifts, it followed that if gifts were not given, nor was access. The giving of gifts was fundamental to the establishment of relations of parity. So, too, was the desired repayment of the monies owed to the Bacris. This was how they continually brought the debt to the center of relations. Whether because of successful lobbying on the family's part, as many consuls and their governments believed, or because they were the dey's creditors, as different deys claimed, the Bacri debt was woven into the relationship between France and the regency. This was a situation of long standing. When the Dey Hassan wrote to the Convention in 1795 to recommend Jacob, who had just established himself in Marseilles, Delacroix, the minister for foreign affairs, responded that Hassan should "be assured" that Jacob would have "nothing but satisfaction in the way in which we will continue to conduct ourselves with him." France would "not miss any opportunity," he went on, "to further strengthen the bonds of this ancient friendship."[69] The debt was also included in the 1801 treaty, signed after the break caused by Napoleon's invasion of Egypt. Article 13 of that treaty stated that "his Excellency the Dey promises to have all sums that might be

67. Price, "What Did Merchants Do?," 278.

68. Aoki Santarosa, "Financing Long-Distance Trade," 691.

69. Charles-François De Lacroix [Minister for Foreign Affairs] to Sidi Hassan, Dey of Algiers, Prairial, June 1796, in Plantet, *Correspondance des Deys d'Alger*, vol. 2, 455–56.

owing to French citizens by his subjects reimbursed, just as citizen Dubois-Thainville makes the commitment, in the name of his government, to have all those [debts] that might be legally claimed by Algerian subjects settled."[70] "Algerian subjects" referred to the Bacris and Busnachs, and for Talleyrand, then foreign minister, this link was so clear, and so powerful, that France, he wrote, could not "hope to succeed fully in our given goals, in our dealings with the Barbary States, unless we deal efficiently with the settlement and reimbursement of the debts."[71] Almost exactly nineteen years after Talleyrand's letter, Deval wrote of the debt in the same terms. An 1817 report, written for King Louis XVIII, explained that while "the refusal to satisfy the Bacri debts" was not the only point of contention between France and the regency, nonetheless, this grievance had always been "predominant as a cause of contestations." For the regency, the Bacri debts were "an engagement from government to government."[72] France's refusal to pay, therefore, was one cause of Algerian corsairing attacks on French ships and their men.[73] Years later, the debt clearly still rankled in Algiers. In 1825, the Algerian admiral Hadgi Ali Capoudan forcibly entered the French consular house in Bona, and searched all the rooms, looking for stores of gunpowder. When Deval protested this treatment, Hussein retorted that as long as he received no response to his letters about the Bacri debt, he would not respond to Deval's complaint.[74] This was the genius of Naphtali Busnach, and the Bacri brothers: to convince a succession of deys that debts owed to them were a matter of diplomacy. As Hussein was insistently pursuing France for payment of the Bacri debt, Jacob was in debt to the regency, and insisting for his part that he could not pay his debts, as France had not yet paid him.

The pursuit of debts through diplomatic channels became standard practice for the Bacri family, even when they were pursuing one another. This was how they had always operated, and how they operated best. In stark contrast to their new diplomacy, foreign

70. *Traité de paix entre la Régence d'Alger et la France, le 17 décembre 1801*, reproduced in Laborde, *Au Roi et aux chambres*, v.

71. AMAE 8CCC/44, p. 97, October 1818, cited in Pierre Deval, *Mémoire analytique*.

72. AMAE 8CCC/43, p. 85, May 1817, "Rapport à Sa Majesté."

73. AMAE 8CCC/43, p. 84, May 1817, "Rapport à Sa Majesté."

74. AMAE 8CCC/47, p. 376, December 30, 1825, Deval to Damas.

governments were pulled into the family's disputes, as Bacris forced their way to the center of relations, maintaining old diplomacy. Family quarrels played out in parliaments, courts, and diplomatic correspondence across Britain, France, and Spain, emphasizing the extent to which all family members understood the personal to be legitimate in the pursuit of a grievance. And disagreements were long-lasting, as the family breakdown was carried over into the next generation. Bad feeling was high between Jacob and his nephews, the sons of Salomon, Joseph, and Abraham. In 1815, after his three brothers and co-associates had died, Jacob wrote to his nephews, inviting them to meet in order to settle the family's accounts. But Jacob and his nephews could not reach any agreement on how those accounts should look, so in 1819, Jacob requested the chief rabbis of Algiers to rule that the family business be disbanded, that Jacob, as sole surviving associate, be declared liquidator, and that the heirs of his fellow associates, or their nominated representative, be called to settle the business accounts before the Jewish tribunal, in Algiers. His brother's heirs chose not to respond to this summons, and over the years that followed, they produced a series of counterclaims. Nathan Bacri, Joseph's son and brother of the murdered David, lived in Paris. He was a particularly persistent litigant. (Nathan was described in the 1811 police report as having "squandered a great deal, and made bad deals." He had been forced to sell his belongings to pay off a debt of seventeen thousand francs. "On this occasion," the report observed, "he found no support, either from his father, or his uncle Salomon; which suggests that they no longer do business together.")[75] Two months after the government pronounced itself liable to the Bacris for seven million francs, in October 1819, Nathan sought to have the sum held as a guarantee for money that Jacob allegedly owed him, by virtue of inheritance. This was refused and he appealed, but the initial refusal was upheld. Nathan was not yet a French citizen (he obtained citizenship in 1823) and the court could not, it stated, pronounce a ruling on a matter between two Algerian subjects. In 1821, Abraham's son David had had the

---

75. AN F/7/6537, dossier 1633, série 2: Busnach et Bacry, négociants algériens à Livourne, arrêtés par ordre de S.M, "Notes sur la famille Bacri d'Alger, de Livourne, de Marseille et ses co-intéressés."

1803 letter from Jacob to Abraham translated and registered at the French consulate, to be used as evidence in David's pursuit of Jacob for sixty thousand francs that he claimed had been owed to his father.

In 1823, Salomon's children, living in Livorno, took up the baton. David, Aziza, Rachel, and Fortunée alleged that Jacob had owed their father 600,000 francs, and the seven million should be withheld as surety for this sum, still unpaid. They had Jacob's French assets, together with sums owed him in France, seized. Once again, it was ruled that a French court could not decide a matter between foreigners, this time by the civil court in Marseilles. Nonetheless, between Nathan's and their appeals, the matter dragged on for seven years.[76] It was probably deep frustration with the court process that led Salomon's four children to publish a pamphlet, where they referred to both Jacob and Michel Busnach in defamatory terms. Busnach was "that faithful assistant of bad faith, always ready to sell both his help and his conscience."[77] Jacob was like Busnach, they went on, "a man without morals or integrity." They accused him, outright, of causing the death of his brother Joseph.[78] Following a complaint by Michel, the Bacri descendants were ordered to suppress this pamphlet. But in France, both Salomon and Joseph's children continued to pursue Jacob and Michel, through the court system, and by petitioning, just as Jacob, a generation earlier, had pursued Michel Busnach.[79]

Hussein's response to the court proceedings in France placed him squarely in Jacob's camp. So angered was he by the ongoing legal battle between Jacob and various Bacri heirs that he called Deval to a meeting, in order to complain, "bitterly," about the French

76. "Nathan Coen Bacri C. Jacob Coen Bacri," *Journal du palais*, July 24, 1826, 719.

77. BNF, p. 6, "Jugement dont est appel rendu par le tribunal de première instance de Marseille, le 25 mai 1832."

78. BNF, p. 8, "Jugement dont est appel rendu par le tribunal de première instance de Marseille, le 25 mai 1832."

79. BNF, Paris, n.d., "Pétition des héritiers Bacri"; BNF, Marseille, n.d., Nathan Bacri, "A Son Excellence, Monsieur le Ministre des Finances." Francesca Trivellato noted that in the late eighteenth century, Jews "pursued the only two roads" open to them in international disputes: a formal lawsuit and a reputational assault. Trivellato, "Sephardic Merchants between State and Rabbinic Courts," 636. A half century later, the situation remained the same.

courts. The Bacri descendants in France were nothing but "a bunch of schemers," being given credence by the French government for a petty squabble.[80] But the family dispute continued to play out on the grand stage of international relations, in ministerial and diplomatic correspondence, as governments found themselves obliged to resolve the sorts of questions raised by Jacob's nieces and nephews, over who should rightfully inherit credits.

As the Bacris cleaved their path through governments and juridical systems, many were pulled into their wake. Spain found itself in a particularly difficult situation with regard to the extended family. The Spanish archive file, tellingly named "Bacri Claims," contains a tale of Spanish diplomatic woes. Deval reported on the same woes, in long letters to his minister Baron Etienne-Denis Pasquier. In Algiers, Joseph had had a close relationship with Spanish diplomats. In 1807, he lent money to Don Pedro Ortiz, the Spanish consul, who was trying to carry out his duties with no funds or payment from his government. Incremental loans from Joseph eventually added up to sixty thousand piasters. When Joseph was exiled from the regency in 1816, Jacob stepped into the relationship with Spain and demanded reimbursement of this sum, with interest. The consul refused to pay and the regency intervened, claiming that the payment of this debt should be made to Jacob, in Algiers. Meanwhile, however, Joseph had arrived in Livorno, and made a claim on the same debt to the Spanish government, which recognized him as the rightful creditor. Joseph died shortly after, and Spain recognized his son Nathan, at that time also in Livorno, as the rightful heir to his father, and thus to the money owed to him. They paid him a deposit of fifteen thousand piasters. The problem, as Deval reported to Pasquier, was that the Spanish government had determined that the rightful payee was Joseph's heir in Livorno, but Jacob, with the regime behind him, insisted that the House of Bacri, now represented in Algiers by Jacob, should receive the repayment.[81] In Algiers, Omar continued to insist that the Spanish government repay the debt in Algiers to Jacob. Hussein brought new energy to the dispute, but as much as

80. AMAE 8CCC/46, p. 282, May 27, 1824, Deval to the Vicomte de Chateaubriand, Ministre des affaires étrangères.
81. AMAE 8CCC/45, p. 309, June 30, 1821, Deval to the Duc de Pasquier, Ministre des affaires étrangères.

he would insist, Madrid remained firm in its refusal. In mid-1821, Hussein wrote to the King of Spain, Ferdinand VII, threatening a rupture between the two states if the debt were not paid as Hussein requested. The Spanish king responded, but however much Spain tried to insist that the nature of Don Pedro Ortiz's debt was personal, and thus only payable to his creditor or the latter's descendants, Hussein maintained his position. King Ferdinand missed the point. In Algiers, the personal was diplomatic. Hussein was conducting international diplomacy the regency way.

Spain and its ally the Netherlands, together with Britain, France, Portugal, and Tuscany all became concerned observers or unwilling participants in this diplomatic contretemps. Deval reported to his minister, Mathieu de Montmorency, that the Dutch consul had been ordered by his government to inform Hussein that, were war to be declared between Spain and Algiers, the Netherlands would be obliged by alliance to join Spain.[82] MacDonell let Hussein know that Portugal, too, would likely be dragged into any war. Hussein remained defiant, and the matter soon escalated. In June 1822, a joint Spanish and Dutch squadron appeared before Algiers, bringing an official letter from the Spanish government to Hussein. Spain had moved to an ultimatum: Hussein was to drop his demands, or the Spanish consul in Algiers would leave, together with all Spanish citizens. Hussein would not budge. The consul departed.

Three years later, in 1825, a Spanish report described Hussein as still making the same "galling, inflated and unreasonable claim" for the sum of three million piasters, for the principal and interest on Joseph's claim, originally lodged in 1813 for the sum of 93,250 piasters. Now, it was Jacob, "protected by the dey," who was claiming the money on the basis of "the blackest perfidy and violent usurpation against his brother Joseph."[83] Nathan, now in Paris, also claimed the debt, and had managed to gain support from the Livornese government, as well as the Austrian minister in the Spanish court. Spain was caught in a quandary: who was the rightful claimant? If it paid, what chance was there that it would be forced to pay the

82. AMAE 8CCC/46, p. 10, March 30, 1822, Deval to Montmorency. AMAE 8CCC/46, p. 28, June 7, 1822, Deval to Montmorency.

83. AHN, AMAE Politica Exterior, dossier 2309, April 28, 1825, "Reclamaciones de los Bacri 1816–1834."

same sum twice? Spain, newly emerged from the wars, tried, like all powers, to insist on the new, dignified international diplomacy. "The government of Spain," the Spanish consul in Tuscany wrote to his minister in Madrid, "despite the fact that it owes nothing to the government of Algiers, should re-establish the peace in the interest of Spanish commerce, but this should strike a balance between economic necessity dictated by circumstances and respect for the decorum of our government's dignity."[84] To that end, a royal decree in April 1825 sent the consul Ortiz de Zugasti back to the regency, to "attempt, definitively, a friendly reconciliation of our differences with the dey." But Zugasti was blocked by Jacob, as he told his minister, the Count of Ofalia: "Jacob Bacri, known in Algiers as the sworn enemy of Christians of all Nations." His "reprehensible schemes" caused "incalculable evil for humanity."[85] Hussein had demanded 500,513 douros to be paid to Jacob, and 100,000 douros for himself, to keep the peace. Until that time, Algiers and Spain would be at war.[86] Zugasti, who had departed, was then sent back, to negotiate once again. He was instructed to propose to Hussein that the Spanish courts determine who was Joseph's rightful heir. He was to offer the dey no more than thirty thousand douros for the settlement of the peace, and to engage to pay 150,000 piasters to Jacob, eighty thousand piasters to the dey, and twenty thousand to his ministers, constituting the final settlement of any debts. Zugasti was to remind Hussein that it was not Spain's fault if Joseph's debt had not been repaid, but rather, it was due to the squabbling between his heirs. Zugasti was to request, "with equal force and resolve," the return of vessels to the value of fifty thousand douros, taken by the Algerians "under the unjust pretext of claiming the said debt."[87] But Jacob proved a determined claimant, and he left nothing to chance in his fight for the Spanish money. By 1826, he had managed to become Tuscan consul general in Algiers. In the same year, he registered an

84. AHN, AMAE Politica Exterior, dossier 2309, May 1, 1824, "Reclamaciones de los Bacri 1816–1834."
85. AHN, AMAE Politica Exterior, dossier 2309, April 28, 1825, "Reclamaciones de los Bacri 1816–1834."
86. AHN, AMAE Politica Exterior, dossier 2309, March 24, 1825, "Reclamaciones de los Bacri 1816–1834."
87. AHN, AMAE Politica Exterior, dossier 2309, November 28, 1825, "Reclamaciones de los Bacri 1816–1834."

act of association at the French consulate between himself and his three brothers, Joseph, Salomon, and Mordecai.[88] Presumably he reasoned that this would make his argument that he should be beneficiary of a personal debt Spain owed to his deceased brother more convincing. It was to take considerable diplomacy for the matter to be settled—in Jacob's favor. It was resolved in the peace treaty, signed in January 1827, between Spain and the regency.

Britain, perhaps enjoying its sense of itself as the victor in the long-drawn-out Napoleonic Wars, settled matters differently. Hugh MacDonell, the British consul, and colonial office bureaucrats and politicians, all agreed that any claim from Jacob was simply without foundation. Britain believed fully that the cake was there to be had, and to be eaten. Not only did they refuse to return to the old version of Mediterranean diplomacy, but they also sought to expand their trade with North Africa. MacDonell had always been scornful of France's approach. Under the bloodthirsty Ali, even as the consuls were in danger of being imprisoned, Deval had "detached himself from the corps [of consuls] and common cause," rendering "degrading homage" to the dey.[89] The French were "favoring the Algerines in a special manner," agreeing to repay the Bacri debt, even though this was "of very doubtful authenticity."[90] This was a misguided approach, MacDonell believed. While France's "minute attention to all the demands of the regency," with the "sedulous" aim of gaining preferential treatment, might in theory bring success, Britain possessed "generally more influence at Algiers, than France, or any other Christian power, or perhaps the whole of them united."[91] MacDonell was clearly drawing on a British view of France as defeated and humiliated, but France did take a different approach. Deval acknowledged that Britain commanded greater respect and suffered less torment in Algiers than France. The British government was "always ready" to protect its honor and carried out its threats promptly. Deval, in contrast, sought to reason with the dey and the elite by means of "gentleness and

88. Haddey, *Le Livre d'or des israélites algériens*, 71.
89. TNA FO 3/20, p. 1, March 10, 1818, MacDonell to Bathurst.
90. TNA FO 3/24, p. 55, September 20, 1822, MacDonell, "A Snapshot of Algiers."
91. TNA FO 3/24, p. 61, September 20, 1822, MacDonell, "A Snapshot of Algiers."

persuasion."[92] This approach earned him the disdain of both the British and American consuls. Shaler was dismissive of France's "absurd and expensive concessions [. . .] unbecoming a great and powerful nation."[93]

That is not to say that Britain did not have its own issues with the regency, and with Jacob. When the regency was demanding the government of Sardinia pay money owed to Jacob and threatening the capture of their ships if they would not pay, the King of Sardinia sought help from his ally, George IV. "Immediately," a frigate was dispatched from London to Algiers, arriving in late October 1824, and bearing a message for the dey: "Great Britain would not tolerate any insult to their ancient ally, and even less, the mortification of their Commerce." Britain offered mediation, in the form of the Governor of Malta, the Marquis of Hastings. "Should His Highness refuse Great Britain's mediation," the message continued, "His Majesty's government should be aware that the Admiral in command of the British forces in the Mediterranean has been issued with the relevant orders to protect the Commerce of the subjects of the ancient ally, His Majesty the King of Sardinia." Hussein needed only three days' reflection before agreeing to these terms.[94] But he retained his rancor. When Britain sent a representative to request some access to Algerian waters for coral fishing, or, conversely, the closure of those waters, Hussein rejected every proposition Britain could make, as a smug Deval noted, "for reasons of high politics."[95]

Jacob was nothing if not persistent when it came to the pursuit of funds. By 1825, MacDonell had departed, and been replaced by Vice-Consul Thomas. Clearly, for Jacob, a new consul was a new opportunity. Shortly after his arrival, Thomas wrote to Earl Bathurst regarding a rather difficult issue that had arisen. Jacob, he reported, was maintaining that the British vice-consul in Oran owed him money, and because he was new to the regency, he added, in explanation: "A rich and powerful Jew who is the real claimant on Sardinia under the mediation to be exercised to His Majesty."

92. AMAE 8CCC/47, p. 377, December 30, 1825, Deval to Damas.

93. Shaler, *Sketches of Algiers*, 162.

94. AHN, AMAE Politica Exterior, dossier 2309, "Reclamaciones de los Bacri 1816–1834," AI. No. 5 of 1825 A.

95. AMAE 8CCC/47, p. 338, October 15, 1825, Deval to Damas.

At the same time, Jacob owed money to MacDonell. However, Jacob, supported by Hussein, was claiming that the money owed to him by the vice-consul in Oran had actually been paid directly to MacDonell, and on that basis, Jacob was no longer liable. This, in Thomas's opinion, and in line with the British approach, was "at best a pretended claim,"[96] and one that called for "strong yet temperate remonstrance" on his part, "against the injustice and chicane" of Hussein's government.[97] Thomas was perhaps a little less than gentle, pointing out to Hussein that he had violated article 14 of a 1686 treaty, in what might be considered a veiled threat. It was with "utter astonishment" that he found Hussein defiant. The matter went to London, was considered at length, and it was decided that since no one knew the actual truth of the matter—that is, whether Jacob was truly owed these funds—it was impossible to arrive at a suitable outcome. MacDonell, now in London, was not surprised. Jacob's power was such, he wrote, that "no chance of an impartial hearing or an equitable adjudication of the case was to be expected."[98]

Jacob did eventually overreach himself, in what might be seen as a feature of his business practice. In fact, he had been in financial trouble since 1824, when he had been forced to ask the British for a loan. Where once he had reached "a point of affluence which is seldom attained," now, he had large debts, both in Algiers and elsewhere. According to gossip, relayed by Shaler, Jacob had failed to pay money he owed the dey, either through joint debts, or in business he contracted on the dey's behalf. Jacob had proposed signing the Spanish debt over to Hussein, but had delayed doing so once too often. There had clearly been a significant shift in the relationship. Hussein, tired of waiting, imprisoned Jacob, and seized his property.[99] In late August 1826, Jacob and all of his male relatives were arrested, and seals were placed on their papers and possessions. They were put in irons. But Jacob had found his way out of catastrophic debt once, and he would do so again. In early 1827, Thomas reported a rumor: the regency was trying to force the

96. TNA FO 3/27, p. 43, March 5, 1825, Thomas to Bathurst.
97. TNA FO 3/27, p. 42, March 5, 1825, Thomas to Bathurst.
98. TNA FO 3/28, p. 1, April 3, 1826, MacDonell to Bathurst.
99. NARA Atlanta M23, roll 13, vol. 11, n.p., August 25, 1826, Shaler, "Extract from the Journal kept in the consulate of the U. States in Algiers."

Tuscan government to oblige its own citizens to pay debts they owed Jacob, by threatening Tuscany with hostilities.[100] Jacob, in debt, had clearly claimed to be waiting for money owed to him to be paid. Somehow, he managed, once again, to make his finances a matter of international diplomacy. In this case, it was Hussein—Jacob's creditor—threatening violence against Tuscany.

Beleaguered and bankrupt, Jacob still managed to elbow his way to the center of diplomacy. In 1827, the Bacri name became visible to the historical record as never before. A difficult meeting between Hussein and Deval over the debt that Hussein believed was still owed led to a diplomatic contretemps that would become significant in the history of the French invasion of the regency. On April 29, Deval paid a ceremonial visit to Hussein on the occasion of Eid, marking the end of Ramadan. Hussein had sent a message asking to see the most recent letter from the Minister for Foreign Affairs, the Baron de Damas, to which Deval had replied that he had received no letters from the most recent ship. Unsuspecting, he arrived at the palace at the specified time. The "deplorable" scene then followed.

Was it true, Hussein asked, that Britain had declared war on France?

Deval replied that this was just a rumor, arising from issues in Portugal. The king's government, he said, had not wished to interfere.

"So", Hussein stated, "the French government gives Britain all that it wants, and nothing at all to me."

"It appears to me, sir, that the king's government has always given you all that it could."

"Why has your minister not replied to the letter I wrote him?"

"I had the honor of bringing you the reply as soon as I received it."

"Why did he not reply to me directly? Am I," Hussein demanded to know, "ranked so lowly? You are the reason I have had no reply from your minister; you are the one who persuaded him not to write to me: you are wicked, an infidel, an idolater."

In a fury, Hussein rose from his seat, delivered three violent blows to Deval's body with the reed of his fan, and told him to leave.[101]

---

100. TNA FO 3/29, p. 27, February 9, 1827, Thomas to Bathurst.

101. AMAE, Mémoires et Documents (hereafter MD) Alger, 2, 61, April 30, 1827, Deval to Damas. Where the debt is concerned, the exact money trail is impossible to follow, but Pierre Deval stated, repeatedly, that the debt had been disbursed. Of the seven million

Thomas told the story of the confrontation rather more fully to Earl Bathurst. It appeared, he wrote

that a warm discussion had arisen between them upon two points— one, connected with a right assumed by the French government to repair and garrison the old fort of La Calle, and the other upon a question arising out of the affairs of a bankrupt Jew of some celebrity in the annals of Algiers, named Bacri. Expressions of a very gross and irritating nature are said to have been indulged in by the consul, which after having been for a time tolerated, excited the dey's indignation to a degree that caused him to forget his own dignity and the mild character for which he was remarkable.[102]

Deval, he noted, had not discussed the affair with any of his fellow consuls, but was "studiously" observing a guarded silence on the matter. William Shaler was characteristically acerbic in his assessment of the French consul. "Imbued with incomprehensible prejudices," and that from a man with plenty of his own, Deval could not "with safety be relied on."[103] Thomas simply watched, and reported, as one month later, a French squadron appeared in the port and Deval, and all French subjects with him, embarked. A schooner then returned to deliver a letter, demanding that Hussein make a public apology to Deval, in the presence of all of the European consuls, who would be invited to observe. Hussein flatly refused.[104] From that point, relations headed downhill.

In the years following the end of the Napoleonic Wars, Austria, Britain, Prussia, and Russia, together with a forgiven France, wished to see themselves as remade, and ready to remake the world in their image. To this end, they held congresses and wrote protocols. They delivered ultimata. But this is only half of the story of the postwar period. When these European powers sought to enact these protocols in the Mediterranean, they encountered roadblocks.

francs owing, he claimed, Michel Busnach (the brother of Naphtali) received 2.5 million, and Jacob, now the last remaining Bacri brother, two million, plus a further 1.5 million, to be paid out to creditors in Algiers. The balance was kept by France, to pay off the House's creditors there. See, for example, a letter from Deval in AMAE 2MD/3, p. 28, February 28, 1828.

102. TNA FO 3/29, pp. 70–71, May, 14, 1827, Thomas to Bathurst.

103. Shaler, *Sketches of Algiers*, 179.

104. TNA FO 3/29, pp. 94–95, June 15, 1827, Thomas to Bathurst.

When the French and British—not to mention the Americans—set out to teach the regency a lesson, they found it less than willing to be schooled. Brute force could bring the regency around for a time, but deys would not submit willingly, or permanently, to infidels. The protocols stopped at the southern shores of the Mediterranean, and holding them back was Jacob Bacri. The contrast between Jacob's situation from the last chapter to this one is striking. Now, Jacob was in his element, able to use the regency structures and norms of gift-giving, as well as the centrality of credit in statecraft, to force his way into the center of diplomatic relations. Methods tried and tested by the entire extended Bacri family worked for them, because France, Britain, the United States, and Spain all needed stable shipping and the raw goods that the regency had to offer. Even when business acumen failed him, Jacob was able to find a way out. But radical changes were on the way. Jacob thrived in the regime of the regency. What would happen to Jacob when France transported its own regime there?

CHAPTER SIX

Invasion

ROBERT WILLIAM ST JOHN arrived in Algiers in late 1827, together with his wife Elizabeth and their four young children. He was to be the last British consul general to the regency, and his was the task of watching, as French troops attacked and invaded Algiers. In his observations, St John was ably seconded by the US consul, Major Henry Lee, and the two men walk us through this chapter, as we observe events on the ground through their eyes, and from their perspective. In this final chapter, the invasion of Algiers becomes a shared story, where a French narrative has to make room for the perspectives of its British and American competitors. Even as France invaded, the contest continued.

This chapter marks an end and a beginning, as well as a continuation. With this chapter, the process that was to lead to France's colonization of the regency, and the creation of Algeria, begins. With it, the existence of the regency ended. So, too, did the great ascendancy of the Bacri family. The Bacris, and their onetime partners, the Busnachs, had thrived in the regency because circumstances in Algiers allowed them to do so: the lack of Christian competition, the space made for Jews that allowed them to form relationships with the elite, the chaos and contest of the war, and the needs of Western powers all combined to create perfect conditions for the two families. They knew how to manipulate local practices, interests, and regulations, as well as circumstances, to their advantage. But as this story has shown, in systems unlike their own, the families could not occupy the same spaces, and thus lost their potential for power.

Most of them failed to understand this difference, and to adapt to it. When France imprisoned family members and sequestered their goods, the Bacris made direct appeals to the highest authority, as had always been the standard practice in their regency. In France, the families' entreaties fell on deaf ears. Even Salomon, who did so well in Livorno, could not escape sequestration, and died during one imprisonment. The Bacris' relationship to the elite in Algiers was not the same as in France, and the prospect of reproducing in France the nature of relationships to power in Algiers was non-existent. Moreover, in France, as the sequestrations showed, their importance in Algiers worked against them. Now France came to Algiers, and the circumstances that had so favored the Bacris as brokers between two parties that misunderstood one another, often profoundly, were to change forever. In this chapter, Jacob no longer occupies center stage. He is no longer the latest Bacri through whom consuls experienced and made sense of their lives and fortunes in the regency, and this is reflected in the bit part he now plays in the story.

With all that was to change in the regency, much stayed the same. France and Britain continued in their relationship of mistrust and uneasy diplomacy, both in close interactions on the ground at the periphery, and in the high politics of the metropoles. The United States continued to seek a foothold in the world of global trade and influence, with ever more confidence. The imperial contest for influence in Algiers had not ended, but its focus moved away from North Africa itself to the centers of power in London and Paris. The question of supply and competition for resources did not go away, but it was to be overtaken by the intense diplomacy raised over the question of precisely what sort of revenge France intended to inflict on the regency for the insult committed against its consul.

By the time Robert St John and Henry Lee were in the regency, Pierre Deval had left, and the Sardinian consul took care of French affairs. The national contest could still flare up at the slightest sense of provocation, betraying its continued intensity. One such provocation was the question of precedence. On the occasion of Eid al-Fitr, marking the end of Ramadan, the consuls were required to go to Hussein as a body, to present their compliments. Hussein gave precedence on this occasion to the British consul, who was allowed to approach him first. Britain's preferential treatment was based on the wisdom that Britain had been the first Christian power to sign a treaty with the regency. This arrangement was agreed to by the other consuls, with two exceptions. Deval, and then his Sardinian stand-in, demurred, predictably, but so did Lee, who joined the fray to be first in line for the dey's attentions, on behalf of the United States, competing as the representative of a nation with all its dignity to play for. The representatives of both France and the United States made a point of staying away on such occasions. In the name of the United States, Lee was offended. To acquiesce in "the pretentions of the British consul," he wrote to his secretary of state, Martin Van Buren, was unthinkable. Lee compromised by proposing to Hussein that he be received on a different day from the visit of the European consuls, a course of action that would also affirm the separation that Lee had sought to establish "between American and European affairs." For the same reasons, he told his minister, he had fixed on presenting gifts on July 4, rather than at the beginning of Ramadan, as was the custom.[1]

Henry Lee IV was born into the American elite. His half brother was Robert E. Lee, later the Confederate commander. His father, Henry "Light-Horse Harry" Lee, was a great hero of the American War of Independence. After the war, Henry Lee senior had pursued a political career, becoming governor of Virginia. Lee junior followed his father into the military and politics. He represented Westmoreland County in the House of Delegates for three terms (1810–13) and entered military service against Great Britain during the War of 1812. He was appointed a major and saw action along the Canadian border. His ambition was to be scuppered by scandal, when he had an affair with his wife's younger sister, who was also his ward. Although he could no longer pursue his own political career, he became close with Andrew Jackson, and in 1829, as Jackson became president, he appointed Lee consul in Algiers. It was with ongoing financial trouble, then, and having to forge a new path, that Lee came to the regency.[2] But for all his difficulties, he

---

1. NARA M23, roll 4, vol. 12, n.p., April 8, 1830, Lee to Van Buren.

2. "Henry Lee (1787–1837)," *Encyclopedia Virginia*, accessed February 10, 2020, https://www.encyclopediavirginia.org/Lee_Henry_1787-1837. Algiers was considered very dangerous, but Lee seemed to relish it. He claimed to keep six pistols, six muskets, and

had lost nothing of his patriotism. For him, the United States was no longer a fledgling power, but rather, it could take its place at the table of global diplomacy alongside France and Britain, or, as it were, apart from them.

Lee was concerned to ensure that his actions set a standard for honorable behavior and US dignity. Shortly after his arrival, as part of the consular present, he presented the captain of the port with a cash gift. The next day, he received a message from the minister of the marine. The other consuls had given more to the captain of the port than he had, and the minister had suggested Lee give thirty or forty dollars extra. Lee would do no such thing, as he told Secretary of State Van Buren. He sent his dragoman, "with orders to say to him that I would allow him nor no-one else to dictate to me what I was to give, that his interference was improper and his message unjustifiable, and that if the captain of the port was dissatisfied with what I had given him, he had only to send it back." The next day he received a profuse apology. His actions, he was pleased to report, were proof of "the elevation to which our national character and influence in this quarter have been advanced." This was thanks to William Shaler's "prudence and ability," as well as to the "good conduct" of US naval commanders in the Mediterranean. Lee paused, in his letter, to single out one particular commander, and to laud his prowess: "In this distant region," he wrote, building to one of the climaxes that tended to punctuate his paragraphs, "on this barbarous shore, in tongues that are strange and various, the name of Decatur is remembered in honor and repeated with respect, his country profiting by his valor, long after his martial frame has moldered into dust, so valuable may be the virtues of one officer to his fellow citizens."[3] Lee's correspondence did not always reach such heights. Earlier in December he had written regarding matters much more prosaic. He needed to find cash, and he wrote to Gibraltar to ask that this be organized for him, as in Algiers "the commercial population" was "limited and Jewish."

---

a Tennessee rifle in his house, and walked the streets armed. But his stay in Algiers was short-lived. On January 30, 1837, Lee died of the flu. He is buried in an unmarked grave in Montmartre.

3. NARA M23, roll 14, vol. 12, n.p., December 20, 1829, Lee to Van Buren.

It is safe to assume that references to Jews and the management of the regency, whether old or new, would include Jacob. By fair means or foul, Jacob had clearly established himself in the regency, and following the invasion, he initially moved quite easily from one regime to another. Numerous memoirs of events place Jacob at their center. He became head of the Jewish community (the *nation hébraïque*), simply transposing his role as *muqaddam* into the new vernacular. He offered his homes for the use of French troops, and hosted parties for them. The French invaders came to trust him, and for this reason, and for the sake of continuity, St John continued to see Jacob as an impediment to the possibilities for trade that he felt were simply waiting for Britain. It was for St John that Jacob, or "Jews" in general, loomed largest, and this is telling. St John was, of course, a partisan observer. His was the perspective of Britain, and he watched and commented on events with a critical eye. St John saw himself as representing France's only true rival for national standing. Even as France invaded, the British consul still imagined Algiers as a trading utopia. The presence of Jacob and others at the heart of the invading competitor was significant grounds for harsh criticism of France's many weaknesses.

While suspicion was maintained on the ground in Algiers, contest and mistrust also continued at the highest levels. In London and Paris, the seats of power, the same competitors performed a delicate dance of uneasy diplomacy. The imperial contest no longer played out in the context of war, but nor had it ever come to a close.[4] More than two decades of war between France and Britain had become busy diplomacy, and the two powers continued to be suspicious of one another's motives. Since 1821, all of Europe had been preoccupied by uprisings and massacres in what were to become the Greek Islands, as Greek nationalists rose up against their Ottoman rulers. By early 1830, European governments began to seek a definitive settlement to the war and the establishment of a settled, recognized regime in Greece. The question of the Greek monarchy was closely followed

---

4. The contest continued to play out in the historiography. In *Restoration and Reaction*, André Jardin and André-Jean Tudesq wrote, of the invasion of Algiers, that "The king and Polignac were able to withstand all attempts at intimidation on the part of the British government, thereby preserving France's future freedom of action in North Africa." Jardin and Tudesq, *Restoration and Reaction*, 96.

by the growing instability of the regime in France, and what might happen if the deeply conservative and increasingly unpopular government of Charles X were overthrown. Fraught diplomacy swirled around Algiers, too, and the question of France's intentions.

Since the events of 1827, when Hussein had struck Deval, the British had been expecting a justified French reprisal. They were uneasy about the form that this might take, a fact of which the French were very much aware. Even as the French had begun planning an attack on Algiers, they knew that London would raise great difficulties. Britain had made it very clear that they saw the Barbary regencies as useful and wished them to remain as they were. As long as they did not attack British ships, Barbary corsairs acted almost as a protective force for British shipping, keeping the boats of lesser powers out of the Mediterranean. The Baron de Boislecomte, a career diplomat, believed that Britain was especially fearful of seeing France establish a colony on the African coast, "perhaps the only place where we might be able to defend a colony against its maritime superiority."[5] So Charles X's regime resolved to "paralyze" the anticipated British opposition. It did so through diplomacy. Lord Aberdeen, the British foreign minister, sent repeated messages to France, requesting that Charles X's foreign minister, Jules de Polignac, communicate France's intentions with regard to Algiers to the British government. Britain wanted France to categorically state that it had no intentions of taking possession of the regency.[6] Polignac, who at that time was the most powerful man in the French government, gave a response that was dressed up in moral garb. He instructed the Duc de Laval, the French ambassador in London, to inform Aberdeen that the king's ambition in invading Algiers was not merely to obtain satisfaction for France's grievances, but to launch an expedition for the good of all Christendom.[7] Perhaps cynically employing the discourse of a decade before, Polignac described France's plan as "a European enterprise," directed at

5. AMAE 2MD/7, p. 198, August 25, 1830, Baron de Boislecomte, "Indication du système suivi par le gouvernement français, dans l'entreprise formée contre les régences barbaresques."

6. British Library (BL) Add MS 43084, Aberdeen Papers, Correspondence of Lord Aberdeen with Charles Stuart, Baron Stuart de Rothesay, p. 27, March 19, 1830.

7. AMAE 2MD/7, p. 37, March 12, 1830, Polignac to Laval.

destroying corsairing. France was prepared to accept "the dangers and the responsibilities for that in which all the powers would share, along with her, the advantages." France showed its face to Europe as "a friendly power," its interests "in perfect harmony with the general interests of the world and of civilization."[8] Britain was stymied; from that moment, Boislecomte wrote, triumphalism seeping out from between the lines, "the London government was obliged to handle us very carefully: several times, it even had to publicly praise an enterprise that wounded it deeply."[9]

On May 12, when the French expedition to the regency was due to depart, the French court sent a circular to all of its European allies. In it, France "prudently" announced that while the projected war was not undertaken with the intention of establishing a colony in Algiers, it "could nonetheless not make any undertakings on the future fate of this country."[10] This was unacceptable for Britain, which demanded more information. In particular, the British government wanted to know what France planned to do *after* it had invaded. Lord Stuart de Rothesay, Britain's ambassador in Paris, explained to Aberdeen that Polignac had assured him that, in undertaking this expedition, France "had never contemplated" territorial acquisition, adding that Polignac had told Rothesay that he "could not better meet the wishes of my government than by rendering the explanations [Britain] had given when Lord Exmouth's fleet attacked Algiers the model of his answer to any further enquiries upon the subject."[11] Aberdeen was having none of it. Here was an "unfailingly courteous" man, who "loathed war," and would prefer to negotiate a compromise than to stir up a conflict.[12] It was perhaps in a spirit of frustrated conciliation that he continued to insist that France give "an entire and frank explanation of the objects of the expedition, especially a renunciation of all views of territorial acquisition or aggrandizement on the part of the French government." Britain, he went on, could not be accused of hostility to France's project, as long as France had not removed

8. AMAE 2MD/7, p. 198, August 25, 1830, Boislecomte, "Indication."

9. AMAE 2MD/7, p. 199, August 25, 1830, Boislecomte, "Indication."

10. AMAE 2MD/7, p. 199, August 25, 1830, Boislecomte, "Indication."

11. BL Add MS 43084, p. 35, March 22, 1830, Rothesay to Aberdeen.

12. Hilton, *A Mad, Bad, and Dangerous People?*, 561.

any uncertainty regarding their aims.[13] France had been clever. Rothesay reported that Polignac had confided to him that Charles X was ready to confer with all interested governments on the best means to prevent piracy, slavery, and the payment of tributes into the future. This prospect, Rothesay felt, must surely make Britain uneasy. If Britain allowed the holding of a congress or conference to regulate the navigation of the Mediterranean, aware as it was of Russian ambitions in the east of that sea, it must fear the "propositions relating to maritime rights which may be brought forward," more "than would have been warranted by the continued occupation of Algiers by French troops."[14]

Thus, the British kept a close eye on French preparations leading up to the invasion. They even placed a spy in Marseilles, whose job it was to give "regular accounts of every circumstance" connected with the expedition.[15] But with no written assurances coming from Paris, by May, what Aberdeen called "the affair of the explanations respecting Algiers" had become "very serious."[16] Running throughout the correspondence between Aberdeen and his ambassador in Paris was the subtext that France could not be trusted. Rothesay, who gained the posting when George IV promised it to him during a day out at Ascot, may have felt defensive. Neither the Prime Minister, the Duke of Wellington, nor Aberdeen had supported his appointment, and Wellington complained constantly about Stuart de Rothesay's "wretchedly bad" information.[17] Rothesay, perhaps conscious of this, or perhaps just as frustrated as his minister, made this explicit when he wrote that he could not "fairly be rendered responsible for the falsehood of the assurances I receive or the failure of M. de Polignac's promises."[18] By May, Polignac had begun to bat Aberdeen's increasingly insistent requests away, with the veiled threat that a dispute with Britain at that time could be fatal to France's monarchy. It was of the highest importance to Britain that their agreeing to France's right to attack Algiers not become

13. BL Add MS 43084, p. 87, April 6, 1830, Aberdeen to Rothesay.
14. BL Add MS 43085, p. 64, July 19, 1830, Rothesay to Aberdeen.
15. BL Add MS 43084, p. 139, April 30, 1830, Rothesay to Aberdeen.
16. BL Add MS 43084, p. 147, May 11, 1830, Aberdeen to Rothesay.
17. Cited in Chamberlain, *Lord Aberdeen*, 235.
18. BL Add MS 43084, p. 149, May 14, 1830, Rothesay to Aberdeen.

an implicit acceptance of France's equal right to acquire the regency as a colony.

In late May, Aberdeen sent Rothesay an official note, to be presented to the French government. The King, Rothesay was to tell the French cabinet, had "long been sensible of the injuries sustained by his most Christian majesty from the Regency of Algiers." It was normal to expect that vengeance would be sought. But Aberdeen, speaking for George IV, also wished to call Polignac's attention to the regency's unique and peculiar situation with regard to its relationship to the Ottoman Porte. If the main object of France's expedition turned out to be conquest, rather than just reparations for injuries, Aberdeen went on, in an increasingly threatening tone, "the undersigned would submit to the serious consideration of the Prince de Polignac what must be the effect of a precedent which thus disposes of the rights of a third party, against whom no complaint whatever has been alleged."[19] This was clearly too much for France. Complaints about English "pertinacity," in politely insisting that France explain their aims, reached Aberdeen from the British ambassador to Austria, Baron Cowley. "All eyes" in Vienna were turned upon the French expedition, he told Aberdeen—and the Count de Rayneval, undersecretary of state for foreign affairs, had complained about Britain to Austria's Prince Metternich.[20]

Right throughout the French diplomatic community, the conviction that Britain was jealous of France's actions in Algiers, and therefore could not be trusted, pervaded. Reports came into Paris from around the Mediterranean regarding the British attitude to France's actions. From Smyrna, consul Adrien Dupré wrote that while the British were "taking part in our success," they were not indifferent to it, nor were they without jealousy.[21] The French consul in Malta described the state of diplomacy there. All awaited the outcome of the attack on Algiers impatiently. Representatives of the nations of Europe on the island did agree that all had an interest in suppressing the "impudence" of the Barbary States, but they "let it be known" that they would prefer that someone other than France achieve this.

19. BL Add MS 43084, pp. 224–25, May 31, 1830, Aberdeen to Rothesay.

20. BL Add MS 43080, Aberdeen Papers, Correspondence with Henry Wellesley, 1st Baron Cowley, Ambassador to Austria, p. 339, June 20, 1830.

21. AMAE CPC 259, p. 174, August 2, 1830, Dupré to Polignac.

To account for their distaste, the consul went on, they circulated the idea that France would not be more successful than Britain had been, when Admiral Sir Harry Burrard-Neale, as commander in chief of the Mediterranean fleet, had presided over the blockade and bombardment of Algiers, in response to an outrage committed against its consul, Hugh MacDonell, in 1824. In the margin of the letter, an administrator had summarized for the benefit of his minister: "The English flatter themselves that the expedition against Algiers will not be more successful than that of Admiral Neal."[22]

Britain still saw Algiers as useful. It continued to imagine the regency as a location for trade. In mid-1828, St John promised to give a full account of the state of affairs, including the regency's "political conduct, power and resources, and the state in which the agents of the different European powers are in relation with it and with each other."[23] Two years later, Sir George Murray, Secretary of State for War and the Colonies, sought a report from St John on how Britain might disseminate specimens or patterns of British manufactures throughout the African interior.[24] Perhaps this was why St John cast himself as the regency's true ally and friend. As Hussein awaited the French invasion, St John became a trusted advisor to the dey. In April 1830, Hussein summoned St John to ask his opinion on "the present posture of affairs." St John replied that "to flatter would not be the part of a friend," and that Hussein's situation was critical. Hussein's response was to protest that in punishing Deval, he had been in the right. St John could not allow this. Deval's conduct might have been "most unjustifiable," but in striking him, Hussein "had certain compromised his dignity and the rights of nations," and this, moreover, "was the sentiment of the civilized world in general."[25]

In one of the centers of the civilized world, Charles X's beleaguered government was hoping that an invasion might provide the distraction it desperately needed from domestic issues, including

22. AMAE Correspondance commerciale 15 bis: Malte 1827, p. 133, June 28, 1827, Consul Miège to Polignac.

23. TNA FO 3/30, p. 64, July 16, 1828, St John to William Huskisson, Secretary of State for War and the Colonies.

24. TNA FO 3/32, p. 89, April 2, 1830, St John to Robert Hay, Under-Secretary of State for the Colonies.

25. TNA FO 3/32, pp. 97–98, April 4, 1830, St John to Hay.

several years of poor harvests, an increasingly unpopular government, and an encroaching economic recession.[26] As Europe eyed
the weakening Ottoman Empire and planned its dismemberment,
Polignac, now president of the Council of Ministers, had sought
an alliance with Russia, on the grounds that this might provide a
counterbalance to British naval preponderance in the Mediterranean.[27] France hoped, also, that such an alliance would allow it to
rearrange the political map of Europe, to give it Belgium and part
of the left bank of the Rhine.[28] But this project collapsed, and on
January 31, 1830, the Council of Ministers in Paris voted to take
direct unilateral action in Algiers. Charles X appointed General
Louis de Bourmont, his minister of war, to lead the expedition.

On May 16, the fleet left Toulon for Algiers. 103 warships and
464 transports carried an army of more than 37,000 men. On
June 14, the army landed at Sidi Fredj, a beachhead to the west of
Algiers. The regency's army was greater in number than the French,
although the janissary corps only numbered around seven thousand men. They were nonetheless unable to stop the French from
landing. The French army advanced, and, by June 29, they were on
the hills surrounding Algiers. "On the anniversary of our glorious
independence," as Lee wrote to Secretary of State Van Buren, the
French bombarded the fortress commanding Algiers (this was the
Borj Mawlay Hasan, known to the French as Fort l'Empereur), and
gained possession of it after six hours.[29] Perhaps it was the military man in Lee that led him to identify with the French forces. "I
do not know," he wrote, "that I ever experienced a prouder glow of
sympathy and triumph, than when I first beheld from the terrace
of our garrison, the victorious Christian troops driving the Barbar-
ian hordes before them, and crowning the heights in full view of
Algiers, their kindred banners streaming proudly to the wind, and
their conquering arms glittering in the morning sun."[30] It was a
letter redolent of Frances Scott Key's poem "The Star-Spangled
Banner," written during the 1812–15 war, in which Lee had served.

26. Sessions, *By Sword and Plow*, 20.
27. McDougall, *A History of Algeria*, 51.
28. Jardin and Tudesq, *Restoration and Reaction*, 95.
29. NARA M23, vol. 14, n.p., July 5, 1830, Lee to Van Buren.
30. NARA M23, vol. 14, n.p., July 15, 1830, Lee to Van Buren.

Lee organized a safe haven for his fellow consuls and their families in a large, fortified house. All the Christians he could find in the city were offered refuge, along with a number of Jews. Lee, given command of the house by unanimous vote, described how he organized everyone in the form of a garrison protected by the American flag. Houses around them were "cruelly plundered," he reported, and lives were lost, but in the fortified house, all were maintained in perfect security. As the French advanced, nonetheless, they requisitioned his house, positioned at a high point with a view over the city. Lee welcomed them as fellow soldiers, and indeed, he informed Van Buren, he found among the officer corps "names which were distinguished in our revolution," including men who had known his father, and "young cavaliers, who seemed to have imbibed the friendship of their fathers for the U. States."[31] Here, again, was the United States, the equal, and in many ways, the brother of the French forces.

On July 5, Hussein signed the capitulation, agreeing to surrender Algiers. Hussein had sought and obtained St John's help, and St John became go-between, as Lee recounted, "at no small risk of his personal safety."[32] As the French surrounded the city, the beleaguered dey had sent for St John, begging the British consul "to go to speak to his people and apprise them that the French will not massacre them or he says they will believe me more than him or the French."[33] St John aided Hussein in negotiating the capitulation, including a delay of two hours to allow Hussein to safely remove his family from the palace to his private house.[34] (St John continued to make himself useful after the surrender. He gave Arabic lessons to the captain of the Zouaves—French light infantry regiments—Louis Juchault de Lamorcière, and was named administrator of Hussein's belongings.)[35] On July 5, at midday, two hours later than originally planned, French troops placed their flag on the walls of the palace.

Hussein soon decided, as he told St John, that he no longer considered himself safe in Algiers, and wished to leave. General de Bourmont, Commander of the invading forces, had urged him to take up

31. NARA M23, vol. 14, n.p., July 15, 1830, Lee to Van Buren.
32. NARA M23, vol. 14, n.p., July 15, 1830, Lee to Van Buren.
33. TNA FO 3/32, p. 155, July 4, 1830, St John to Murray.
34. TNA FO 3/32, pp. 213-14, July 28, 1830, St John to Hay.
35. Redouane, "La Présence anglaise," 15.

residence in France, but Hussein had "a decided objection" to this option, and wished instead to go to Malta. He "begged" St John to procure Bourmont's consent to his going there and staying while he decided on a place of permanent residence. St John obtained this consent, and agreed to have a British brig, the *Ferret*, accompany the French ship of the line in which Hussein and his family would travel, to mitigate the latter's distaste at sailing under the French flag.[36] St John attached great significance to his role. He was not simply acting as an individual. He was acting in the name of, and on behalf of Britain. St John might have reported that he was careful to insist to Bourmont that his visits to French headquarters were made "merely as the private friend of the dey," but his daily letters to Sir George Murray made it clear that he never wavered from his role. He did not stop being the British consul. In particular, he watched the French invasion with a highly critical, and competitive eye. The French were untrustworthy occupiers. They were both perfidious and incompetent. High on the list of their mistakes was their misplaced trust of Jacob. "No good," St John wrote censoriously, could come "of following the advice of such Jews as are now about the French commander in chief."[37]

Following the invasion, Jacob, so used to being at the center of diplomacy, simply placed himself there once again. In accounts of the early days of the invasion, Jacob's name appears time and again. Claude-Antoine Rozet, an army captain and engineer-geographer, wrote that since the army had been in Africa, "we haven't been able to do without the Jews."[38] He described Jacob as "the richest and most respected of the Jews in Algiers." Jacob regularly invited French officers to his home to take part in his soirées.[39] In November of 1830, Jacob Bacri was afforded a position of high importance by the French; named head of the Jewish nation—the *nation hébraïque*—in Algiers, he was invested with the powers of policing and surveillance of that town's Jewish community. He was to carry out any judgements handed down by the Tribunal, and took responsibility for the collection of taxes. He reported to the general

36. TNA FO 3/32, pp. 158–59, July 6, 1830, St John to Murray. Hussein changed his mind more than once, and ultimately sailed to Naples.

37. TNA FO 3/32, p. 167, July 11, 1830, St John to Murray.

38. Rozet, *Voyage dans la régence d'Alger*, vol. 2, 231.

39. Rozet, *Voyage dans la régence d'Alger*, vol. 2, 258.

in chief.[40] Jacob does seem to have gained the complete trust of the French administration. When General Bourmont was fighting resistors outside Algiers, he took refuge in Jacob's country house. It was judged too far from battle to make a suitable headquarters, but Bourmont stayed there long enough to take "badly-needed refreshment."[41] Jacob was also supplying cattle to the army.[42] Characteristically, he remained a controversial figure.

Jacob had not enjoyed his power and influence six months before members of the Jewish community addressed a petition to Alexis-Adolphe Bligny, Baron Bondurand, military intendant to the occupying force, demanding that Jacob be relieved of his position. Jacob, it would appear, continued to behave as though he were in a corrupt and corrupting regime. Among the petitioners was an Amar, the traditional allies of the Bacris, and a Durand, the family's great enemies. The signatories to the petition claimed to speak on behalf of the entire Jewish nation, and they listed a litany of misbehavior. Jacob had used the welfare fund to pay those in his employ; he had retained in his possession a sum of money belonging to the community; he was in debt to a very large number of people and being pursued judicially by several of them; his belongings had been seized and sold by the courts; he had sought to intervene in rabbinic judgements, and three rabbis had resigned their posts because of his meddling; several members of the community had spoken to him about his behavior, and instead of listening to them, he had responded by having any member of the elite who sought to address him arbitrarily imprisoned, "with no regard for principles." Many of the elite had chosen to leave Algiers, rather than to remain at the pleasure of Jacob Bacri, and this was doing damage to the entire community. Jacob, the petitioners wrote, had been ordered to stand down from his position by the Baron Volant, predecessor to Baron Bondurand. For the sake of his dignity, Jacob had been given time to resign. Meanwhile, however, Volant had left Algiers, and Jacob had profited from the change of staff to remain in place. Now they asked that he be well and truly dismissed and replaced

40. Martin, *Les Israélites algériens*, 44–45.
41. Bartillat, *Relation de la campagne d'Afrique en 1830*, 82.
42. Bartillat, *Relation de la campagne d'Afrique en 1830*, 208.

by three or four administrators.[43] Through ineptitude, and perhaps also corruption and bad will, Jacob repeatedly got into trouble, and then refused absolutely to shoulder any of the responsibility for his situation. This places his brothers' reactions to him, and his nieces' and nephews' pursuit of him, in perspective.

As St John saw it, the combination of French rule and Jacob's scheming promised to be nothing less than disastrous for the regency's inhabitants, as well as for the other European powers. That the French placed trust in "sundry Jews and Moors" was a sign of a significant weakness. The French allowed themselves to be influenced, and even controlled, by these local inhabitants. Even though Bourmont had made the proclamation that a Turkish government would be maintained, they had sent all unmarried members of the Turkish elite away. (In fact, members of the Ottoman establishment of Algiers, together with many of the janissaries, were deported to Izmir.)[44] St John was convinced that it was because of certain "Jews and Moors" that these Turks were sent from the regency, in "dreadful" circumstances. The *Hasnagi* or prime minister, an old friend to Britain in the regency, had come to St John for help in organizing a passage for himself in an English brig of war. While the two men were together, word came that twenty-five of the Turkish elite had been sent for, accused of having intrigued against the French, and immediately transferred to a French ship. The *Hasnagi* was seized and conveyed on board. The order was given for all the accused Turks to sail. Among them were dragomen and guardians of the various consuls. It took a joint resistance on the part of the consuls as a united body to obtain permission for them to remain. The actions of the French army in sending so many Turks away constituted nothing less than "a gross breach of promise," and St John was outraged. Wives and children were left behind,

43. Archives nationales d'outre-mer (ANOM), Aix-en-Provence, GGA/1H/1, June 12, 1831, "Petition from members of the Jewish community of Algiers." Cited in McDougall, *A History of Algiers*, 53.

44. McDougall, *A History of Algiers*, 52. Muslim refugees from the Spanish Inquisition were often referred to as "Moors" by European travellers and diplomats, including St John. McDougall calls them "Andalusis" (McDougall, *A History of Algiers*, 30). I will use the term "Moor" as quoted or paraphrased, but otherwise, I will substitute the term "Muslim" to describe the descendants of those who fled the Iberian Peninsula, and "Turkish" to describe the elite imposed from Constantinople.

unprotected, and many of them starving. He was convinced, and he had tried to convince Marshal Bourmont, that the Jews and Muslims were behind this: these Turks had lent them money, and this was a convenient way to avoid repayment.[45] Not that the channels of communication were open. St John's sense that the French were being less than diplomatic with him began soon after the latter arrived. He was "induced," he said, to write "anxiously" to Sir George Murray, as a promised communication from French authorities had not been made. General Bourmont had assured him that any action France decided to take in the long term in Algiers would be with Britain's approval. He promised to give St John further information as soon as he received replies to his letter announcing the regency's capitulation. But he had "long since" received those replies, and St John had heard nothing more.[46] St John could only deduce that either some suspicion of Britain existed, or there was some matter about which Bourmont wished to keep Britain in the dark. A month later, he reported that his position in Algiers "had become more disagreeable," as many of the French believed that he was stirring up the Muslims against them. He had foreseen this, but it was nonetheless unpleasant.[47] Early in the next month, Bourmont was replaced by General Bertrand Clausel. The mistrust between France and Britain continued. Clausel told the Danish consul that "the English consul would do all he could to impede their progress," as the British government "constantly" made its agents abroad oppose them.[48]

Even as they led what St John saw as a botched and vindictive campaign, the French settled matters to their advantage wherever possible. They sought to block, or, at the least, disadvantage British trade. St John was sure that the French would extend the monopoly they had enjoyed at Bona to the entire country, thus excluding merchants from the various Italian states. This would be a problem for Britain, as they disposed of "a tolerable quantity" of their manufactures through these channels.[49] Real, as opposed

45. TNA FO 3/32, pp. 221–22, August 4, 1830, St John to Murray.
46. TNA FO 3/32, p. 200, July 23, 1830, St John to Murray.
47. TNA FO 3/32, p. 234, August 25, 1830, St John to Murray.
48. TNA FO 3/32, p. 282, October 23, 1830, St John to Murray.
49. TNA FO 3/32, p. 99, April 4, 1830, St John to Murray.

to anticipated problems, were already surfacing. The French had laid a ten-day quarantine on Gibraltar for no reason that St John could discover "except it be to favor the French commerce to our prejudice."[50] Later, Clausel went further. He raised the duty on British produce from five to eight percent (French merchants only paid four percent). When St John remonstrated with the general, he got nowhere, and "all the benefit which Europe was promised" from the French action against the regency "is a total insecurity from the natives along the coast, and a heavy drag on our commerce."[51] Then, in early 1831, a decree was issued prohibiting the export of wheat from all the ports of Algiers, for any destination other than France, until further orders.[52] For France, of course, this was a ruling that provided a solution to a problem that had dogged the country for decades. In 1794, they had signed an agreement with the Bacris and Busnachs for the supply of desperately needed wheat. Now, almost forty years later, that need was no less desperate. 1830 was the last of three years of poor grain harvests. Scarcity had first been felt in late 1826, with the first of several poor harvests. By 1827, credit was tight, and demand for manufactured goods plunged. This led to a run of bankruptcies and commercial failures.[53] The price of a hectoliter of wheat had risen by fifty percent in those years and was to remain high until 1832. In a repeat of the events of 1817, shortages and high prices had led to civil unrest throughout the country. With this monopoly over the trade of grain, decades of Franco-British contest for this precious resource came to an end, with a stunning French victory.

In Algiers, meanwhile, the French were pulling down streets, and the consuls of Spain, Sweden, Denmark, and Holland had been notified that their country houses were required by France. In Bona, French troops outraged the British vice-consul, Mr. Fraser. They made free with his papers, and "even seized and read" them. They drank his wine.[54] If their indecency were not enough, the French were also literally filthy. The squalor they created around them

50. TNA FO 3/32, p. 210, July 28, 1830, St John to Murray.

51. TNA FO 3/32, p. 424, October 13, 1830, St John to Murray.

52. TNA FO 3/33, p. 7, January 8, 1831, St John to Murray.

53. Miller, *Mastering the Market*, 264.

54. TNA FO 3/32, p. 245, September 2, 1830, St John to Murray.

was such, that St John fully expected "some serious sickness in the country—if not the plague." This, together with their "extreme indecency of conduct, and depredations," had made all "regret their uncivilized predecessors."[55] The British would, of course, have done a better job of invading and occupying the regency. And the locals, bristling under French rule, would welcome the benevolent British. "If it should be your wish that the French should not remain here," he wrote to Sir George Murray, "the whole country could be stirred up in a moment," much to the benefit of Britain.[56] Oran, in particular, would be of considerable value as a trading post for Gibraltar and commerce with the interior. (Murray's response, which must have disappointed the ambitious St John, was to maintain strict neutrality, and to avoid stirring up the locals or helping the French army, as the latter had only a "temporary possession" of Algiers.)[57] Those same locals were telling St John that they would live under a British government. They told him that after Lord Exmouth's expedition, Britain could have done what France had now done, "but we proved ourselves their real friends in not doing so."[58] Even some French were suggesting to St John that the British join them in occupying the regency.[59] St John was an amateur military strategist. He saw countless fertile approaches that the French had missed. The coast, he advised, could be "governed easily and quietly" by Europeans.[60] The French had sent the Turks away, leaving "mere Moors" in charge, an "imprudent" strategy because of their weakness.[61] A Muslim government "would be overturned instantly."[62] The Turks were "the only Mahometans with energy sufficient to restrain these wild tribes." If the "wild tribes" did attack French forces, Britain could take the regency "with ease and be received as saviors."[63] As long as St John remained

55. TNA FO 3/32, p. 224, August 4, 1830, St John to Murray.
56. TNA FO 3/32, p. 234, August 25, 1830, St John to Murray.
57. TNA FO 8/9, October 9, 1830, Murray to St John.
58. TNA FO 3/32, p. 235, August 25, 1830, St John to Murray.
59. TNA FO 3/32, p. 233, August 25, 1830, St John to Murray.
60. TNA FO 3/32, p. 202, July 23, 1830.
61. TNA FO 3/32, p. 167, July 11, 1830, St John to Murray; TNA FO 3/32, p. 208, July 26, 1830, St John to Murray.
62. TNA FO 3/32, p. 208, July 26, 1830, St John to Murray.
63. TNA FO 3/32, p. 208, July 23, 1830, St John to Murray.

in Algiers, the "natives" would not give up hope of British protection.[64] St John's fantasies were to be put to the test—and shown to have merit—when news of the July Revolution reached Algiers. Troops were recalled to Algiers from Bona and Oran. In Oran, the bey "immediately declared himself independent," and sent for the local British vice-consul, a Mr. Welsford, to make known his readiness to make a treaty with the British.[65]

In St John's fantasy, only a few Muslims and Jews, who had got power over the French, would fail to welcome a British force.[66] If the French were to desert, it would be, St John anticipated, "without providing a protection to the town against the Arabs."[67] Algiers would be pillaged. St John, secure in the certainty of British superiority, was not concerned for his own safety in the event of a British invasion. It would fall to him, he was certain, to "arrange matters" among the inhabitants—Jew, Turk, and Muslim—and all parties would be anxious to secure a British alliance.[68] The Jews alone would be in a bad way, but this would be no less than they deserved. They certainly did not deserve pity. Since the arrival of the French in Algiers, they had become "insolent and revengeful." St John could not think of any villainy "on the face of the Earth," that matched theirs, and, with outraged emphasis, he underlined, "without one single exception."[69] Jews continued to get in the way of St John's fantasies of British superiority.

On July 11, St John received an official communication from Bourmont, informing him that he was henceforth to communicate with the commander in chief through the French consul—Alexandre Deval, the son of Pierre—and only with regard to commercial affairs. As far as the French were concerned, St John's political functions had "ceased."[70] In fact, this instruction was given to all of the European consuls, and St John reported that it caused "great offense."[71]

64. TNA FO 3/32, p. 427, October 13, 1830, St John to Murray.

65. TNA FO 3/32, p. 245, September 2, 1830, St John to Murray.

66. TNA FO 3/32, p. 208, July 23, 1830, St John to Murray.

67. TNA FO 3/32, p. 283a, October 23, 1830, St John to Murray.

68. TNA FO 3/32, p. 283a, October 23, 1830, St John to Murray.

69. TNA FO 3/32, p. 283a, October 23, 1830, St John to Murray.

70. TNA FO 3.32, p. 168, July 11, 1830, St John to Murray.

71. TNA FO 3/32, p. 201, July 23, 1830, St John to Murray.

Lee, however, far from being greatly offended, saw these events as an opportunity for another display of US dignity. He described to Van Buren how he paid a ceremonial visit to the French consul, Alexandre Deval, to acknowledge his appointment. He also visited Bourmont, but, he took care to note, unlike his colleagues, he waited to visit until Hussein's deposition had been completely effected. "Even then," he wrote, "I thought it more consonant to the free and magnanimous character of the United States, to visit the fallen prince, before I called on the successful general, sure to pay the same respect to the former in misfortune, which I had been accustomed to show him in the height of his power." He was gratified by the "deep emotion" his visit aroused.[72]

St John was more interested in finding fault with France than in enacting British superiority. The new ruling by Bourmont was an "odd" undertaking, one that St John attributed to Jacob. Bourmont was "so fond of the presence of the Jews at his headquarters," and it was "so much in their interest to prevent his getting any information from the consuls," that St John saw this as the reason for Bourmont avoiding them.[73] The marshal was, after all, "entirely advised by the Jews."[74] They were even able to sway France's policy regarding Hussein's exile. The French had first attempted to persuade Hussein to go to Paris. He refused and nominated Malta as his destination. Eventually he went to Naples, departing Algiers on July 10, 1830, and arriving on July 31. In November 1830, St John wrote to Hay that he had news from that city. Hussein, he wrote, had "fallen into the hands of the Jews at Leghorn," and he was to move there. St John had no doubt that he would be "picked pretty clean."[75] In characteristic contrast, US consuls were much less invested in these events, and thus much more pragmatic in their assessment of them. David Porter, the US naval captain who served as consul in Algiers for a brief period in 1830, reported similar news to Secretary of State Martin Van Buren in November: that the former dey was now in Leghorn. In Porter's version, Hussein was in complete control of

72. NARA M23, vol. 14, n.p., July 15, 1830, Lee to Van Buren.

73. TNA FO 3/32, p. 204, July 23, 1830, St John to Murray.

74. TNA FO 3/32, p. 225, August 4, 1830, St John to Murray.

75. TNA FO 3/32, p. 294, November 14, 1830, St John to Hay.

his destiny. The dey had, he wrote, "formed a connection with some Jews," and planned to establish himself in that town as a banker,[76] thus effectively resuming the business relationship he had had with members of the Bacri family, when he was Dey of Algiers.

The French settled in to their occupation of Algiers, but their long-term projects in the regency remained unclear. By late July, St John believed that everything suggested very strongly that the French intended to retain possession of Algiers permanently. Just a month later, however, in late August, St John was reporting that the French generals had begun "to see the difficulty of retaining this country." St John thought they would be obliged to evacuate. Here they were, in a land that was "extremely rich, the climate perhaps the finest in the world and cotton, silk and barilla would grow admirably," unable to guarantee their possession. But, St John concluded philosophically, "the French always act without solid thought."[77] He could well have had the July Revolution in mind when he wrote those words.

In 1829, as prices were rising, Charles X had dismissed his interior minister, the Viscount de Martignac, and appointed three ultra-royalist ministers to positions of power. His close friend, the Prince de Polignac, was given the foreign ministry, and later promoted to the presidency of the council of ministers. Parliament resumed in March 1830, and opponents of the king's new government had their first opportunity to voice their displeasure. A motion of no confidence in the government was passed by a majority of deputies. Charles dissolved parliament and announced an election. Elections were duly held, on June 23 and July 3. 428 deputies were elected, of whom a majority—270—were liberals, compared with 145 royalists. For Charles, the overwhelming liberal victory raised the specter of revolution, and he decided to seize the initiative. News of the triumph in Algiers had reached Paris on July 9. Charles, overestimating the patriotism the news would arouse, allowed himself to be persuaded by ultra-royalist ministers that the newly elected liberals were so dangerous, he was fully justified in invoking the emergency decree powers given him by article

76. NARA M23, roll 14, vol. 12, n.p., November 19, 1830, Porter to Van Buren.
77. TNA FO 3/32, p. 425, October 13, 1830, St John to Rothesay.

14 of the constitutional charter. As king, he had personal legislative power to be used in an emergency, allowing him to declare existing laws invalid, and issue decrees or ordinances in their place. This was what Charles did. He believed that an emergency had been created by the result of the election, and he hoped that the signing of the ordinances would bring this emergency to an end. Instead, the publication of the ordinances in the official government organ, the *Moniteur*, on July 16 was the catalyst for three days of street fighting. Protests were stirred up by the angry response of the liberal press to the ordinances, combined with a Parisian laboring poor, resentful at continued deprivation in the face of the economic depression, and anxious about the political crisis. This potent mix led to revolution. Aberdeen watched events from London with great concern. On July 31, amid passages of rapid change, he wrote a concerned letter to Rothesay, very much aware that France could once again become a republic.[78] But Britain's fears were not to be realized on this occasion. Charles fled, and his cousin, Louis-Philippe of the house of Orléans, replaced him, as a constitutional monarch.

David Porter informed Van Buren in September 1830 that France seemed determined to colonize Algiers, and he thought they would do so, "if the other cabinets of Europe permit it."[79] In the wake of the latest revolution, the other cabinets of Europe were inclined to act prudently. No one wished to stir up domestic unrest in France, or to pick a quarrel.[80] Britain, in particular, had its own concerns. For some years, British politics had faced a series of changes and challenges that preoccupied both the government and the nation. In 1825, the British stock market crashed, an event described by Boyd Hilton as "the first and worst [crash] of the century."[81] Banks failed and bankruptcies abounded. Food prices rose, but a shortage of specie meant that wages were not paid, and this provoked riots. In 1828, parliament passed the repeal of the Test and Corporation Acts, giving Protestant nonconformists the right to take a public office. Close behind this broadening of conditions for inclusion in public

78. BL Add MS 43085, pp. 70–71, July 31, 1830, Aberdeen to Rothesay.
79. NARA M23, vol. 14, n.p., September 25, 1830, Porter to Van Buren.
80. Schroeder, *The Transformation of European Politics*, 669.
81. Hilton, *A Mad, Bad, and Dangerous People?*, 398.

life came the campaign for Catholic emancipation. Under great pressure from the Catholic majority in Ireland, the government passed the Catholic Emancipation Act in April 1829, but this was not without controversy, and politics was "confused" for some time after, as angry opponents of the idea that Catholics could be their equal in British society split the governing conservative coalition.[82]

In mid-1830, two events marked a shift in the British political scene. On June 26, George IV died, necessitating an election. Two days later, the July Revolution erupted in Paris. When Algiers fell to French troops, Wellington's policy had been to wait. In part, this was because the British government was in disarray. As Ambassador Stuart de Rothesay pointed out on July 16, it was safer for Britain, her Dutch ally, and Europe generally to have France seek military glory on the North African coast, rather than in Belgium or along their eastern border.[83] The desire to contain French ambition and prevent popular uprising was foremost. But France was no longer a natural enemy, and with the ascension of Louis-Philippe to the throne, Britain could be magnanimous. A constitutional monarchy could be accommodated. Louis-Philippe had been an émigré to Britain during the first revolution. For Wellington, Louis-Philippe was an acceptable option.[84]

British politics was preoccupied, too, with Belgium. Revolution had broken out in Brussels on August 25, and after a failed attempt by the prince of Orange to regain the city by force, a provisional Belgian government declared independence on October 4. St John wrote in November that "the peace of the whole world" now depended on the outcome of events in Belgium. He reported that the French army in Algiers were hoping that Prussia would interfere in Belgium and "give France what they call a right in self defense to *aller en avant*."[85] All the European powers were concerned by the prospect of an aggressive France, loose in Europe once again.[86] From his perspective across the Mediterranean, St John was less

82. Briggs, *The Age of Improvement*, 233.

83. Cited in Redouane, "British Attitudes to the French Conquest of Algeria," 3.

84. Schroeder, *The Transformation of European Politics*, 669.

85. TNA FO 3/32, p. 295, November 14, 1830, St John to Hay. Original emphasis.

86. Schroeder has discussed the gap between this idea as a perception of France, and the reality of July Monarchy politics, in *The Transformation of European Politics*, 676–79.

worried. The French, he thought, were "fully aware" that if it came
to war with Britain, they would lose Algiers.[87] By November 1830,
when he wrote that letter, St John was the last remaining foreign
consul in Algiers, and he was awaiting permission to depart. All
other powers had either abolished their consulate entirely or had
simply allowed the acting consul to retire. US consul in Algiers
David Porter told Van Buren that "the arrangement made by the
commander in chief, which cuts off all direct communication
between him and the consuls and reduces them to the level of mere
commercial agents forbids their continuance in Algiers." In these
difficult circumstances, it was "the subject of pride" that Henry Lee,
the American consul, had been the first "to give proofs of his disin-
clination to submit to the degradation, an example which has been
followed by all the rest."[88] As the situation moved and changed
around him, St John returned time and again to the contest, and
the reassurance of French inefficiency and British ascendancy. For
Porter, this was an opportunity to repeat and rehearse a narrative of
US dignity and moral superiority. British and US consuls were still
coming to know their nation through their actions and relations
on the Algerian periphery, but this was no longer filtered through
the actions of and their relations with members of the Bacri family.

The question of France in Algiers returned to the fore in 1833.
Louis-Philippe had decided to colonize the regency, and this provoked strong reactions in the British parliament and press. The
Times drew on the narrative of contest, and eternal French short-
comings. "We do not envy France a colony which she has obtained
by a fraud," the editorial went,

> and which she can only retain at enormous sacrifices. We are convinced
> that the French government would find it now unsafe to abandon its
> onerous conquest.[89]

Discussion in the House of Lords was more concerned with the
implications of such an action for Britain. Aberdeen, no longer in
the governing party, was particularly concerned to make clear to his

87. TNA FO 3/32, p. 295, November 14, 1830, St John to Hay.
88. NARA M23, vol. 14, n.p., November 19, 1830, Porter to Van Buren.
89. *The Times*, May 21, 1833, p. 5, cited in Redouane, "British Attitudes to the French Conquest of Algeria," 4.

fellow peers "the advantage that must be held by any power possessing a line of five or six hundred miles of coast at the entrance of the Mediterranean [. . .] and above all when such an advantage was in possession of such a power as France."[90] With Algiers once again a topic for discussion in parliament, so were its Jews. In 1833, parliament was debating the removal of legal disabilities for Britain's Jews, including barriers to public office and elite institutions. Robert Inglis, known for his conservatism and staunch opposition to any measure that might weaken the Anglican Church, rose to oppose any such motion. For Inglis, it was established that "Christianity was part and parcel of the Law of Britain." Given that, Jews would be "incompetent and unworthy" to hold "all the dearest interests" of Britain in their custody. Moreover, they themselves would not wish to be placed in a position where they were required to renounce their distinct national character. "Place them in Poland, in Prussia, in France, in Algiers, in China, they still regard themselves as a separate nation, and they would resist the conferring of any benefit upon them, founded upon a renunciation upon their parts of that claim to a distinct national character."[91] It would be a stretch to imagine that Jacob's notoriety had reached quite so far, but those who knew him would have recognized him in Inglis's words.

By the time Inglis rose to bring a particularly conservative note to that particular debate, Jacob had lost the leadership of his community. Nonetheless, he remained at the forefront of contention, as his nieces and nephews took up the financial disputes between the brothers and kept them alive. The family fight for Jacob's money continued into 1832. Salomon's heirs, including his son David, his daughters Aziza and Rachel, together with their husbands Moses Bacri and Moses Nacmani, and Salomon's youngest daughter, Fortunée, brought the matter to the County Court of Marseilles, hoping to bring the issue to a close with a victory. They hoped that Algiers might now be found to be within the jurisdiction of the French legal system. They asked the court to find that Busnach and

90. House of Lords debate, vol. 17, p. 902, May 3, 1830, https://api.parliament.uk /historic-hansard/lords/1833/may/03/occupation-of-algiers.

91. House of Commons debate, vol. 17, p. 223, April 17, 1833, http://api.parliament.uk /historic-hansard/commons/1833/apr/17/emancipation-of-the-jews. I am grateful to Ira Katznelson for bringing this quote to my attention.

Jacob came under their jurisdiction, that Jacob's debt of 600,000 francs to Salomon, and thus to his heirs, be duly recognized, and both he and Busnach jointly condemned to pay this amount with interest calculated from July 23, 1811. Once again, the court found against the Bacri heirs, and on the same basis as before. The court proceedings, dry as they are, reveal some facts about Jacob that take us closer to an understanding of him. Jacob was always a terrible manager of money. He lost his Marseilles house (in fact, the court record refers to more than one), and his ship, *l'Africain*, which were sold to pay off debtors. As Salomon's heirs took up proceedings, other—external—parties sought to intervene in the matter. A stockbroker and a company of bankers, and a merchant in Marseilles, all wished to urge the court to pass judgement on Jacob, so that he might be found liable for sums he owed them. Wherever he went, Jacob left a string of debts behind him.

Details of Jacob's death are elusive. Some sources claim that he died in Paris in 1836. The destruction of records in 1871 in fires set by the Paris communards make this impossible to verify. His name is not listed among deaths of Bacris (of whom there were many) in Algiers. Those records begin in 1838, so it is entirely possible, and probably more likely, that he died in Algiers, before this date. He would have been in his early seventies. In Algiers, his legacy continued through his daughter Aziza, born in 1815. Aziza, who married Alexandre Benjamin Foa, was renowned for her beauty. She was known in Algiers as "the pretty daughter of the Bacris." She quickly became a regular figure, dressed in French style, at balls held by the invaders. Henri Klein, the teacher and general secretary of the *Comité du vieil Alger* who wrote about her, claimed that she was the first of the Jewish community to take part in French festivities. In 1860, when Napoleon III and the Empress Eugénie visited Algiers, Aziza Bacri served as interpreter to the Empress.[92]

By then, of course, Algeria was French, and was to be so for another century to come. As the invasion progressed, Britain maintained its naval presence in the Mediterranean. British trade was increasing, and the packet service from Britain to India via the Mediterranean and overland to the Red Sea had been established.

92. Klein, "Souverains, souveraines, présidents," 8.

As the British government saw it, they had to keep the control of sections of Mediterranean coastline by a rival such as France to a minimum.[93] The British consular presence remained in place, too, and in fact, St John stayed on as consul in Algeria for another two decades, until 1851. Contest in the Mediterranean dissipated, but it did not disappear.

As Aziza's story suggests, Bacris remained in Algiers. There were those who, like Aziza, maintained the Bacri family position as brokers. After the invasion, French authorities laid claim to a cemetery in Algiers, known as Ayoun Skakna (Hot Springs). It was on land purchased by the five brothers in the early days of the French Revolution, and Naphtali Busnach, as well as other family members, had been buried there. A David Bacri, stating himself to be the son of Mordecai, who was working as a court interpreter, claimed the cemetery as his family's property. His assertion was accepted as valid. There were still Bacris in Algiers, and there was still a sense of what it meant to be a Bacri. But under French rule, being a broker came to mean something different. The space that Jacob and his brothers had occupied so successfully when Algiers had been a regency eventually ceased to exist. It was replaced by the same framework that had once defeated Jacob, where relations were largely impersonal and professional, clientelism was available to a select few, and middle spaces offered little opportunity for the sort of creative license and mobility that the Bacris had so successfully employed.

93. Bartlett, *Great Britain and Sea Power*, 61.

Conclusion

LAYERS OF THE past remain in Algiers. The Casbah, or old city, clings to the hills that rise up from the port. It is almost unchanged; its streets and alleyways climb and snake with the topography. Here, in the Casbah, stands the palace of Mustapha Pasha, once the Dey of Algiers. Here you can walk the corridors where Thainville and Cartwright raced one another to be the first to kiss his hand. The rooms where Mustapha lived and ruled are empty now, but their extravagant decoration hints at the life that once animated them: tiles from Tunisia, their colors still vibrant, line the walls, alongside more muted, but highly prized tiles from Delft.

Of the Bacris and their relatives the Busnachs, there is just one trace. This is a small, blue star of David at the apex of an arched doorway. Today, this doorway forms the entrance to the National Museum of Popular Arts and Traditions, created by the Algerian government in 1987. It stands inauspiciously on a corner in the Casbah. Once it was *dar Bakri*: the Bacri house. The change in the building's function tells the story of the Bacri family's ultimate displacement from the central position they had enjoyed. The house where first Joseph, then Jacob lived, became an official building of the colonial regime, the system that took over from the one that had served them so well. Trading Jews such as the Bacris had been able to adapt to new circumstances in the Mediterranean by drawing on the personal relationships that they were able to establish as Jews. In an absolutist state with apparently endless funds to be put to the cause of mercantilism, "an unprecedented level of opportunities awaited the enterprising Jewish merchant and financier."[1] The Bacris' Jewishness gave them proximity to power in the regency, and legitimate occupation of the sorts of spaces occupied by traders and brokers. But when they found themselves in a different structure of power, such as in France, where the rule of law prevailed, as opposed to personal rule, and when that state imposed its structure on Algiers, they floundered.

The Bacris floundered, also, because of a complete lack of trust in one another, and because of intense contest in the community of which they were a part. Sarah Stein's point, regarding the role of commerce as "a resilient thread" in the weaving together of modern Jewry is important.[2] Trust, however, was clearly much more fragile. The Bacris show us that trust cannot be assumed, nor can the strength of family, or even community ties. Trust broke down between the brothers, perhaps when Jacob, deep in debt, went to Salomon in Livorno for the first time in 1803. That was when he wrote the letter to his brother Abraham, protesting his older sibling's lack of faith in his ability to recoup the monies owed to the family by France. For their part, the Busnach brothers appear to have had no faith in Michel at all. David Busnach, in Livorno, made an agreement with Salomon that neither would bail out their brothers, although David did eventually help pay Michel's debts. The example of the Bacris tells us solidarity amongst kin, or even coreligionists, cannot be assumed to be a given. It does not take "a wild leap of imagination," as Francesca Trivellato has argued, "to consider the possibility that social and emotional proximity could also ignite acrimonious rivalries."[3] No one should be truly surprised to find that the five brothers did not all—or always—see eye to eye.

Nor was trust a binding factor in the broader community—far from it. In Algiers, the community elite created factions—pro-Bacri, or pro-Duran—and this was a bitter rivalry. After Naphtali's assassination, when Joseph and David were imprisoned, David Duran became *muqaddem*. When Joseph and David were eventually

1. Schroeter, *The Sultan's Jew*, 3.
2. Stein, *Plumes*, 152.
3. Trivellato, "Sephardic Merchants between State and Rabbinic Courts," 627; Trivellato, *The Familiarity of Strangers*, 276, 277.

released, they were obliged to stay in Duran's home, an arrangement that must have pleased the latter, who was bent on the Bacris' humiliation and destruction. The same David Duran was, according to some commentators, behind David Bacri's sudden execution. When Duran also met his death at the hands of the dey, nine months later, the dey accused him of having caused David Bacri's execution through his intrigues. The rivalry between the Bacris and the Durans was quite literally fought to the death. Whatever else people might have imagined Jewishness to be, it was not, necessarily, a quality that guaranteed cohesion.

A glance into the inner workings of the Bacri clan can tell us, also, what it was to be a trading Jew in the early nineteenth-century Mediterranean. We cannot take the Bacris as typical. Theirs was a unique and extraordinary trajectory. No other trading Jews were able to leverage their position in the regency to reach such heights of fame. From their story we can, however, generalize about what it took to trade successfully in their time and place. It required agility: the networks to receive information about prices and demand as quickly as was possible in a war-plagued sea, and the courage to make snap decisions on the basis of that information. It required the ability, the creativity, and the chutzpah to take advantage of the chaos brought on by the war: to stretch the law and continue to trade to forbidden, although lucrative ports, using neutral ships. It required the ability to forge vital personal relationships, for favorable trade decisions, and for a diplomatic champion who would take your side when, for example, an irate government confiscated the goods you had sent to the forbidden port on said neutral ship. It required the ability to profit from what it was to be a Jew in the regency of Algiers: to see the great advantages to be had from the middle space that Jews could occupy. The bitter fighting between Bacris and Durans offers an insight into just what benefit could be gained from occupying the top spot of *muqaddem* in that middle space.

It mattered that the Bacris were Jews because their Jewishness was a prism through which consuls and ministers understood and misunderstood them. Those who interacted with the Bacris had a knowledge of Jews, learned through Church teachings, and experiences and structures in their own lands. They brought this to the regency. The Bacris posed a problem to foreign powers, who used the Bacris' Jewishness—drawing on tropes and prejudice—to explain the challenges and setbacks they faced. For the Bacris themselves, Jewishness was not about being or believing, but doing. Jewishness was enacted through the observance of law and ritual. Their Jewishness was, also, a means to an end, in that it allowed them to access power in the regency, and thus wealth. The mismatch between understandings of Jewishness, as a mode of action, and as a quality that explained the same actions, has been a constant throughout this book.

The Bacris were able to succeed because the nature of rule and power in the regency enabled it. Their situation invites a comparison with the court Jews of the early modern German states. The usefulness of comparison is limited, of course, as the contexts differ so greatly from one another. However, placing both situations side by side allows structures of government to become visible—in particular, the way the needs of elites created space for Jews, not within those structures, but in a legitimate liminal space where they enjoyed extraordinary license, as well as great vulnerability.[4] We see the function of Jews in both cases, of closing a virtuous circle, where they enriched themselves, as well as the elites who enabled them. In both cases, it was Jews who could thrive outside the bounds of standard rules and customs, and it was Jews, above all, who could be trusted close to power, as figures who would not seek that power for themselves. This was not the case, however, in the new ideas of statehood developing across the Mediterranean and the Atlantic.

Trading successfully in the early nineteenth-century Mediterranean also required the ability to overcome the challenge of working across different systems. This was where the Bacris showed their weakness. They did not stop being brokers. Indeed, a century after the Napoleonic Wars ended, Bacri brothers were to rise again, establishing a highly successful business as antique collectors and dealers—brokers—in early twentieth-century Paris. They are most famous, perhaps, for the Bacri-Clark Sickle-Leaf carpet, a sixteenth-century Persian carpet renowned for its beauty. (Its owner William Clark, an industrialist and US senator, had donated

---

4. See Penslar, *Shylock's Children*, 20–21; and for a survey of different court Jews in early modern Europe, Israel, *European Jewry in the Age of Mercantilism*, 101–18.

it to the Corcoran Gallery on his death in 1925. The rug subsequently sold at auction in 2013 for almost 34 million US dollars.) It is fascinating that the Bacri name is still attached to the carpet, cementing their role in the rug's history. They were still acting as traders, but distant, now, from the days of Ottoman absolutism. To be a broker in twentieth-century Paris meant something different: a removal from power and implantation in the world of business. Even in the decades immediately following the French invasion of the regency, members of the Bacri family found that the nature of the space they had occupied so happily in the regency was changing. Jacob did deal with the authorities, and a Busnach acted as go-between in peace negotiations with the bey of Constantine. But after the invasion, Bacris appear in the record, increasingly, as interpreters, now occupying a different sort of space, one that no longer offered access to wealth and influence. When the rule of law replaced personal rule, the scope for brokers changed. Nonetheless, it is interesting— and important—to note, as Joshua Schreier has shown, that Jacob Lasry, another elite Jewish trader operating in Oran, further west along the coast, was able "profoundly" to shape that port city in the early years of French colonial rule.[5] This reinforces the point regarding brokers, or trading Jews, that these are histories that beg a differentiated analysis, rather than over-generalization.

The Bacris' failures should take nothing away from their great success, however fleeting. They took full advantage of their context, and they had the wherewithal to extend their reach, spreading out around the Mediterranean. So good were they at involving themselves with the great and the mighty that for a few decades they became, arguably, the best-known Jews in the Mediterranean. And here is their greatest triumph, from the perspective of the historian, and the question at the core of this book: What happens when we let their story interact with the histories of the great and the good surrounding it? What becomes visible?

When we follow the Bacris' interactions with would-be imperial powers and their representatives, we gain fresh perspectives on a series of established narratives. For the history of Jewish trading networks, we find that their activity did not screech to a halt in the

5. Schreier, *The Merchants of Oran*, 155.

mid-eighteenth century, but rather, extended into the nineteenth century and beyond. Indeed, given the extraordinary agility and enterprise of those first refugees from the Spanish Inquisition, we ought to give their descendants more credit. The scope of Jewish activity across the Ottoman Empire, in particular, opens up a world of meaningful interactions. Jews did not just engage in trade. Jews in the Ottoman Empire who worked as intermediaries often became translators or financial agents for one or another power. They facilitated diplomacy. Here, again, is where the Bacris went further than their coreligionists had done. They were unique in this sense because they offered their services broadly.

The Bacris might have presented a constant irritation for the three significant powers who feature in this book, but in their activities, they bring them together. Through the Bacris, we find Britain firmly in the Mediterranean, competing with France for trade, ascendancy, and dignity. We know, of course, that it was France that ended up colonizing the regency, but in the first decades of the nineteenth century, the British did not, and Algiers was a key port in an important sea. Nor, of course, did the French themselves know. French diplomatic interactions with the Bacris allow us to forget, to circumvent a teleology whereby Ottoman Algiers is a regime destined to end. Instead, we see a relationship of would-be imperial influence. Through US diplomatic interactions with the Bacris, we are able to give shape to a young, self-conscious, and uncertain United States of America, seeking to make its way as a trading nation on the world's seas, and learning the "perils and responsibilities" of their newfound liberty.[6]

In bringing together these three powers in contest, helplessness, and irritation, the Bacris become a focal point external to the national paradigms and perspectives that have traditionally bound the histories of imperial contest and international relations. This allows us, in particular, to bring together the histories of French and British imperialism, almost always tangled together, yet almost always told in a way that teases them apart. The Bacris cared nothing for national pride or belonging. The way they tried to argue for being French when it suited their needs tells us just how instrumental was their

6. Peskin, *America*, 298.

attitude toward the idea of citizenship. The Bacris allow us, then, to go beyond the national, to write a history that is truly entangled. This was their world: the shifting imperial and local worlds of the Western Mediterranean, and the chaos of that sea amidst the Revolutionary and Napoleonic Wars. Here is where they lived, operated, and prospered. National histories cannot contain them.

The relations between consuls and the extended Bacri family allow us to explore how the imperatives of war, imperialism, and international relations played out, and were adapted and reshaped, far from the metropole. We access this history when our vantage point is the southern shore of the Mediterranean looking north, where this book began. The prevailing belief among all diplomatic and many government staff that the Bacris were inordinately powerful is key. In Algiers, French, British, and American consuls were convinced that the Bacris always worked to favor their competitor, to their own disadvantage. It shaped French, British, American, and even Spanish perceptions of what they could achieve in the regency, and against one another. Diplomatic and governmental perceptions of what could and could not be accomplished in the regency—how they saw roadblocks in the way—tells us what the different powers sought to achieve—for themselves, and also against one another. The Bacris show us the representatives of nascent nations far from home, coming to know themselves as global national powers through interactions with liminal figures, little—but deeply significant—people on the ground. Kings, in their time, of Algiers.

REFERENCES

Archival Sources

DENMARK

Departementet for de Udenlandske Anliggender, Algier: Sager vedrørende baron
Rehbinders embedsførelse som dansk konsul i Algier, 2867, Rigsarkivet,
Copenhagen

FRANCE

Archives du ministère des affaires étrangères, la Courneuve
Archives nationales, Pierrefitte
Archives départementales des Bouches-du-Rhône, Marseille
Archives nationales d'outre-mer, Aix-en-Provence
Bibliothèque nationale de France, Paris

ITALY

Archivio di Stato di Firenze, Florence
Archivio della Comunità Ebraica di Livorno, Livorno
Archivio di Stato di Livorno, Livorno

SPAIN

Archivo General de la Administración, Alcalá de Henares
Archivo Histórico Nacional, Madrid

UNITED KINGDOM

The National Archives, Kew
The British Library, London
The London Municipal Archives, London
House of Lords debate, volume 17
House of Commons debate, volume 17

UNITED STATES OF AMERICA

National Archives and Records Administration (RG Series), College Park, Maryland

State Department Consular Despatches, Algiers Series, Atlanta, Georgia (M23)

Tobias Lear Papers (1791–1817), Clements Library, University of Michigan, Manuscripts Division

Journal du commerce, de politique et de littérature

Journal du palais

Le Moniteur universel

The Times

Printed Sources

Abun-Nasr, Jamil M. *A History of the Maghrib in the Islamic Period*. Cambridge: Cambridge University Press, 1987.

Adams, Michael. *Napoleon and Russia*. New York: Continuum, 2006.

Ageron, Charles-Robert. *Modern Algeria: History from 1830 to the Present*. Translated and edited by Michael Brett. London: Hurst & Co., 1991.

Aghib Levi d'Ancona, Flora. "The Sephardi Community of Leghorn (Livorno)." In *The Sephardi Heritage: Essays on the Historical and Cultural Contribution of the Jews of Spain and Portugal*, edited by Richard D. Barnett and W.M. Schwab, 180–202. Vol. 2. London: Vallentine-Mitchell, 1989.

Albert, Phyllis. *The Jewish Oath in Nineteenth-Century France*. Spiegel Lectures in European Jewish History. Tel Aviv University, 1982.

Alderman, Geoffrey. *Modern British Jewry*. Oxford: Clarendon Press, 1992.

Allardyce, Alexander, *Memoir of the Honourable George Keith Elphinstone, K.B.: Viscount Keith, Admiral of the Red*. Edinburgh: Blackwood and Sons, 1882.

Allen, Gardner W. *Our Navy and the Barbary Corsairs*. Boston: Houghton Mifflin, 1905.

Allison, Robert J. *The Crescent Obscured: The United States and the Muslim World, 1776–1815*. Oxford: Oxford University Press, 1995.

Allison, Robert J., ed. *Narratives of Barbary Captivity: Recollections of James Leander Cathcart, Jonathan Cowdery, and William Ray*. Chicago: The Lakeside Press, 2007.

Allison, Robert J. *Stephen Decatur: American Naval Hero, 1779–1820*. Boston: University of Massachusetts Press, 2005.

Altès, F. *Traité comparative des monnaies, poids et mesures, changes, banques et fonds publics entre la France, l'Espagne et l'Angleterre*. Marseille: Barile et Boulouch, 1832.

American State Papers: Documents, Legislative and Executive, of the Congress of the United States. Washington: Gales and Seaton, 1833. Vol. 1.

Anderson, Matthew Smith "Great Britain and the Barbary States in the Eighteenth Century." *Bulletin of the Institute of Historical Research* 29 (1956): 87–107.

Aoki Santarosa, Veronica. "Financing Long-Distance Trade: The Joint Liability Rule and Bills of Exchange in Eighteenth-Century France." *Journal of Economic History* 75, no. 3 (September 2015): 690–718.

Aprile, Sylvie. *La Révolution inachevée: 1815–1870*. Paris: Belin, 2010.

Au conseil des prises: Mémoire pour les capitaine et armateur du corsaire français le Brutus*: Contre les capitaine et propriétaires de la cargaison du navire soi-disant le* Rachel. [Paris]: De l'Imprimerie de Laurens ainé, rue d'Argenteuil, [1801?].

Ayoun, Richard. "Les Juifs livournais en Afrique du Nord." *Rassegna mensile di Israel* 50, no. 9/12 (1984): 650–706.

Ayoun, Richard, and Bernard Cohen. *Les Juifs d'Algérie: Deux mille ans d'histoire*. Paris: J. C. Lattès, 1982.

Bacri, Nathan. "A Son Excellence, Monsieur le Ministre des Finances." Marseille, n.d.

Baghdiantz McCabe, Ina. *A History of Global Consumption, 1500–1800*. New York: Routledge, 2015.

Bamford, Paul W. "The Barbary Pirates: Victims and the Scourge of Christendom." *The James Ford Bell Lectures, Number 10*. Minneapolis, MN: University of Minnesota, 1972.

Barker, Nancy Nichols. *The French Experience in Mexico, 1821–1861: A History of Constant Misunderstanding*. Chapel Hill, NC: University of North Carolina Press, 1979.

Barnard, Sophia. *Travels in Algeirs* [sic], *Spain &c. &c. With a Faithful and Interesting Account of the Algerines, Amongst whom the Authoress Resided Some Time, and from her Access to whom she had Many Opportunities of Discovering and Appreciating their Customs, Ceremonies, Pursuits, Costume, &c. Which no Historian has Before Detailed, with a Minuteness due to that Extraordinary and Interesting Race of People: Also a Copious Description of Her Residence in Andalusia, Abounding in Remarkable Events, Anecdotes of Persons, Places, Produce, &c*. London: Goyder, [1820].

Barnby, Henry. *The Prisoners of Algiers: An Account of the Forgotten American-Algerian War, 1785–1797*. London: Oxford University Press, 1966.

Bartillat, Marquis de. *Relation de la campagne d'Afrique en 1830*. 2nd ed. Paris, 1832.

Bartlett, C. J. *Great Britain and Sea Power, 1815–1853*. Oxford: Clarendon Press, 1963.

Bartolomei, Arnaud. "Introduction." In *De l'utilité commerciale des consuls: L'Institution consulaire et les marchands dans le monde méditerranéen (XVII-XX siècle)*, edited by Arnaud Bartolomei et al. Rome and Madrid: Publications de l'École française de Rome, 2017.

Bartolomei, Arnaud et al., eds. *De l'utilité commerciale des consuls: L'Institution consulaire et les marchands dans le monde méditerranéen (XVII-XX siècle)*. Rome and Madrid: Publications de l'École française de Rome, 2017. http://books.openedition.org/efr/3253

Bayly, Christopher. *Imperial Meridian: The British Empire and the World, 1780–1830*. London: Longman, 1989.

Bell, David A. *The First Total War: Napoleon's Europe and the Birth of Modern Warfare*. London: Bloomsbury Publishing, 2008.

Benbassa, Esther, and Aron Rodrigue. *Sephardi Jewry: A History of the Judeo-Spanish Community, 14th–20th Centuries.* Berkeley: University of California Press, 2000.

Benichou Gottreich, Emily, and Daniel J. Schroeter, eds. *Jewish Culture and Society in North Africa.* Bloomington: Indiana University Press, 2011.

Bénot, Yves, and Marcel Dorigny, ed. *Rétablissement de l'esclavage dans les colonies françaises, 1802: Ruptures et continuités de la politique coloniale française, 1800–1830. Aux origines d'Haïti: Actes du colloque international tenu à l'Université de Paris VIII les 20, 21 et 22 juin 2002.* Paris: Maisonneuve et Larose, 2003.

Bertier de Sauvigny, Guillaume de. *The Bourbon Restoration.* Translated by Lynn M. Case. Philadelphia: University of Pennsylvania Press, 1966.

Bew, John. *Castlereagh: A Life.* Oxford: Oxford University Press, 2012.

Biale, David. *Cultures of the Jews: A New History.* 3 Vols. New York: Schocken, 2002.

Biale, David. *Power and Powerlessness in Jewish History.* New York: Schocken, 1986.

Black, Jeremy. *British Diplomats and Diplomacy, 1688–1800.* Exeter: University of Exeter Press, 2001.

Bloch, Isaac. *Inscriptions tumulaires des anciens cimetières israélites d'Alger, recueillies, traduites, commentées et accompagnées de notices biographes, par Isaac Bloch, Grand Rabbin d'Alger.* Paris: Durlacher, 1888.

Bloch, Isaac. *Les Israélites d'Oran de 1792–1830, d'après des documents inédits.* Paris: Durlacher, 1886.

Borutta, Manuel, and Sakis Gekas. "A Colonial Sea: The Mediterranean, 1798–1956." *European Review of History: Revue européenne d'histoire* 19, no. 1 (2012): 1–13.

Braude, Benjamin. "The Myth of the Sephardi Economic Superman." In *Trading Cultures: The Worlds of Western Merchants: Essays on Authority, Objectivity, and Evidence.* Edited by Jeremy Adelman and Stephen Aron. Belgium: Brepols, 2001.

Bregoli, Francesca. *Mediterranean Enlightenment: Livornese Jews, Tuscan Culture, and Eighteenth-Century Reform.* Stanford, CA: Stanford University Press, 2014.

Brett, Edwin J. *Brett's Illustrated Naval History of Great Britain, From the Earliest Period to The Present Time; A Reliable Record of the Maritime Rise and Progress of England.* London: Publishing Office, 1871.

Bridge, Roy. "Allied Diplomacy in Peacetime: The Failure of the Congress 'System,' 1815–23." In *Europe's Balance of Power, 1815–1848,* edited by Alan Sked, 34–53. London: Macmillan, 1979.

Briggs, Asa. *The Age of Improvement, 1783–1867.* London: Longman, 1959.

Brilli, Catia. "Coping with Iberian Monopolies: Genoese Trade Networks and Formal Institutions in Spain and Portugal during the Second Half of the Eighteenth Century." *European Review of History: Revue européenne d'histoire* 23, no. 3 (2016): 456–85.

Broughton, Elizabeth. *Six Years Residence in Algiers.* London: Saunders and Otley, 1839.

Boyd, Julian P. et al, eds. *The Papers of Thomas Jefferson.* 40 volumes. Princeton, NJ: Princeton University Press, 1950–.

Buel, Richard, Jr. *Joel Barlow: American Citizen in a Revolutionary World.* Baltimore, MD: Johns Hopkins University Press, 2011.

Byrne, Michael. *Britain and the European Powers, 1815–1865*. London: Hodder and Stoughton, 1998.

Calafat, Guillaume. "L'Indice de la franchise: Politique économique, concurrence des ports francs et condition des juifs en Méditerranée à l'époque moderne." *Revue historique* 2, no. 686 (2018): 275–320.

Calafat, Guillaume. "Les Juridictions du consul: Une Institution au service des marchands et du commerce? Introduction." In *De l'utilité commerciale des consuls: L'institution consulaire et les marchands dans le monde méditerranéen (XVIIe-XXe) siècle*, edited by Arnaud Bartolomei, Guillaume Calafat, Mathieu Grenet, et al. Rome and Madrid: Publications de l'Ecole française de Rome, 2017.

Camps, Miquel Àngel Casasnovas. "Minorca: The First United States Naval Base in the Mediterranean and the American Consulate at Port Mahon." In *Rough Waters: American Involvement with the Mediterranean in the Eighteenth and Nineteenth Centuries*, edited by Silvia Marzagalli, James R. Sofka, and John J. McCusker, 135–60. St. John's, Newfoundland: International Maritime Economic History Association, 2010.

Cannadine, David, ed. *Empire, the Sea and Global History: Britain's Maritime World, c. 1760–c. 1840*. London: Palgrave, 2007.

Cantor, Milton. "Joel Barlow's Mission to Algiers." *The Historian* 25, no. 2 (February 1963): 172–94.

Caron, François. *An Economic History of Modern France*. Translated by Barbara Bray. New York: Columbia University Press, 1979.

Carrière, Charles. *Négociants marseillais au XVIIIe siècle: Contribution à l'étude des économies maritimes*. 2 vols. Marseille: Institut historique de Provence, 1973.

Carrière, Charles et al. *Banque et capitalisme commercial: La Lettre de change au XVIIIe siècle*. Marseille: Institut historique de Provence, 1976.

Chamberlain, Muriel E. *Lord Aberdeen: A Political Biography*. London: Longman, 1983.

Chia Yin Hsu, Thomas Luckett, and Erika Vause, eds. *The Cultural History of Money and Credit: A Global Perspective*. Lanham, MD: Lexington Books, 2016.

Clancy-Smith, Julia. *Mediterraneans: North Africa and Europe in an Age of Migration, c. 1800–1900*. Berkeley: University of California Press, 2011.

Cogliano, Francis D. *Emperor of Liberty: Thomas Jefferson's Foreign Policy*. New Haven, CT: Yale University Press, 2014.

Coller, Ian. *Arab France: Islam and the Making of Modern Europe, 1798–1831*. Berkeley: University of California Press, 2010.

Colley, Linda. *Britons: Forging the Nation 1707–1837*. New Haven, CT: Yale University Press, 1992.

Colley, Linda. *Captives: Britain, Empire, and the World 1600–1850*. New York: Pantheon Press, 2002.

Cooper, Frederick, and Ann Laura Stoler, eds. *Tensions of Empire: Colonial Cultures in a Bourgeois World*. Berkeley: University of California Press, 1997.

Correspondance de Napoléon Ier, publiée par ordre de l'empereur Napoléon III. Vol. 6, *1799–1801*. Paris: Bibliothèque des introuvables, 2006.

Correspondance inédite, officielle et confidentielle, de Napoléon Bonaparte avec les cours étrangères, les princes, les ministres et les généraux français et étrangers, en Italie, en Allemagne et en Egypte. Vol. 7. Paris: Panckoucke, 1820.

Crouzet, François. "Angleterre et France au XVIIIe siècle: Essai d'analyse comparée de deux croissances économiques." *Annales: Economies, Sociétés, Civilisations* 21, no. 2 (1966): 254–91.

Crouzet, François. *Britain, France, and International Commerce: From Louis XIV to Victoria.* Aldershot, UK: Ashgate Variorum, 1996.

Crouzet, François. "Wars, Blockade, and Economic Change in Europe, 1792–1815." *Journal of Economic History* 24, no. 4 (December 1964): 567–88.

Curtis, James. *A Journal of Travels in Barbary in the Year 1801 with Observations on the Gum Trade of Senegal.* London: D. N. Shury, 1803.

Daly, Gavin. "Anglo-French Sieges, the Laws of War, and the Limits of Enmity in the Peninsular War, 1808–1814." *English Historical Review* 135, no. 574 (2020): 572–604.

Davis, Robert C. *Christian Slaves, Muslim Masters: White Slavery in the Mediterranean, the Barbary Coast, and Italy, 1500–1800.* New York: Palgrave MacMillan, 2003.

De Goey, Ferry. *Consuls and the Institutions of Global Capitalism, 1783–1914.* New York: Routledge, 2016.

De Goey, Ferry. "Les Consuls et les relations internationales au XIXe siècle." Translated by Silvia Marzagalli. In "Les Consuls dans tous leurs états: Essais et bibliographie (avant 1914)." Special issue, *Cahiers de la Méditerranée* 93 (2016): 61–75.

De Lange, Erik. "The Congress System and the French Invasion of Algiers, 1827–1830." *The Historical Journal* 64, no. 4 (2021): 940–62.

Dehérain, Henri. "La mission du commissaire-général Dubois-Thainville auprès du dey d'Alger." *Revue de l'histoire des colonies françaises* 14 (1926): 75–100.

Denzel, Markus A. *Handbook of World Exchange Rates, 1590–1914.* Farnham, UK: Ashgate, 2010.

Devoulx, Albert. *Les Archives du consulat général de France à Alger: Recueil de documents inédits concernant soit les relations politiques de la France soit les rapports commerciaux de Marseille avec l'ancienne régence d'Alger.* Alger: Bastide, 1865.

Dickinson, H. T., ed. *Britain and the French Revolution, 1789–1815.* London: Macmillan, 1989.

Dietz, Peter. *The British in the Mediterranean.* London: Brassey's, 1994.

Duffy, Michael. "British Policy in the War against Revolutionary France." In *Britain and Revolutionary France: Conflict, Subversion and Propaganda,* edited by Colin Jones. Exeter: University of Exeter Press, 1983.

Dureau de la Malle, Adolphe, ed. *Peysonnel et Desfontaines: Voyages dans les régences de Tunis et d'Alger.* Vol. 1. Paris: Gide, 1838.

Dzanic, Dzavid. "France's Informal Empire in the Mediterranean, 1815–1830." *The Historical Journal* 65, no. 3 (2022): 663–64.

Eisenbeth, Maurice. "Les Juifs en Algérie et en Tunisie à l'époque turque (1516–1830)." *Revue Africaine* 46 (1952): 114–187, 343–384.

Eldem, Edhem. *French Trade in Istanbul in the Eighteenth Century.* Leiden: Brill, 1999.

ElGaddari, Sara. "His Majesty's Agents: The British Consul at Tripoli, 1795–1832." *Journal of Imperial and Commonwealth History* 43, no. 5 (2015): 770–86.

Elphinstone, George Keith, First Viscount Keith. *The Keith Papers: Selected from the Letters and Papers of Admiral Viscount Keith*. Edited by Christopher Lloyd. 3 vols. London: Navy Records Society, 1927–1955.

Endelman, Todd. *Radical Assimilation in English Jewish History, 1656–1945*. Bloomington, IN: Indiana University Press, 1990.

Enthoven, Victor. "'From the Halls of Montesuma, to the Shores of Tripoli': Antoine Zuchet and the First Barbary War, 1801–1805." In *Rough Waters: American Involvement with the Mediterranean in the Eighteenth and Nineteenth Centuries*, edited by Silvia Marzagalli, James R. Sofka, and John J. McCusker, 117–34. St. John's, Newfoundland: International Maritime Economic History Association, 2010.

Esquer, Gabriel. *Collection de documents inédits sur l'histoire de l'Algérie après 1830, III: Reconnaissance des villes, forts et batteries d'Alger par le Chef de Bataillon Boutin (1808), suivie des Mémoires sur Alger par les consuls de Kercy (1791) et Dubois-Thainville (1809)*. Paris: Honoré Champion, 1927.

Esquer, Gabriel. *Les Commencements d'un empire: La Prise d'Alger (1830)*. Paris: Larose, 1929.

Fenton, Paul. "Mardochée Najjar: Un Juif tunisien à Paris au début du XIXe siècle et son rôle de correspondant de savants européens." In *Entre Orient et Occident. Juifs et Musulmans en Tunisie*, edited by Denis Cohen-Tannoudji. Paris: Eclat, 2007.

Fenton, Paul, and David Littman. *Exile in the Maghreb: Jews Under Islam, Sources and Documents, 997–1912*. Madison, NJ: Fairleigh Dickinson University Press, 2015.

Field, James A. *America and the Mediterranean World, 1776–1882*. Princeton, NJ: Princeton University Press, 1969.

Filippini, Jean Pierre. "Una famiglia ebrea di Livorno tra le ambizioni mercantili e le vicissitudini del mondo mediterraneo: i Coen Bacri." *Richerche Storiche* 2 (1982): 288–344.

Filippini, Jean Pierre. "Juifs émigrés et immigrés dans le port de Livourne pendant la période napoléonienne." *East and Maghreb* 4 (1983): 31–91.

Filippini, Jean Pierre. "Les Séfarades en méditerranée occidentale." *Histoire, économie et société* 12, no. 3 (1993): 345–49.

Finn, Margot. *The Character of Credit: Personal Debt in English Culture, 1740–1914*. Cambridge: Cambridge University Press, 2003.

Fisher, Godfrey. *Barbary Legend: War, Trade and Piracy in North Africa, 1415–1820*. Oxford: Clarendon Press, 1957.

Fleury, Georges. *Comment l'Algérie devint française, 1830–1848*. Paris: Perrin, 2004.

Fukasawa, Katsumi. *Toileries et commerce du Levant d'Alep à Marseille*. Paris: CNRS, 1987.

Fusaro, Maria. "Cooperating Mercantile Networks in the Early Modern Mediterranean." *Economic History Review* 65, no. 2 (2012): 701–18.

Gale, Caitlin M. "Barbary's Slow Death: European Attempts to Eradicate North African Piracy in the Early Nineteenth Century." *Journal for Maritime Research* 18, no. 2 (2016): 139–54.

Gale, Caitlin M. "Beyond Corsairs: The British-Barbary Relationship during the French Revolutionary and Napoleonic Wars." PhD diss., University of Oxford, 2016.

Gash, Norman. *Aristocracy and People: Britain 1815–1865*. London: Edward Arnold, 1979.

Gautier, Antoine. "Les Drogmans des consulats." In *La Fonction consulaire à l'époque moderne: L'Affirmation d'une institution économique et politique (1500–1800)*, edited by Jörg Ulbert and Gérard Le Bouëdec, 85–103. Rennes, France: Presses universitaires de Rennes, 2006.

Girard, Albert. "La Saisie des biens des Français en Espagne en 1625." *Revue d'histoire économique et sociale* 19, no. 3 (1931): 297–315.

Goldsborough, Charles W. *The United States Naval Chronicle*. Vol. 1. Washington, DC: Wilson, 1824.

Gregory, Desmond. *Minorca, the Illusory Prize: A History of the British Occupations of Minorca between 1708 and 1802*. Cranbury, NJ: Associated University Presses, 1990.

Grenet, Mathieu. "Consuls et 'nations' étrangères: Etat des lieux et perspectives de recherche." *Cahiers de la Méditerranée* 93 (2016): 25–34.

Guiral, Pierre, and Paul Amargier. *Histoire de Marseille*. Paris: Mazarine, 1983.

Haddey, J. M. *Le Livre d'or des israélites algériens: Recueil de renseignements inédits et authentiques sur les principaux négociants juifs d'Alger pendant la période turque*. Alger: Impr. A. Bouyer, 1871.

Hancock, David. *Citizens of the World: London Merchants and the Integration of the British Atlantic Community, 1735–1785*. Cambridge: Cambridge University Press, 1995.

Harding, Nicholas B. "North African Piracy, the Hanoverian Carrying Trade, and the British State, 1728–1828." *The Historical Journal* 43, no. 1 (2000): 25–47.

Haynes, Christine. *Our Friends the Enemies: The Occupation of France after Napoleon*. Cambridge, MA: Harvard University Press, 2018.

Heinsen-Roach, Erica. *Consuls and Captives: Dutch-North African Diplomacy in the Early Modern Mediterranean*. Rochester, NY: University of Rochester Press, 2019.

Hildesheimer, Françoise. "Grandeur et décadence de la maison Bacri de Marseille." *Revue des Etudes juives* 86, nos. 3–4 (July–December 1977): 389–414.

Hilton, Boyd. *A Mad, Bad, and Dangerous People? England 1783–1846*. Oxford: Oxford University Press, 2006.

Hirschberg, H. Z. *A History of the Jews in North Africa*. Vol. 2, *From the Ottoman Conquests to the Present Time*. Edited by Eliezer Bashan and Robert Attal. Leiden: Brill, 1981.

Hoffman, Philip T., Gilles Postel-Vinay, and Jean-Laurent Rosenthal. *Priceless Markets: The Political Economy of Credit in Paris, 1660–1870*. Chicago: University of Chicago Press, 2000.

Hoffman, Philip T., Gilles Postel-Vinay, and Jean-Laurent Rosenthal. "Private Credit Markets in Paris, 1690–1840." *Journal of Economic History* 52, no. 2 (June 1992): 293–306.

Hopkins, Antony G. "Back to the Future: From National History to Imperial History." *Past & Present* 164 (1999): 198–243.

Horden, Peregrine, and Nicholas Purcell. *The Corrupting Sea: A Study of Mediterranean History.* Oxford: Blackwell, 2000.

Horn, David Bayne. *The British Diplomatic Service, 1689–1789.* Oxford: Clarendon Press, 1961.

Howe, Anthony. "Restoring Free Trade: The British Experience, 1776–1873." In *The Political Economy of British Historical Experience, 1688–1914,* edited by Donald Winch and Patrick K. O'Brien, 193–213. Oxford: Oxford University press, 2002.

Hunter, F. R. "Rethinking Europe's Conquest of North Africa and the Middle East: The Opening of the Maghreb, 1660–1814." *Journal of North African Studies* 4, no. 4 (1999): 1–26.

Islamoğlu-Inan, Hurí, ed. *The Ottoman Empire and the World Economy.* Cambridge: Cambridge University Press, 1987.

Israel, Jonathan. *Diasporas within a Diaspora: Jews, Crypto-Jews, and the World of Maritime Empires (1540–1740).* Leiden: Brill, 2002.

Israel, Jonathan. *European Jewry in the Age of Mercantilism, 1550–1750.* London: Vallentine Mitchell, 1998.

Jardin, André, and André-Jean Tudesq. *Restoration and Reaction, 1815–1848.* Translated by Elborg Forster. Cambridge: Cambridge University Press, 1983.

Jarrett, Mark. *The Congress of Vienna and its Legacy. War and Great Power Diplomacy after Napoleon.* London: I. B. Tauris, 2013.

Jasanoff, Maya. *Edge of Empire: Lives, Culture and Conquest in the East, 1750–1850.* New York: Vintage, 2005.

Jefferson, Thomas. "Report of the Secretary of State Relative to the Mediterranean Trade." National Archives online, December 28, 1790, https://founders.archives.gov/documents/Jefferson/01-18-02-0139-0004.

Jones, Colin, ed. *Britain and Revolutionary France: Conflict, Subversion and Propaganda.* Exeter: Western European Studies Centre, University of Exeter, 1983.

"Jugement dont est appel, rendu par le tribunal de première instance de Marseille, le 25 mai 1832, entre les héritiers de feu M. Salomon-Coën Bacri, le Sieur Jacob-Coën Bacri, et le Sieur Michel Busnach." Paris: Baudillon, n.d. [Bibliothèque nationale de France, May 25, 1832.]

Julien, André. *Histoire d'Algérie contemporaine: La conquête et les débuts de la colonisation.* 2 vols. Paris, 1964.

Jurien de la Gravière, Pierre Roch. *Souvenirs d'un Amiral, par le contre-amiral Jurien de la Gravière.* Paris, 1860.

Kagan, Richard L., and Philip D. Morgan. *Atlantic Diasporas: Jews, Conversos, and Crypto- Jews in the Age of Mercantilism, 1500–1800.* Baltimore, MD: Johns Hopkins University Press, 2009.

Kalman, Julie. *Orientalizing the Jew: Religion, Culture, and Imperialism in Nineteenth-Century France.* Bloomington: Indiana University Press, 2017.

Kämpe, Fredrik. "Competition and Cooperation: Swedish Consuls in North Africa and Sweden's Position in the World, 1791–1802." In *Traces of Transnational Relations in the Eighteenth Century,* edited by Tim Berndtsson et al., 37–51. Uppsala, Sweden: Uppsala University Press, 2015.

Kaplan, Yosef. *An Alternative Path to Modernity: The Sephardi Diaspora in Western Europe*. Leiden: Brill, 2000.

Kardasis, Vassilis. *The Greeks in Southern Russia, 1775–1861*. Lanham, MD: Lexington Books, 2001.

Karp, Jonathan. *The Politics of Jewish Commerce: Economic Thought and Emancipation in Europe, 1638–1848*. New York: Cambridge University Press, 2008.

Kennedy, Charles Stuart. *The American Consul: A History of the United States Consular Service, 1776–1924*. 2d ed. Washington, DC: New Academia Publishing, 2015.

Khoja, Sidy Hamdan ben Othman. *Aperçu historique et statistique sur la régence d'Alger*. Paris, 1833.

Klein, Henri. "Souverains, souveraines, présidents," *Feuillets d'El-Djezaïr* 10 (1921): 4–30.

Kortepeter, Carl Max. "Jew and Turk in Algiers in 1800." In *The Jews of the Ottoman Empire*, edited by Avigdor Levy, 327–352. Princeton: Darwin, 1994.

Kortepeter, Carl Max. "The United States Encounters the Middle East: The North African Emirates and the U.S. Navy (1783–1830)," *The Ottoman Turks: Nomad Kingdom to World Empire*. Piscataway, NJ: Gorgias Press, 2010.

Kroen, Sheryl. *Politics and Theater: The Crisis of Legitimacy in Restoration France, 1815–1830*. Berkeley: University of California Press, 2000.

Laborde, Alexandre de. *Au Roi et aux chambres, sur les véritables causes de la rupture avec Alger et sur l'expédition qui se prépare*. Paris, 1830.

Laget, Francis. "Le Serment 'sur le coude' more judaïco." Etudes et recherches en Baronnies, Actes des Rencontres du Garde-Notes Baronniard, La Motte-Chalançon, October 23, 1993, 117–20.

Landes, David S. *The Unbound Prometheus: Technological Change and Industrial Development in Western Europe from 1750 to the Present*. Cambridge: Cambridge University Press, 1972 [1969].

Lee, Hilda. "The Supervising of the Barbary Consulates, 1768–1836." *Bulletin of the Institute of Historical Research* 23 (1950): 191–99.

Lehmann, Matthias. "A Livornese 'Port Jew' and the Sephardim of the Ottoman Empire." *Jewish Social Studies* 11, no. 2 (2005): 51–76.

Levy, Avigdor, ed. *The Jews of the Ottoman Empire*. Princeton: Darwin Press, 1994.

Lévy, Lionel. *La Nation juive portugaise: Livourne, Amsterdam, Tunis 1591–1951*. Paris: Harmattan, 1999.

Lévy-Leboyer, Maurice. "La Croissance économique en France au XIXe siècle: Résultats préliminaires." *Annales. Histoire, Sciences Sociales* 23, no. 4 (July–August 1968): 788–807.

Lewis, Bernard. "Corsairs in Iceland." *Revue de l'Occident musulman et de la Méditerranée* 16 (1973): 139–44.

Ligou, Daniel. *Jeanbon Saint-André, membre du Grand Comité de salut public (1749–1813)*. Paris: Messidor, 1989.

Lloyd, Christopher. *English Corsairs on the Barbary Coast*. London: Collins, 1981.

Lopez, Olivier. "Travailler chez l'autre, vivre avec? En Barbarie avec les employés de la compagnie royale d'Afrique au XVIIIe siècle." *Revue d'histoire maritime* 21 (2015): 307–18.

Lord, Walter Frewen. *England and France in the Mediterranean, 1660–1830*. London: S. Low, Marston and Co., 1901.

Löwenheim, Oded. "'Do Ourselves Credit and Render a Lasting Service to Mankind': British Moral Prestige, Humanitarian Intervention, and the Barbary Pirates." *International Studies Quarterly* 47 (2003): 23–48.

Lyons, Martyn. *Napoleon Bonaparte and the Legacy of the French Revolution*. London: Macmillan, 1994.

Mackesy, Piers. "Strategic Problems of the British War Effort." In *Britain and the French Revolution, 1789–1815*, edited by H. T. Dickinson, 147–64. London: Macmillan, 1989.

Mackesy, Piers. *The War in the Mediterranean, 1803–1810*. Cambridge: Cambridge University Press, 1957.

Malkin, Irad, ed. *La France et la Méditerranée: Vingt-sept siècles d'interdépendance*. Leiden: Brill, 1990.

Mantran, Robert. "Le Statut de l'Algérie, de la Tunisie et de la Tripolitaine dans l'Empire ottoman." *L'Empire ottoman du XVIe au XVIIIe siècle: Administration, économie, société*, 3–14. London: Variorum Reprints, 1984.

Marjolin, Robert. "Troubles provoqués en France par la disette de 1816–1817." *Revue d'histoire moderne et contemporaine* 8, no. 10 (1933): 423–60.

Martin, Claude. *Les Israélites algériens de 1830 à 1902*. Paris: Herakles, 1936.

Marzagalli, Silvia. "American Shipping and Trade in Warfare, or the Benefits of European Conflicts for Neutral Merchants: The Experience of the Revolutionary and Napoleonic wars, 1793–1815." *Kyoto Sangyo University Economic Review* 1 (March 2014). http://ksurep.kyoto-su.ac.jp/dspace/bitstream/10965/1043/1/KSUER_1_1.pdf.

Marzagalli, Silvia. "American Shipping into the Mediterranean during the French Wars: A First Approach." In *Rough Waters: American Involvement with the Mediterranean in the Eighteenth and Nineteenth Centuries*, edited by Silvia Marzagalli, James R. Sofka, and John J. McCusker, 43–62. St. John's, Newfoundland: International Maritime Economic History Association, 2010.

Marzagalli, Silvia. "De l'intérêt des périphéries pour les puissances atlantiques: Les Etats-Unis et la navigation en Méditerranée, fin XVIIIe—début XIXe siècle." In *Cinq Continents: La Mémoire et l'héritage de Tibor Wittman: Les Cahiers du Département d'histoire moderne et contemporaine no 2013/2*. Budapest: Université Eötvös Loránd, 2015.

Marzagalli, Silvia. "Les Etats-Unis en Méditerranée: Modalités et enjeux d'une nouvelle présence atlantique dans la mer intérieure." *Revue d'histoire maritime* 13 (2011): 71–100.

Marzagalli, Silvia. "Etudes consulaires, études méditerranéennes: Eclairages croisés pour la compréhension du monde méditerranéen et de l'institution consulaire à l'époque moderne." In "Les Consuls dans tous leurs états: Essais et bibliographie (avant 1914)." Special issue, *Cahiers de la Méditerranée* 93 (2016): 11–23.

Marzagalli, Silvia. "'However Illegal, Extraordinary or Almost Incredible Such Conduct Might Be': Americans and Neutrality Issues in the Mediterranean during the

French Wars." *The International Journal of Maritime History* 28, no. 1 (2016): 118–32.

Marzagalli, Silvia. "Le Négoce maritime et la rupture révolutionnaire: Un Ancien débat revisité." *Annales historiques de la Révolution française* 352 (April/June 2008): 183–207.

Marzagalli, Silvia. "Le Réseau consulaire des Etats-Unis en Méditerranée, 1790–1815: Logiques étatiques, logiques marchandes?" In *De l'utilité commerciale des consuls. L'institution consulaire et les marchands dans le monde méditerranéen (XVII-XX siècle)*, edited by Arnaud Bartolomei et al. Rome and Madrid: Publications de l'École française de Rome, 2017.

Marzagalli, Silvia. "Was Warfare Necessary for the Functioning of Eighteenth-Century Colonial Systems? Some Reflections on the Necessity of Cross-Imperial and Foreign Trade in the French Case." In *Beyond Empires. Global, Self-Organizing, Cross-Imperial Networks 1500-1800*, edited by Cátia Antunes and Amelia Polónia, 253–77. Leiden: Brill, 2016.

Marzagalli, Silvia, James R. Sofka, and John J. McCusker, eds. *Rough Waters: American Involvement with the Mediterranean in the Eighteenth and Nineteenth Centuries.* St. John's, Newfoundland: International Maritime Economic History Association, 2010.

Marzagalli, Silvia, and Leos Müller. "'In Apparent Disagreement with All Law of Nations in the World': Negotiating Neutrality for Shipping and Trade During the French Revolutionary and Napoleonic Wars." *The International Journal of Maritime History* 28, no. 1 (2016): 108–17.

Marzagalli, Silvia, Maria Ghazali, and Christian Windler, eds. *Les Consuls en Méditerranée, agents d'information, XVIe-XXe siècle.* Paris: Classiques Garnier, coll. Les Méditerranées, 2014.

Masson, Paul. *Histoire des établissements et du commerce français dans l'Afrique barbaresque (1560-1793) (Algérie, Tunisie, Tripolitaine, Maroc).* Paris: Hachette, 1903.

McCranie, Kevin D. *Admiral Lord Keith and the Naval War against Napoleon.* Gainesville, FL: University Press of Florida, 2006.

McDougall, James. *A History of Algeria.* Cambridge: Cambridge University Press, 2017.

McPhee, Peter. *The French Revolution, 1789-1799.* Oxford: Oxford University Press, 2001.

Meeks, Joshua. *France, Britain, and the Struggle for the Revolutionary Western Mediterranean.* Cham, Switzerland: Palgrave, 2017.

Melissen, Jan, and Ana Mar Fernandez, eds. *Consular Affairs and Diplomacy.* Leiden: Martinus Nijhoff, 2011.

Meyer, Jean, Jean Tarrade, Annie Rey-Goldziguer, and Jacques Thobie. *Histoire de la France Coloniale.* Vol. 1, *Des origines à 1914.* Paris: Armand Colin, 1991.

Mézin, Anne. *Les Consuls de France au siècle des lumières (1715-1792).* Paris: Imprimerie nationale, 1997.

Middleton, Alex. "French Algeria in British Imperial Thought, 1830–70." *Journal of Colonialism and Colonial History* 16, no. 1 (Spring 2015): n.p.

Miller, Judith. *Mastering the Market: The State and the Grain Trade in Northern France, 1700-1860.* Cambridge: Cambridge University Press, 1999.

Ministère de la guerre. *Tableau de la situation des établissements français dans l'Algérie (Années 1838-1855)*. Paris: Imprimerie royale, n.d.

Moalla, Asma. *The Regency of Tunis and the Ottoman Porte, 1777-1814: Army and Government of a North African Ottoman Eyelet at the End of the Eighteenth Century*. London: Routledge Curzon, 2004.

Monk, Winston Francis. *Britain in the Western Mediterranean*. London: Hutchinson House, 1953.

Morgan, Iwan. "French Policy in Spanish America: 1830-48." *Journal of Latin American Studies* 10, no. 2 (1978): 309-28.

Morgan, Kenneth. "Mercantilism and the British Empire, 1688-1815." In *The Political Economy of British Historical Experience, 1688-1914*, edited by Donald Winch and Patrick K. O'Brien, 165-91. Oxford: Oxford University press, 2002.

Mori, Jennifer. *Britain in the Age of the French Revolution, 1785-1820*. Harlow: Pearson, 2000.

Mori, Jennifer. *The Culture of Diplomacy: Britain in Europe, c. 1750-1830*. Manchester: Manchester University Press, 2010.

Mösslang, Markus, and Torsten Riotte, eds. *The Diplomat's World: A Cultural History of Diplomacy, 1815-1914*. Oxford: Oxford University Press, 2008.

Mösslang, Markus, and Torsten Riotte. "Introduction: The Diplomats' World." In *The Diplomat's World: A Cultural History of Diplomacy, 1815-1914*, edited by Markus D Mösslang and Torsten Riotte, 1-20. Oxford: Oxford University Press, 2008.

Muldrew, Craig. *The Economy of Obligation: The Culture of Credit and Social Relations in Early Modern England*. London: Macmillan Press, 1998.

Müller, Leos. *Consuls, Corsairs, and Commerce: The Swedish Consular Service and Long-Distance Shipping, 1720-1815*. Uppsala, Sweden: Uppsala University Press, 2004.

Naval Documents Related to the United States Wars with the Barbary Powers. 6 vols. Published under direction of the Secretary of the Navy. Prepared by the Office of Naval Records and Library, Navy Department, under the supervision of Captain Dudley W. Knox, U. S. Navy (ret.). Washington, DC: U.S. Government Print Office, 1939-45.

Newsam, Frank, Sir. *The Home Office*. London: George Allen and Unwin, 1955.

Nicolas, Nicholas Harris, Sir, ed. *The Dispatches and Letters of Vice Admiral Lord Viscount Nelson*. 7 vols. London: Henry Colburn, 1844-46.

Noah, Mordecai. *Travels in England, France, Spain, and the Barbary States, in the Years 1813-14 and 15*. New York: Kirk and Mercein, 1819.

Northcote Parkinson, C. *Britannia Rules: The Classic Age of Naval History 1793-1815*. London: Weidenfeld and Nicolson, 1977.

Northcote Parkinson, C. *Edward Pellew, Viscount Exmouth: Admiral of the Red*. London: Methuen, 1934.

Oberg, Barbara B. et al., eds. *The Papers of Thomas Jefferson*. Vol. 34, *1 May to 31 July 1801*. Princeton, NJ: Princeton University Press, 2007.

Oberg, Barbara B. et al., eds. *The Papers of Thomas Jefferson*. Vol. 35, *1 August to 30 November 1801*. Princeton, NJ: Princeton University Press, 2008.

Oberg, Barbara B. et al., eds. *The Papers of Thomas Jefferson*. Vol. 36, *1 December 1801 to 3 March 1802*. Princeton, NJ: Princeton University Press, 2009.

Oliel-Grausz, Evelyne. "Communication and Community: Multiplex Networks in the 18th Century Sephardi Diaspora." *Early Modern Workshop: Jewish History Resources*. Vol. 7, *Jewish Community and Identity in the Early Modern Period*. Middletown, CT: Wesleyan University Press, 2010.

Oliel-Grausz, Evelyne. "Networks and Communication in the Sephardi Diaspora: An Added Dimension to the Concept of Port Jews and Port Jewries." *Jewish Culture and History* 7, nos. 1–2 (2012): 61–76.

Panzac, Daniel. *Les Corsaires barbaresques: La Fin d'une épopée, 1800–1820*. Paris: CNRS, 1999.

Panzac, Daniel, ed. *Histoire économique et sociale de l'empire ottoman et de la Turquie (1326–1960): Actes du sixième congrès international tenu à Aix-en-Provence du 1er au 4 juillet 1992*. Paris: Peeters, 1995.

Parker, Richard Bordeaux. *Uncle Sam in Barbary: A Diplomatic History*. Gainesville, FL: University Press of Florida, 2004.

Pennell, C. R. "The Social History of British Diplomats in North Africa and How it Affected Diplomatic Policy." In *The Diplomat's World. A Cultural History of Diplomacy 1815–1914*, edited by Markus Mösslang and Torsten Riotte, 347–79. Oxford: Oxford University Press, 2008.

Pennell, C. R. "Treaty Law: The Extent of Consular Jurisdiction in North Africa from the Middle of the Seventeenth to the Middle of the Nineteenth Century." *Journal of North African Studies* 14, no. 2 (2009): 235–56.

Penslar, Derek. *Shylock's Children: Economics and Jewish Identity in Modern Europe*. Berkeley: University of California Press, 2001.

Perrin, W. G., ed. *The Keith Papers: Selected from the Letters and Papers of Admiral Viscount Keith*. 2 vols. London: Navy Records Society, 1950.

Peskin, Lawrence A, and Edmund F. Wehrle. *America and the World: Culture, Commerce, Conflict*. Baltimore, MD: Johns Hopkins University Press, 2011.

Peskin, Lawrence A. "The Lessons of Independence: How the Algerian Crisis Shaped Early American Identity." *Diplomatic History* 28, no. 3 (June 2004): 297–319.

Petersen, Christian. *Bread and the British Economy, c. 1770–1870*. Edited by Andrew Jenkins. Hants, UK: Ashgate, 1995.

"Pétition des héritiers Bacri." Paris, n.d.

Philipp, Thomas. "The Farhi Family and the Changing Position of the Jews in Syria, 1750–1860." *Middle Eastern Studies* 20, no. 4 (October 1984): 37–52.

Philipp, Thomas. "French Merchants and Jews in the Ottoman Empire During the Eighteenth Century." In *The Jews of the Ottoman Empire*, edited by Avigdor Levy, 315–26. Princeton, NJ: Darwin, 1994.

Pilbeam, Pamela. *The 1830 Revolution in France*. London: Macmillan, 1991.

Pitts, Jennifer. *A Turn to Empire: The Rise of Imperial Liberalism in Britain and France*. Princeton, NJ: Princeton University Press, 2005.

Plantet, Eugène. *Les Consuls de France avant la conquête, (1579–1830)*. Paris: Messageries Hachette, 1930.

Plantet, Eugène. *Correspondance des Deys d'Alger avec la Cour de France 1579–1833*. 2 vols. Paris: Alcan, 1889.

Platt, D.C.M. *The Cinderella Service: British Consuls since 1825*. London: Longman, 1971.

Playfair, Robert Lambert, Sir. *The Scourge of Christendom: Annals of British Relations with Algiers Prior to French Conquest*. London: Smith Elder, 1884.

Post, John D. *The Last Great Subsistence Crisis in the Western World*. Baltimore, MD: Johns Hopkins University Press, 1977.

Potter, Simon J., and Jonathan Saha. "Global History, Imperial History and Connected Histories of Empire." *Journal of Colonialism and Colonial History* 16, no. 1 (2015).

Price, Jacob M. "What Did Merchants Do? Reflections on British Overseas Trade, 1660–1790." *Journal of Economic History* 49, no. 2 (June 1989): 267–84.

Price, Roger. *An Economic History of Modern France, 1730–1914*. London: Macmillan, 1981 [1975].

Redouane, Joelle. "British Attitudes to the French Conquest of Algeria, 1830–71." *The Maghreb Review* 15, nos. 1–2 (1990): 2–15.

Redouane, Joelle. "British Trade with Algeria in the Nineteenth Century: An Ally Against France?" *The Maghreb Review* 13, nos. 3–4 (1998): 175–82.

Redouane, Joelle. "La Présence anglaise en Algérie de 1830 à 1930." *Revue de l'Occident musulman et de la Méditerranée* 38 (1984): 15–36.

Resnick, Daniel P. *The White Terror and the Political Reaction after Waterloo*. Cambridge, MA: Harvard University Press, 1966.

Reuveni, Gideon, and Sarah Wobick-Segev, eds. *The Economy in Jewish History: New Perspectives on the Inter-Relationship between Ethnicity and Economic Life*. New York: Berghahn, 2011.

Rosenstock, Morton. "The House of Bacri and Busnach: A Chapter from Algeria's Commercial History." *Jewish Social Studies* 14, no. 4 (October 1952): 343–64.

Ross, Frank E. "The Mission of Joseph Donaldson, Jr., to Algiers, 1795–97." *The Journal of Modern History* 7, no. 4 (December 1935): 422–33.

Rousset, Camille. *La Conquête d'Alger*. Paris: E. Plon et Cie, 1879.

Rozet, Claude-Antoine. *Voyage dans la régence d'Alger, ou description du pays occupé par l'armée française en Afrique; contenant des observations sur la géographie physique, la géologie, la météorologie, l'histoire naturelle, etc. suivies de détails sur le commerce, l'agriculture, les sciences et les arts, les mœurs, les coutumes et les usages des habitans de la régence, de l'histoire de son gouvernement, de la description complète du territoire, d'un plan de colonisation, etc.* 3 vols. Paris: Bertrand, 1833.

Schechter, Ronald. *Obstinate Hebrews: Representations of Jews in France, 1715–1815*. Berkeley: University of California Press, 2003.

Schreier, Joshua. *The Merchants of Oran: A Jewish Port at the Dawn of Empire*. Stanford, CA: Stanford University Press, 2017.

Schroeder, Paul W. *The Transformation of European Politics, 1763–1848*. Oxford: Clarendon Press, 1994.

Schroeter, Daniel. *The Sultan's Jew: Morocco and the Sephardi World*. Stanford, CA: Stanford University Press, 2002.

Schwarzfuchs, Simon. "Réalités et déclin du *Herem* dans la France d'Ancien Régime." *Archives Juives* 44 (2011/2012): 16–25.

Sears, Christine. "'In Algiers, the City of Bondage': Comparative Slavery in the Urban Context." In *Commodification, Community and Comparison in Slave Studies*, edited by Jeff Forret and Christine Sears, 201–18. Baton Rouge: Louisiana State University Press, 2015.

Sears, Christine. "'Tyra[n]nical Masters Are the Turks': The Comparative Context of Barbary Slavery." In *Slavery in the Islamic world: Its Characteristics and Commonality*, edited by Mary Ann Fay. New York: Palgrave Macmillan, 2019.

Semmel, Stuart. *Napoleon and the British*. New Haven, CT: Yale University Press, 2004.

Sessions, Jennifer. *By Sword and Plow: France and the Conquest of Algeria*. Ithaca, NY: Cornell University Press, 2011.

Shaler, William. *Sketches of Algiers, Political, Historical, and Civil: Containing an Account of the Geography, Population, Government, Revenues, Commerce, Agriculture, Arts, Civil Institutions, Tribes, Manners, Languages, and Recent Political History of that Country*. Boston: Cummings, Hilliard, and Company, 1826.

Shuval, Tal. "The Ottoman Algerian Elite and its Ideology." *International Journal of Middle Eastern Studies* 32, no. 3 (August 2000): 323–44.

Sluga, Glenda. "'Who Hold the Balance of the World?' Bankers at the Congress of Vienna, and in International History." *American Historical Review* 122, no. 5 (2017): 1403–30.

Sofka, James R. "'The Jeffersonian Idea of National Security' Revisited." In *Rough Waters: American Involvement with the Mediterranean in the Eighteenth and Nineteenth Centuries*, edited by Silvia Marzagalli, James R. Sofka, and John J. McCusker, 161–83. St. John's, Newfoundland: International Maritime Economic History Association, 2010.

Spang, Rebecca. *Stuff and Money in the Time of the French Revolution*. Cambridge, MA: Harvard University Press, 2015.

Stein, Sarah Abrevaya. *Plumes: Ostrich Feathers, Jews, and a Lost World of Global Commerce*. New Haven, CT: Yale University Press, 2008.

Stern, Philip J., and Carl Wennerlind, eds. *Mercantilism Reimagined: Political Economy in Early Modern Britain and its Empire*. New York: Oxford University Press, 2013.

Stoler, Ann Laura. "Tense and Tender Ties: The Politics of Comparison in North American History and (Post) Colonial Studies." *The Journal of American History* 88, no. 3 (December 2001): 829–65.

Swain, James Edgar. *The Struggle for the Control of the Mediterranean prior to 1848: A Study in Anglo-French Relations*. New York: Russell and Russell, 1973.

Taieb, Jacques. *Sociétés juives du Maghreb moderne (1500–1900): Un Monde en mouvement*. Paris: Maisonneuve et Larose, 2000.

Teller, Adam, and Rebecca Kobrin, eds. *Purchasing Power: The Economics of Modern Jewish History*. Philadelphia: University of Pennsylvania Press, 2015.

Temimi, Abdeljelil. "Documents turcs inédits sur le bombardement d'Alger en 1816." *Revue de l'Occident musulman et de la Méditerranée* 5 (1968): 111–33.

Thomson, Ann. *Barbary and Enlightenment: European Attitudes towards the Maghreb in the 18th Century*. Leiden: Brill, 1987.

Toaff, Ariel, and Simon Schwarzfuchs, eds. *The Mediterranean and the Jews: Banking, Finance, and International Trade (XVI-XVIII Centuries)*. Ramat-Gan, Israel: Bar Ilan University Press, 1989.

Todd, David. "A French Imperial Meridian, 1814–1870." *Past and Present* 10 (February 2011): 155–86.

Todd, David. *L'Identité économique de la France: Libre-échange et protectionnisme (1814-1851)*. Paris: Grasset, 2008.

Todd, David. "Retour sur l'expédition d'Alger: Les faux-semblants d'un tournant colonialiste français." *Monde(s)* 10 (November 2016): 205–22.

Todd, David. "Transnational Projects of Empire in France, c. 1815–c. 1870." *Modern Intellectual History* 12, no. 2 (2015): 265–93.

Todd, David. *A Velvet Empire: French Informal Imperialism in the Nineteenth Century*. Princeton, NJ: Princeton University Press, 2021.

Tonnelé, Jean. *L'Angleterre en Méditerranée*. Paris: C. Lavauzelle, 1952.

Touati, Ismet. "L'Algérie au 'siècle du blé' (1725–1815)." Le Carnet des Glycines: Conférence donnée aux Glycines, January 23, 2014. https://glycines.hypotheses.org/93.

Touati, Ismet. *Le Commerce du blé entre l'Algérie et la France, XVIe-XIXe siècles*. Paris: Editions Bouchène, 2018.

Tracy, James D., ed. *The Rise of Merchant Empires: Long-Distance Trade in the Early Modern World, 1350-1750*. New York: Cambridge University Press, 1990.

Trivellato, Francesca. *The Familiarity of Strangers: The Sephardic Diaspora, Livorno, and Cross-Cultural Trade in the Early-Modern Period*. New Haven, CT: Yale University Press, 2009.

Trivellato, Francesca. "Sephardic Merchants between State and Rabbinic Courts: Malfeasance, Property Rights, and Religious Authority in the Eighteenth-Century Mediterranean." In *From Florence to the Mediterranean and Beyond: Essays in Honor of Anthony Molho*, edited by Diogo Ramada Curto, Eric R Dursteler, Julius Kirshner, and Francesca Trivellato, 625–48. Vol. 2. Florence: Leo Olschki, 2009.

Trivellato, Francesca. "Sephardic Merchants in the Early Modern Atlantic and Beyond: Toward a Comparative Historical Approach to Business Cooperation." In *Atlantic Diasporas: Jews, Conversos, and Crypto-Jews in the Age of Mercantilism, 1500-1800*, edited by Richard L., Kagan and Philip D. Morgan, 99–120. Baltimore, MD: Johns Hopkins University Press, 2009.

Ulbert, Jörg. "A History of the French Consular Services." In *Consular Affairs and Diplomacy*, edited by Jan Melissen and Ana Mar Fernandez, 303–24. Leyde and Boston: Martinus Nijhoff, 2011.

Ulbert, Jörg. "Introduction: La Fonction consulaire à l'époque moderne: Définition, état des connaissances et perspectives de recherche." In *La fonction consulaire à l'époque moderne: L'affirmation d'une institution économique et politique (1500-1800)*, edited by Jörg Ulbert and Gérard Le Bouëdec, 9–20. Rennes, France: Presses universitaires de Rennes, 2006.

Ulbert, Jörg, and Gérard le Bouëdec, eds. *La Fonction consulaire à l'époque moderne: L'Affirmation d'une institution économique et politique (1500–1800)*. Rennes, France: Presses universitaires de Rennes, 2006.

Valensi, Lucette. *Juifs et musulmans en Algérie, VIIe–XXe siècle*. Paris: Tallandier, 2016.

Valensi, Lucette. "Multicultural Visions: The Cultural Tapestry of the Jews of North Africa." In *Cultures of the Jews: A New History*, edited by David Biale, 887–932. New York: Schocken, 2002.

Valensi, Lucette. *On the Eve of Colonialism: North Africa Before the French Conquest*. Translated by Kenneth J. Perkins. New York: Africana Publishing Company, 1977.

Van Krieken, Gérard. *Corsaires et marchands: Les relations entre Alger et les Pay-Bas 1604–1830*. Paris: Editions Bouchène, 2002.

Venture de Paradis. *Alger au XVIIIe siècle*. Algiers: Jourdan, 1808.

Veve, Thomas D. "France and the Allied Occupation, 1816–1818." *Consortium on Revolutionary Europe 1750–1850: Proceedings* 20 (1990): 411–16.

Veve, Thomas D. "Wellington and the Army of Occupation in France, 1815–1818." *The International History Review* 11, no. 1 (February 1989): 98–108.

Vick, Brian. *The Congress of Vienna: Power and Politics after Napoleon*. Cambridge, MA: Harvard University Press, 2014.

Vick, Brian. "Power, Humanitarianism and the Global Liberal Order: Abolition and the Barbary Corsairs in the Vienna Congress System." *The International History Review* 40, no. 4 (2018): 939–60.

Vlami, Despina. *Trading with the Ottomans: The Levant Company in the Middle East*. London: I. B. Tauris, 2015.

Weiss, Gillian. *Captives and Corsairs: France and Slavery in the Early Modern Mediterranean*. Stanford, CA: Stanford University Press, 2011.

White, Eugene N. "Making the French Pay: The Costs and Consequences of the Napoleonic Reparations." *European Review of Economic History* 5 (2001): 337–65.

Williams, Greg H. *The French Assault on American Shipping, 1793–1813: A History and Comprehensive Record of Merchant Marine Losses*. Jefferson, NC: McFarland, 2009.

Winch, Donald, and Patrick K. O'Brien, eds. *The Political Economy of British Historical Experience, 1688–1914*. Oxford: Oxford University Press, 2002.

Windler, Christian. "Diplomatic History as a Field for Cultural Analysis: Muslim-Christian Relations in Tunis, 1700–1840." *Historical Journal* 44, no. 1 (2001): 79–106.

Windler, Christian. *La Diplomatie comme expérience de l'autre: Consuls français au Maghreb 1700–1840*. Geneva: Droz, 2002.

Windler, Christian. "Du privilège à la souveraineté: Les ressortissants français et leurs consuls dans les échelles du Levant et du Maghreb (1700–1840)." In *La mobilité des personnes en Méditerranée de l'Antiquité à l'époque moderne. Procédures de contrôle et documents d'identification*, edited by Claudia Moatti, 699–722. Rome: Ecole française de Rome, 2004.

Windler, Christian. "Representing a State in a Segmentary Society: French Consuls in Tunis from the Ancien Régime to the Restoration." *Journal of Modern History* 73 (2001): 233–74.

Windler, Christian. "Tributes and Presents in Franco-Tunisian Diplomacy." *Journal of Early Modern History* 4, no. 2 (2000): 168–99.

Wolf, John B. *The Barbary Coast: Algiers under the Turks, 1500–1830.* New York: W. W. Norton & Co., 1979.

Wood, Alfred C. *A History of the Levant Company.* Oxford: Oxford University Press, 1935.

Woolf, Jeffrey R. *The Fabric of Religious Life in Medieval Ashkenaz.* Leiden: Brill, 2015.

Wright, Louis B, and Julia H. MacLeod. *The First Americans in North Africa: William Eaton's Struggle for a Vigorous Policy against the Barbary Pirates, 1799–1805.* Princeton, NJ: Princeton University Press, 1945.

Zamoyski, Adam. *Rites of Peace: The Fall of Napoleon and the Congress of Vienna.* New York: Harper Collins, 2007.

Zhou, Xiaolan. "La Crise économique française de 1816 à 1817: La Dernière crise d'Ancien régime?" *Revue française d'histoire économique* 2, no. 2 (2014): 86–108.

Zwierlein, Cornel. *Imperial Unknowns: The French and British in the Mediterranean, 1650- 1750.* Cambridge: Cambridge University Press, 2016.

Zytnicki, Colette. *Les Juifs du Maghreb: Naissance d'une historiographie coloniale.* Paris: Presses de l'Université Paris-Sorbonne, 2011.

A NOTE ON THE TYPE

THIS BOOK has been composed in Miller, a Scotch Roman typeface designed by Matthew Carter and first released by Font Bureau in 1997. It resembles Monticello, the typeface developed for The Papers of Thomas Jefferson in the 1940s by C. H. Griffith and P. J. Conkwright and reinterpreted in digital form by Carter in 2003.

Pleasant Jefferson ("P. J.") Conkwright (1905–1986) was Typographer at Princeton University Press from 1939 to 1970. He was an acclaimed book designer and AIGA Medalist.

The ornament used throughout this book was designed by Pierre Simon Fournier (1712–1768) and was a favorite of Conkwright's, used in his design of the *Princeton University Library Chronicle.*